The Montana Cree

Raining Bird
Mystic, Philosopher, Friend
(Courtesy Museum of the Rockies
Photo-archive, Montana State University)

The Montana Cree

*A study
in religious persistence*

by

VERNE DUSENBERRY

Foreword by Lynne Dusenberry Crow

University of Oklahoma Press
Norman

To Mrs. James Willard
(Jessie L. Donaldson) Schultz
whose inspirational teaching
stimulated my interest in the
North American Indian

Library of Congress Cataloging-in-Publication Data

Dusenberry, Verne, 1906–1966.
    The Montana Cree : a study in religious persistence / by Verne
Dusenberry ; foreword by Lynne Dusenberry Crow.
        p.   cm.
    Originally published: Stockholm : University of Stockholm/Almquist
& Wiksell, 1962, in series: Acta Universitatis Stockholmiensis.
Stockholm Studies in Comparative Religion.
    Includes bibliographical references and index.
    ISBN 0-8061-3025-3 (alk. paper)
    1. Cree Indians—Religion.   2. Indians of North America—
Montana—Religion.   I. Title.
E99.C88D87   1998
299'.783—dc21   97-43208
                                                                      CIP

The paper in this book meets the guidelines for permanence and dura-
bility of the Committee on Production Guidelines for Book Longevity of
the Council on Library Resources, Inc. ∞

The Montana Cree originally was published as number 3 in the Stockholm
Studies in Comparative Religion, published by the University of Stockholm
and printed in Sweden by Almquist & Wiksells.

1   2   3   4   5   6   7   8   9   10

TABLE OF CONTENTS

LIST OF ILLUSTRATIONS

FOREWORD
by Lynne Dusenberry Crow

It is May 1997. At the Blackfeet Community College campus on the Blackfeet Indian Reservation, I and many others have gathered to honor a member of the Blackfoot confederacy for her recent doctoral degree from Montana State University. Professors, elders, and Blackfeet tribal chairman Earl Old Person are in attendance. As our meal concludes, I speak with June Tatsey, Director of Blackfeet Tribal Health. She is delighted to learn that *The Montana Cree* is being reprinted and remembers when Verne was a visiting instructor at Northern Montana State College in Havre: "In 1953 I was the only Native student on campus. Verne really helped me."

"What did he do?" I ask.

"He gave me a confidence I didn't know I could have . . . a lot of encouragement. . . . I was feeling lonely and out of place; it was my first time off the reservation. He made me feel comfortable. He shared warmth that I needed to continue [staying in school]. He made me feel I could really do it."

The honoring ceremony begins with short remarks from Chairman Old Person and an educator from the university. Then a group of elderly men and one woman stand to sing a series of honoring songs, and the entire group rises in respect for the event. Women in the audience voice the ancient trills—a victory sound that long ago struck terror into the hearts of the enemy.

We sit, and I lean over to June and remark, "Things have changed so much. Imagine this scene in 1953!"

"It could never have happened," she replies, and we talk about the emergence of Blackfeet Community College as an Indian-controlled institution dedicated both to academic standards and to the incorporation of Blackfeet cultural studies into its curriculum. Verne Dusenberry's activities come up again—the first Native Studies classes in

Montana and his advocacy of Native students—and I assure her, "I'm not saying Verne was responsible for this."

"No," she agrees, "but he broke the trail for it."[1]

Thus is Verne Dusenberry remembered in Blackfoot country today. He was a cross-cultural mentor, a respected historian, and an inspirational teacher to students from all cultures. In his personal life, he was a charismatic storyteller, a dedicated spiritual seeker, and a thorny puzzlement to many of his colleagues, who made belittling remarks about "Verne's Indians." Some aspects of his life remain a mystery even to me. I was only twenty-one when he died, and since then I have endeavored to track down his story.

Verne was born in Carl, Iowa, on April 7, 1906, the only child of Dutch-Irish farmers George Robinson and Maggie Garrett Dusenberry. An educator before her marriage, Maggie instilled in Verne a love of books and a respect for education. In 1909 the family homesteaded in Kelly Canyon, near Bozeman, Montana. Curious about Indians, Verne roamed the hills finding arrow points and hid to watch wagons go by as "real Indians" (probably from the Flathead Reservation) passed near the farm on traditional fall trips eastward. Filled with common stereotypes of the time, he was afraid of them.

In 1919 the mortgaged homestead was lost after a severe drought, and the family moved to the outskirts of Bozeman. Verne worked his way through both high school and the local Montana State College, graduating in 1927 with a B.S. in Education. For several years he taught English in small-town high schools in western Montana. Then, after spending a year in the state tuberculosis sanitarium and emerging to discover a depressed job market for teachers, he found employment as a branch manager with a small seed company in Ronan, Montana, on the Flathead Indian Reservation. Acquaintances in the predominantly non-Indian town discouraged his curiosity about the Indian people living nearby, but he persisted.

Here follows Verne's own account of how he first crossed the cultural boundary and met Mose and Adelaide Michelle:

> I was fortunate to make the acquaintance of the Pend d'Oreille. . . . Although I had been living on their reservation for two years and had wanted to meet them, I had never approached them. One Sunday morning

---

[1] Many thanks to June Tatsey for her permission to document our conversation of May 14, 1997.

in the fall of 1937, I drove to the home of an Indian whose wife had been recommended to me as a good craftsman. I wanted a pair of moccasins.

She took my order, but told me that her husband was so sick she could not ask me to come in. I looked in the cabin and saw the man lying there, obviously quite ill. As one would do with any person in distress, I inquired if I could be of any assistance. He spoke no English; his wife said they had tried to get the government doctor the day before, but that he refused to come because it was Saturday.

I returned to town and called the [government] doctor. He curtly dismissed my plea. I went then to an elderly doctor living in the town who had retired from the Indian Service many years before. While it was against his principle to treat Indian patients (because of their preference for him), he agreed to do so in this instance after I had told him the circumstances. Consequently, I returned to the Indians' home accompanied by the doctor. En route, I learned from the doctor that the patient, Mose Michelle, was the hereditary chief of the Pend d'Oreille tribe and a highly respected man.

The chief was happy to see the old doctor, who talked to him in his own language. The condition was nothing serious, just a severe stomach upset. The doctor left some pills but said that Mose should have a prescription for another medication. So I took the doctor back to town, purchased the medicine, and returned for the third time to Mose's home.

During the two weeks that followed, I went several times to see Mose. Each time I brought some fruit or some small inexpensive gift with me. Each day, he seemed more touched by my thoughtfulness, and when at last he recovered, he brought out his beaded jacket and offered it to me. I declined. Then, rather puzzled, he asked what I did want. I told him I would like to hear some of the stories of the old-time Indians, and that I hoped perhaps sometime he would tell me some. This he immediately promised to do. About three weeks later, he came to my office with a note written by his wife. I was to come to his place that night. They would have some old men there to visit with me.

I went out about seven o'clock and stayed until midnight. I learned that Mose that day had hitched his horses to the spring wagon, put a pallet in the wagon box, and had driven about three miles to the home of old Quee-quee-soo and had put him on the pallet and had brought him home. The old man was reputedly 105 years old at that time. En route home, they had stopped for Little Martin, another ancient Pend d'Oreille, and had brought him along. Still in the same thoughtful manner, Mose had sent for his cousin, Frank Michelle, who (when he wasn't in jail) proved to be my best and most trustworthy interpreter during the next five years that I lived on the reservation.[2]

---

[2] J. Verne Dusenberry, "Samples of Pend d'Oreille Oral Literature and Salish Narratives," in *Lifeways of Intermontane and Plains Montana Indians,* Occasional Papers of the Museum of the Rockies No. 1, ed. Leslie B. Davis (Bozeman: Montana State University, 1979), 109. Used by permission.

That simple act of kindness by a white man stood out as unusual for the People, as did his interest in the stories. Verne further demonstrated his sincerity by rapidly learning the Salish language, thus becoming able to participate more fully with the old people. Within the year, Mose took Verne as his son, giving him the name "Many Grizzly Bears." This had been Mose's grandfather's name, the man who signed the 1855 treaty as representative chief of the Pend d'Oreille.

In 1976 my return to the Flathead Reservation was welcomed as natural by elders, who recognized my family place in the circle and made sure I understood the meaning of Verne's experience. According to individuals who remembered those times, Mose had lived with several different women during his life, but he never had children from his own body.[3] An heir was crucial to the continuation of his hereditary chieftainship. By the 1930s, official political power was no longer involved, but the Pend d'Oreille and their Salish co-inhabitants of the Flathead Reservation understood the continuity-based implications of that adoption. Verne always emphasized to me the distinction between being adopted or given a name by a *tribe*—done to honor an outsider—and Verne's personal family experience with the Michelles.

When Mose and Adelaide Michelle acquired their new adult son, the old-timers—people then in their sixties and older—did not regard him as "Indian" rather than "white." He was simply their son, with the family and community implications that that involved. He was welcomed into the ceremonies throughout the year—the winter medicine dances and the sweat lodges—and he shared in the stories, laughter, and daily family life. Even many years later, he was remembered by those who knew him in the 1930s as a fun person, a friend, and as a white man who was unusually comfortable, respectful, and nonintrusive among them. He was also remembered as an ally. Mary Combs Felsman, daughter of Salish leaders, recalled in 1976: "He helped a lot of people get jobs. It was really hard for Indians to find work—white people wouldn't hire us—but he found work for many people. Some people also hocked their beadwork to him; it was the depression, we were poor. He was generous."[4] Today at the Flathead Reservation, the younger generations remember Verne in his later years as a professor, when he organized university conferences and promoted Indian culture on Montana's campuses. Few seem to

---

[3] Agnes Vanderburg and Etta Adams, personal communications, Arlee, Mont., 1976-85.
[4] Personal communication, St. Ignatius, Mont., 1976.

know of his role as the son of a chief, helping and taking care of the people as befitted his family's status.

When World War II emerged, Verne was declared 4-F by the army because of his history of tuberculosis, so he decided to serve the war effort in another way—he accepted a personnel position with a civilian company that was constructing the Alaska highway under contract with the U.S. military. He married Margaret Hellweg in Montana in 1943, and they spent their first year of marriage in Alaska and the Yukon, returning to Montana in the fall of 1944. There Verne again began teaching English. In 1945 I was born—their only child—and two years later they settled in Bozeman, Montana, where Verne took a position with the English Department at Montana State College (later Montana State University).

According to former [non-Indian] students' recent remarks to me, he was an inspiring teacher who not only taught them to write with thoughtful care, but also took a personal interest in their academic development. Montana historian Merrill Burlingame wrote in 1979 that Verne "stimulated classes en masse, but he also had the interest and took the time to work with individuals as they engaged in original thinking and creative work that often led to careers in Anthropology or English."[5] For example, one of Verne's star students, Leslie B. Davis, is currently curator of archaeology and ethnography in the Museum of the Rockies at Montana State University.

Verne's Indian parents had died while he was in Alaska, but in 1948 he reconnected with people from the Flathead Reservation. Between 1952 and 1955 he became personally acquainted with elders and their families at Rocky Boy, Fort Belknap, Crow, and Fort Peck and among both the Blackfeet and the Northern Cheyenne, the latter giving him the honor of membership in their traditional Council of Forty-four. Most of these journeys he made at his own expense and always in his unique personal style. During the same period, he also resumed his spiritual involvement, participating in sweat lodges, activities of the Native American Church, the Sun Dance, and other ceremonies. He also pursued cultural liaison efforts, helping various tribes communicate with government officials and encouraging education for young people.

In the 1950s, with the publication of various articles relating to Montana history, Verne emerged as a leading regional historian. His

---

[5] Merrill G. Burlingame, "Verne Dusenberry: 1906-1966," in *Lifeways of Intermontane and Plains Montana Indians*, 4.

work on the historical and modern Métis stands as a vital historical record, useful to these "landless" Indians in their continuing struggle for federal recognition as a People.[6]

Verne had begun graduate studies at several universities, but each time health, economics, or war had forced him out. By 1955, when he enrolled as a masters' candidate at the University of Montana in Missoula, his focus had shifted to anthropology as a result of his expanding relationships with Indians. Anthropology seemed a field that could validate his advocacy and give him a way to organize his diverse interests. He completed his master's degree in 1956. His unpublished thesis, "The Varying Culture of the Northern Cheyenne," illustrates cultural continuity (contradicting the then-prevailing anthropological attitude of "get the information before the Indians vanish"). In the same year he organized the Montana Indian Symposium in Missoula, in which tribal representatives spoke on campus to scholars, an event remembered by Blackfeet tribal chairman Earl Old Person as a significant breakthrough in intercultural understanding. It is the direct ancestor of the now week-long Kyi-Yo Conference held each year in late April at the University of Montana.[7]

Returning to the Montana State College English department in the fall of 1956, Verne negotiated to teach two courses outside his department: Indians of North America and Indians of Montana. (No anthropology department existed at the time.) These were the first "Native American studies" courses taught in the state. Indian families began sending their young people to Bozeman to college because he was there to mentor them. By 1957 he had established an official Indian Club on campus to provide a meeting ground for students who were homesick and in culture shock. The club also established the Indian presence on campus through participation in mainstream campus events, such as having a float in the Homecoming Parade. At the same time, Verne deepened his relationships among Montana's Indian people through friendship and increasing personal spiritual participation.

Verne spent a summer session at Brandeis University, in Massachusetts, in 1958. There he had the privilege of studying with Paul Radin, and also met Åke Hultkrantz, from Stockholm. Correspondence with Dr. Hultkrantz resulted in Verne's enrolling as a doctoral candi-

---

[6] Robert Peregoy (Montana Salish), Native rights lawyer, personal communication, 1996.

[7] Personal communication, Browning, Mont., 1995.

4

date at the University of Stockholm. (Joseph Epes Brown, coauthor, with Black Elk, of *The Sacred Pipe*, would be the second American student to pursue a doctorate with Dr. Hultkrantz.)

After initial course readings and program development by correspondence, Verne spent a residence semester in Sweden in the spring of 1960. He returned to Montana State College and continued teaching both English and "Indian Studies" (the growing disgruntlement among some of his colleagues at his split in focus leading to derogatory remarks about "Indian lovers" and "mail-order degrees"). He pursued his dissertation research at Rocky Boy and kept in touch with Stockholm via many transatlantic packets and telephone calls. In June 1962, when his dissertation, *The Montana Cree: A Study in Religious Persistence*, was finished and in process of publication, he returned to Stockholm for several examination requirements and participated in the "fil. doktor" ceremonies there.

In 1965, after he had taught in the anthropology department at the University of Montana for two years, Verne accepted an offer from the Glenbow Foundation in Calgary, Alberta, and became the first Director of their Indian Studies Institute. The position included teaching responsibilities at the University of Calgary. In December 1966, however, he succumbed to cancer, and died.

I first read *The Montana Cree* in 1973 during the period of my own return among Indian people. I remember being irritated by my sense of two styles. There was the warm, storyteller dad, relating things he had seen or been told. This style included a characteristic tone of warm personal response to those events and facts. But with that was an irritating overlay: "anthropology" stuck on like an edging around the tales. It seemed an intrusion into the narrative. Clearly Verne found it necessary to satisfy his dissertation committee, but the scholarly apparatus sat unblended to my eye, obscuring the cultural information.

Twelve years later, as a master's candidate in linguistic anthropology at the University of Calgary, I reread this book and once again sensed that intrusion. Even to my modest anthropological awareness, the analytic comments and vocabulary seemed superficial, even arrogant, when contrasted with the ethnographic material and with what I knew about Verne's deep involvement with the People and their religious beliefs. Obviously Verne needed to complete his degree and, like many a graduate student before him, inserted "dissertationese" to satisfy the requirements, drawing from an apparently limited grasp of the anthropology of his time. In reality, he was a historian and a storyteller endeavoring to achieve academic respectability for the purpose of furthering public understanding and acceptance of Native peoples.

Why did the anthropologists of the University of Stockholm let him get away with it? Certainly the volume documented religious persistence when academia was still in the thrall of the Vanishing American myth. But the answer, I believe, is that although the anthropology is weak, the ethnography is exquisite. The learned Swedes chose to honor Verne's unique and diligent pursuits. He didn't write an account of a brief visit to Indian country, laden with theory and light on experience. He went there—deeply—far beyond the call of fieldwork duty, and he shared what happened with the blessings of the local community. The enduring value of this book, then, is the detailed and compassionate ethnography, written with Verne's remarkable ability to cross the cultural boundaries. Verne, as ethnographer and friend, took his "informants" seriously, as intelligent people living legitimately within their cultural contexts—a notion still in heavy anthropological debate.[8]

Between 1953 and 1962, when Verne was developing friendships, deepening his own personal quest, and completing his doctoral work, I was between eight and seventeen years old; the latter part of that time I was primarily with my mother owing to their divorce. On several occasions I did meet Four Souls and the Gardipee family, and in 1962, a few days before Verne and I traveled to Sweden for his dissertation defense, Art Raining Bird personally prayed over us, for our safety and for the success of Verne's venture.

In 1975, while searching for my own threads of relationship in Indian country and attempting to unravel the mystery of my dad's life, I traveled to Tom and Ruth Gardipee and stayed in their home on several extended visits. Tom told me very directly, "I am your dad now." When I expressed my puzzlement, he elaborated, "Your dad and I took each other as brothers. Now that he's gone, Ruth and I are your mom and dad. Our children are your brothers and sisters." In anthropological terminology this is sometimes called "fictive kinship," but within the fabric of Indian life there is nothing fictitious about it. It continues through time. Tom and Ruth's children and grandchildren relate to me and my daughter as family, both in words and in behavior. Their youngest son, Vern (born during my father's last years, and named for

---

[8] See "Part III: Taking Our Informants Seriously," in *Being Changed by Cross-cultural Encounters: The Anthropology of Extraordinary Experience*, eds. David E. Young and Jean-Guy Goulet (Broadview Press, Peterborough, Ontario, 1994), 197ff.

him), has a son, Vern Jr., and a daughter, Lavern. This continuity, going forward now into a third generation with our children, has taught me—more than any other circumstance—the depth of my father's human involvement with the People of Rocky Boy.

In 1994 a young woman from Rocky Boy, active in cultural and political issues, criticized a current trend among some Native individuals of withholding cultural knowledge from white people. "They still talk about your dad at Rocky Boy," she told me. "His name comes up when there are arguments about whether non-Indians should be allowed to attend ceremonies. Older people will get up and tell this story: Verne participated in the Sun Dance preparation lodge—he was in that sacred tipi for the whole time, and you know they stay in there for several days. After all the prayers, right before they come out and start the Sun Dance itself, anyone may speak to the group. Verne stood up and said, 'We are all full bloods.' That really surprised everybody. No one had ever thought that a white person could see the full humanity of all people, let alone remind them of it. They're still marveling over what he said."

Verne Dusenberry was a controversial figure. Before humanistic anthropology was an acceptable approach, he integrated the personal into his professional perspective. Anthropology was still trying to become an objective science in the early 1960s, and he was heavily criticized: "What do you mean, you pray with those people? How can you maintain objectivity?" Simultaneously, the first reactions against perceived exploitation by anthropologists were murmuring through Indian country: "What do you mean, you're an anthropologist? How can we trust you now?" It was a lose/lose situation in both cultures, an apparent personal, spiritual, and professional dead-end. He experienced confusion and despair, and did not live to see the time come when a scholar could write: "To seek through interviews what [the Northern Athapaskan] Dene expect the investigator to learn through personal experience and observation will *simply not do*" (my emphasis).[9] But his pioneering efforts, and those of many others, bore fruit over time, with Native American studies now an academic discipline, clubs and drop-in centers for Native students present on

---

[9] Jean-Guy Goulet, "Ways of Knowing: Towards a Narrative Ethnography of Experiences Among the Dene Tha," *Journal of Anthropological Research* 50 (1994): 113-19. For additional perspectives on personal experience being vital to understanding other cultures, see also the writings of J. Okely, R. Ridington, R. and S. B. K. Scollon, and B. and D. Tedlock, among others.

many campuses, and personal-cultural experiences more legitimate in anthropology.[10]

Robert M. Pirsig (*Zen and the Art of Motorcycle Maintenance*) was one of Verne's supportive colleagues in the Montana State College English department. He was also a personal friend. Verne appeared as the pivotal thematic figure in Pirsig's subsequent book, *Lila: An Inquiry into Morals*. Prior to publication, Pirsig sent me an advance copy, commenting that "Verne was misunderstood and underestimated both as a person and as a scholar. I hope this helps to set the record straight." Today the keepers of Verne's unpublished notes at the Montana State University Library Special Collections tell me that researchers often come to use his work.

I remember Verne as a laughing, indulgent father (though strict in matters literary), one who took a curious, interested child on magical excursions deep into Indian Country. Those trips became the basis of my own lifetime involvement with Native people in Montana and Alberta, a tradition being continued by my only child, Rachel. *The Montana Cree* reveals a living people, written by a personal human ally lightly masked as a scholar. Verne Dusenberry *experienced* relevance and legitimacy in Native American culture. He ventured into the prejudiced atmosphere of his own ethnic heritage, and battled for recognition of that legitimacy.

Basin, Montana
May 1997

---

[10] See the discussions in Young and Goulet, eds., *Being Changed by Cross-cultural Encounters*, as theorists struggle to find acceptable academic forms to include personal paranormal events in their ethnographies.

ACKNOWLEDGEMENTS

For twenty-five years, I have been closely associated with the Indians of Montana. My friendship began with the now nearly-extinct and almost-forgotten Pend d'Oreille. Since the time in 1935 when the last hereditary chief of that tribe, the late Mose Michelle, took me as his son and gave me the name of his grandfather, I have enjoyed my friendship with Indian people, appreciated their generous and warm hospitality, and have been permitted to attend and to participate in many of their tribal functions. As the years have passed, my area of travel and of association has broadened until I feel equally at home among the Flathead-Salish, the Assiniboine, the Gros Ventre, the Crow, the Northern Cheyenne, and those residents of the Rocky Boy reservation whom I have chosen to call the "Montana Cree" in this study. The first acknowledgement I wish to make, then, is to the Indian people of Montana who have so graciously accepted me as their friend and have accorded me their hospitality.

It was in 1952 that I first met any of the residents of the Rocky Boy reservation. When I had inquired of local white citizens in the nearby town of Havre about the tribal identity of these people, I received the casual reply that they were "Rocky Boy Indians." Published sources revealed little more, so I started doing some research in the old newspapers and government records. In 1954, I published a brief account of their historical background in *Montana, the Magazine of Western History*. (Much of the same material is included in Chapter I of this work.) The Cree who read the article seemingly were pleased with what I had written about them, and as a result have been cordial in their attitude to me since. During the years that followed, I have visited their reservation many times and have learned to know the tribal members well.

Material for this present work has been obtained during the last three years from informants on the Rocky Boy reservation, where I have spent as much of my time as my schedule would permit. And during those years the people there have been extremely cooperative. Working without pay and generous in their willingness to share their beliefs with me, the informants have patiently explained their views, and have taught me the rudiments of their language to the point where I can understand them as they converse in their own tongue. While I am indebted to many of the individuals and families on the Rocky Boy reservation, I am particularly grateful for the long hours that Raining Bird, Ruth and Tom Gardipee, and Four Souls have given me. Sitting in their homes hour after hour, sharing their meals, and frequently staying over night with them are now pleasant memories—memories that are lightened by their rich humor and their warm hospitality. To them, I can only express my gratitude and my hope that they will approve of what I have written about them.

Others too must be given credit for whatever worth this book has. During the last year of his life, I had the privilege of studying with the late Dr. Paul Radin at Brandeis University. It was at his insistence that I began delving into the religion of the Cree, and his encouragement led me to make a serious study of the religion of one Indian tribe. To Dr. Åke Hultkrantz of the University of Stockholm I am particularly grateful and must express my special thanks. To many of my compatriots, as well as to numerous Swedish people whom I met, the idea of an American citizen studying the religion of a North American Indian tribe in Sweden seemed incongruous. I went to Sweden that I might study with Dr. Hultkrantz, a man whom I consider to be the greatest living authority on the religion of the North American Indians. I met him first when he was a visiting professor at an Institute in Anthropology at Brandeis University. Later, I studied with him in Stockholm, and his willingness and patience in directing my work—both there and through trans-Atlantic correspondence—have been of inestimable value. If I had not met him and Dr. Radin, this work would never have been accomplished.

I owe a special debt of gratitude to a man whom I have never met, Mr. F. E. Peeso of Libby, Montana. Mr. Peeso came to Montana in 1905 fresh from the University of Pennsylvania. His first residence in Montana was in Butte, and there by chance he found the forebears of the present Cree camped near the dump grounds of that city. He became acquainted with them, learned their language, inspired their respect, and recorded much valuable material about their life. His friendship and association with them lasted throughout their roaming days. Through a mutual acquaintance, I learned of this material, wrote him, and received a copy of his manuscript. He mentioned in his letter that since he is now a man in his eighties and unlikely to revise his material for publication he hoped that his work would be of help to someone else. To Mr. Peeso, whom I hope someday to meet personally, I can only say that my gratitude is sincere and deeply felt.

Rocky Boy reservation is isolated, and living accommodations are non-existent for a field worker there. Present and former employees of the Bureau of Indian Affairs have not only helped me by giving me access to material in the sub-agency office, but have provided me with housing, meals, baths, as well as their friendship and encouragement. To them, then, I am deeply obligated, particularly Mr. Allan Crain, Mrs. Iradell Andrews, Mr. Harry Anderson, Mr. Robert Crawford, Mr. and Mrs. C. R. Pilgeram, and Mr. and Mrs. Holly Williamson.

Colleagues at Montana State College and Montana State University have encouraged and helped me. To Mr. Paul Grieder, Mrs. Sarah Vinke, Mr. George Douglas, and Mr. Robert Pirsig of the college and to Mr. F. H. Brown, Jr. and Dr. Mason Griff of the university go my special thanks. Three of my former students, Leslie B. Davis, John Fryer, and Rodney L. Jones, have also been particularly helpful. Other friends, too, have assisted—especially those living in the Havre, Montana, area who have fed and housed me while I have been collecting material on the reservation. My thanks go to Mr. and Mrs. Alvin J. Lucke, Mr. and Mrs. M. M. Moores, Mr. and Mrs. M. M. Matheson, and to the Rev. L. Kohlman, S. J., for all the hospitality they have accorded me. In Stockholm, Mrs. Kim Vintilescu, Mrs. Ingrid Samson and Mrs Gerry Hultkrantz have been of great assistance and to them, too, I express my appreciation. To Jan Vintilescu I want to voice my gratefulness for managing all of the business details pertinent to the publication of this book as well as for doing the hundreds of other jobs he has so cheerfully performed for me. I also extend my gratitude to miss Florence Vilén who has compiled the index.

My friend and former student, Emanuel Milstein of New York City, drew the maps and the language chart for this book. My indebtment to him for this and all other favors—especially those in Paris—is sincerely conveyed.

Dr. Carling Malouf, Associate Professor of Anthropology at Montana State University, deserves special commendation from me. It was he who first introduced me to the discipline of anthropology and who has encouraged me to continue in that field. I want to thank him publicly for his encouragement, assistance, and patience.

I wish to express my appreciation to the Chancellor of the University of Sweden for permitting me to matriculate at the University of Stockholm, and to the faculty of that institution for allowing me to study for the doctorate there.

To the Association on American Indian Affairs and its executive director, Miss LaVerne Madigan, I acknowledge with appreciation the financial assistance given me.

I am inadequate in the expression of my gratitude to Mrs. Ethel Hawkins for typing and re-typing this work. Often she worked until the late hours of the night. I wish to say a special thank you to her, not only for the excellence of her work but for her patience and cheerfulness while doing the task.

Stockholm, March 31st, 1962.

PREFACE

To evaluate the worth of any publication, a reader has the right to know what method the investigator used to arrive at his findings. This preface, then, deals with the way I have worked with the Indians on the Rocky Boy reservation to secure the information that I am presenting in this book.

This study has been based on the interview method. I have classified my informants into two types: the leaders and the knowledgeable. My own position is that of a participant-observer, a role that I have been able to achieve through eight years of association with these Indians. Because of my acquaintance with other Plains Indians, I have also been able to set up a control, rough as it may seem, by observing the attendance at various religious functions and noting the difference between the Rocky Boy residents and those on other reservations.

During the years that I have known these people, I have talked with many of them about varying aspects of their culture or their history. In this work, I have drawn from that knowledge, but I have concentrated on my interviews with nineteen people. Four of these I classify as "leader-informants", men who not only can give the information that is necessary, but whose opinions reflect those of their society. Of course, this practice is based upon the assumption that a leader in a democratic society knows the cultural pattern of his people. This method has been used successfully in studies of white culture; I think that the American Indians are sufficiently democratic to warrant the use of the method. Furthermore, I believe because of the face-to-face contacts of a folk society, Indian leaders are closer to the thinking of their people than are many so-designated leaders in white society. Three of the four men whom I have categorized as "leader informants" are or have been elected to the business committee of the tribe. Deference is paid to these people at meetings which I have attended—meetings that have concerned future development of the reservation, educational policies, or plans for religious or secular celebrations.

The other fifteen informants I classify as "knowledgeable informants". In using this terminology, I do not wish to imply that my leader-informants do not possess a thorough knowledge of their culture—especially their religious values—for they do. But I have separated them purposely because not all of my informants are leaders in any sense. In several instances, I have had the good fortune to secure the assistance of some informants who are quite retiring and shy. Their knowledge of their culture and their religion has depth of perception, but their introversive natures restrain them from becoming leaders.

The following information about the informants who have assisted me with the study gives some idea about the group:

Number of informants who are quoted in this study	19
Average age of informants	52.8
Range of ages—20–75	
Sex	
Male	17
Female	2
Veterans	7
World War I 1	
World War II 5	
Korean 1	
Employment (Male)	
Full time (yearly job)	1
Seasonal	13
Leave reservation during summer	7
Self-employed (farming or ranching)	2
Over-age	2
Education	
Estimated average years of formal education completed	6
Range in education completed	0–12
Number unable to speak English	2
Church Affiliation	
Nominally Christian (baptized)	13
Native American	8

In my opinion, informants are representative of residents of the reservation.

In supporting my contention that my role has been that of participant-observer, I stress again the length of time that I have known these people and they have known me. In my earliest years with them, passivity characterized my behavior. I recall the 1953 Sun Dance, the first one that I attended. During those three days, I stood near the entrance to the Sacred Lodge, watched the participants, but asked no questions. In 1954, I did much the same, but before the dance ended the Cree were talking to me. I have attempted to remain passive as I have encountered each new ceremonial since then. Time for questioning can come later, I believe. And so as my rapport has grown with the Cree Indians of Montana, my role has changed from a white observer of an alien culture to that of a participant in some ceremonials.

As I have participated I have likewise met and talked with many different individuals beyond the mere nineteen whom I have listed. For example, when one of my informants invites me to sweat with him, there are usually at least six or eight other men present. The bonds of friendship are strengthened; I am not an outsider but one of them. And my knowledge of the group grows as my acquaintanceship widens. Driving the car carrying the scouts for the sacred pole at the 1960 Sun Dance meant meeting five young men whom I had not known before. Their reticence as we went out in search of the pole was in marked contrast to the friendly conversation of the group as we returned or to their friendliness to me since. And so it has gone—I have made friends, I have talked to many different individuals, I have participated in several activities, and I have intuitively absorbed much information about these people—much more than is possible for me to analyze. For rapport is an elusive thing to view scientifically.

Yet I feel that I have established a rapport with these people. One instance illustrates my belief. One morning when I was sitting in the cabin of one of my informants visiting with the man and woman and writing the information in my notebook, a young tribal member who considers himself a "fullblood" but whose auburn-red hair, blue eyes and Nordic features would never identify him as an Indian, entered the room without knocking, as Indians always do. He lay down on one of the beds and listened to our conversation for awhile.

"What are you giving that white man all that information for?" he asked. "All he'll do with it is to write a book and make a lot of money on it. You ought to keep it to yourself and make your own money."

Unknown to him, I had learned sufficient of the Cree language to understand him. My own hosts were not sure that I could understand, but their defense of me and their repudiation of him were eloquent.

I regret that I have no formal means of maintaining a control study. Again, I have to depend upon my own observation. But Sun Dance participation gives some clue to the vitality of religion on the Rocky Boy reservation. And this vitality is especially significant when compared to the ceremony among other tribes. The following chart gives some indication: (Attendance figures are informants and mine; enrollment from BIA). The smaller number in 1961, consistent among all three tribes, may be explained by the fact that the season was a very bad one for forest fires. Trained Indian fire fighters from all three reservations were away from the reservation working to combat that emergency when the Sun Dance was being held.

Tribe	Number of Dances Per Season	Number Dancing 1960	1961	Total Enrollment
Cheyenne	2	23	17	2,100
Crow	2	75	52	4,500
Cree	2	152	131	1,450

A questionnaire might have been helpful and would perhaps have produced impressive statistical results, but I rejected the idea of using such a device purposely. I have tried to get the depth of feeling of the Crees' religious values as well as a picture of the world view of their religion. From a short questionnaire, I felt that I would be unable to do so. Furthermore, rapport is necessary in any case, for without the rapport, the results of a questionnaire might be severely questioned. Indians tend to become suspicious of filling in blanks for strangers; many times they resent doing so even when they know the person in charge. And more important to me, they are likely to give the answer they feel the investigator wants rather than their own honest responses. And lastly, I have felt that such a questionnaire as I would necessarily prepare could easily be interpreted as an intrusion into their private beliefs. Some of the tribal members, especially those who belong to the Native American Church, might easily have become hostile and thus jeopardized my entire work. Consequently, I have not used a questionnaire.

Replies of my informants, observations of my own, and intuition—these have been the elements with which I have worked on this study. One phenomenon I have discovered is that none of the customary factors that make for heterogeneity among peoples seems to affect the religious values of the Montana Cree. Age levels, work experience away from the reservation, war service, even formal education does not seem to affect their values. Approximately eighty percent of the inhabitants of the reservation seem intent upon preserving the primitive beliefs and values.

During these years that I have been with the Indians, I have seen young boys grow into manhood; I have witnessed the return of the Korean veterans to the reservation; I have seen the adjustment of World

War II veterans to civilian life; I have watched men grow older, but with the exception of the so-called "breeds"—those who are farming and ranching—I have seen the people remain close to the values and religious beliefs that served their ancestors.

It is no accident or anachronism to see, on the Rocky Boy reservation of Montana, an elderly man with braids standing directly beside a boy in his early teens as both of them dance the Sun Dance. Or to see a veteran of World War II standing to the left of the Sun Dance Leader and know that he is acting as the leader's assistant. Or to recognize one of the keepers of the pipes during the ceremony as being one of the men who has returned to the reservation, either from work in the fields of neighboring farmers or from an industrial job with the smelter in Great Falls, one-hundred miles away. Or to look at the lodges and tents in the circle surrounding the Sacred Lodge and to learn that many of these people who live there during the ceremony are fasting and praying and have come primarily for religious reasons. And in time, one is not surprised even to see the mixed bloods, the young successful operators, standing among the spectators in front of the Sacred Lodge.

Experience away from the reservation, age, formal training, association with the members of the dominant white culture—none of these seems significant. That is why I am intrigued with the persistence of these people to practice their religion. That is why I made this study.

INTRODUCTION

A study of North American Indian religion, especially that type of religion as practiced in the latter half of the twentieth century, poses many problems. One recalls immediately the long years of association with the dominant white culture and the subsequent disintegration of the native religion; one looks for evidences of diffusion or of syncretism. Certain aspects of Indian religion manifest these factors—in some instances so strong that one can suspect that very little of the original belief is left. More discouraging, however, is the fact that so many Indians seem to be living in a religious wasteland—the values of the past are gone; the Christian missions stand empty, sometimes deserted and abandoned, or else are struggling along with but a miniscule percentage of Indians in attendance at their services. Why, then, has religion which has always been a vital core in the life of mankind everywhere been so lost or weakened with the American Indian?

Before one can begin to answer that question, he has to examine, if only briefly, the attitude of the Christian conqueror with whom the Indian has been in contact for three-hundred and fifty years. Unfortunately for the Indian, the basic assumption of the Christian has militated against him. With the idea that his was the only religion, the colonist intolerantly and harshly chose every weapon at his command to eliminate Indian religion and to superimpose his own. Let us then review very briefly, and as kindly as possible, to see what has happened in North America regarding the treatment of the American Indian.

We can begin with the New England colonists. Schooled as they were to a world of order, they took one look at the Indians whom they met and immediately saw what happened to man once he was outside the refining influence of Christianity. The aboriginal Americans whom the Puritans saw were little better than animals; they "live in Caves of earth, and hunt for their dinners or praye, even as the beare or other wild beastes do. . . ."[1]

Not only was the Indian a sub-human, he was also an instrument of

---

[1] Richard Hakluyt, *The Principal Navigations* (Glasgow, 1904), Vol. VII, p. 224.

Satan. Satan possessed the Indian as witnessed by his beast-like actions; Indian worship, then, was Satan worship. And to the Puritan, inured as he was to the belief in witchcraft, the Indian provided an excellent example. In his dress, in his action, in his worship he was a living example of the Englishman's notion of a witch. The rattles, the dance, the near-nudity, the concern with ritual and the healing practices of the native doctors exemplified the work of the devil. That the Indian soon became identified with the witchcraft is evidenced by the following statement:[2]

In 1662 in Connecticut Robert Sterne saw 'two black creatures like two Indians, but taller'; as he was at a little distance it is probable that he took a plumed or horned headdress to be the same as the Indian headgear.

This association of the Indian with witchcraft had to be destroyed.

The task of the colonist was a great one. He saw his duty, though, and proceeded to do it: Christianize the Indian. For by Christianizing him he would arise from his animal nature, he would be rescued from the manipulations of Satan, he would find his place in the ordered world in which God had intended man to live. "An ordered life was the basic condition of a holy life; civilization was properly a means to holiness. The Civil and the Holy Covenants of man with God were parts of a cosmic principle of order."[3]

Despite their efforts, the task was hard. No basic understanding existed. No attempt was made to realize that the Indian might have a set of values from which he gained spiritual as well as communal strength. Instead, the philosophy was to wipe out the Indian belief. To kill the practice was to triumph over Satan. Even the way was unimportant if the end justified the means. Paying Indians to attend Christian churches was tried in Massachusetts, yet even that inducement was not successful:[4]

They convert Indians by hiring them to come & heare Sermons; by teaching them not to obey their Heathen Sachims, & by appointing Rulers amongst them over tenns, twenties, fifties, &c. The lives, Manners, & habits of those, who they say are converted, cannot be distinguished from those who are not, except it be by being hyred to hear Sermons, which the more generous natives scorne.

---

[2] From John Taylor, *The Witchcraft Delusion in Colonial Connecticut*, quoted in Margaret Murray, *Witchcult in Western Europe* (Oxford: University Press, 1921), p. 43.

[3] Roy H. Pearce, *The Savages of America* (Baltimore: The Johns Hopkins Press, 1953), p. 29.

[4] Maine Historical Society Collections (1889), Vol. IV, Series 2, p. 294.

And so the years followed, tragic and bloody. The settler received the lands he coveted; the Indians were forgotten in the background. As the settlement pattern continued across the continent, the same basic idea prevailed. Take the lands away from the Indian because in his savagery he was not using them. Christianize him and he would become a farmer. The lands were usurped; the religion ignored. Yet the logic of the Caucasian continued the same. There must be order. There must be reason. Give the Indian an opportunity, he would grasp these obvious values.

But he didn't. The missionaries tried hard enough. They established churches among all of the Indians of the United States; often, they preceded the United States army. They spent millions of dollars in an effort to convert the "heathen" on this continent, yet they never felt assured that their task was appreciated or accomplished. They became involved in politics and were instrumental in securing an infiltration into the administrative posts. Because of the missionaries, President Ulysses S. Grant issued a Peace Proclamation in 1872[5] whereby Indian reservations were to be divided among the various Christian denominations, and no other sect save the one designated by the Indian Service could offer religious services on a specified reservation. More insidious yet was the clause in the Peace Policy that insisted that the Church Boards nominate the agent for the reservation—the representative of the Department of the Interior who was responsible for the welfare of the Indian wards.

And when that policy failed and was revoked in 1885, the missions continued building schools and forcing the Indian children to attend them. Again aided by the government of the United States, the denominations secured federal aid to supplement the offerings of their members. The Indian children attended the schools, many times under threat of starvation of the parents did they not conform,[6] yet the child did not comply entirely with the teachings of the Christian churches. Despite his being forcibly retained away from the home where the influence was considered pagan and detrimental, the Indian child—bewildered and lost—still retained some of his old belief. Practices that have endured could not have done so had all belief been destroyed.

Generally, the Roman Catholic Church has had a greater degree of

[5] James P. Richardson, *Messages and Papers of the Presidents* (New York, 1913), Vol. VI, pp. 4063–4064.

[6] Verne Dusenberry, *The Northern Cheyenne*, Montana Heritage Series No. 6 (Helena: Montana Historical Society Press, 1955), p. 17.

success among the Indians than have the Protestant denominations. At least, on the surface, the Catholics have made greater strides. Part of their success stems from the ritual of the service itself. The Indian has always insisted that everything must be done in exactly the same manner whenever he is addressing his Creator or is performing any of his sacred rites. The unchanging drama of the Catholic Mass appeals to him for the same reason. Just as his religious leaders sing the same songs the same number of times as they are unwrapping a sacred bundle, so does the Catholic priest go through the same ritual each time he celebrates the Mass.

The authority of the Church accounts also for a more ready acceptance, outwardly at least, by the Indian than of the more prosaic Protestant teachings. In the Roman Catholic Church, the priest supplies the doctrine and interpretation. The Indian did not have to read the Bible or to listen to an account of its being read in a language and about a culture he could not understand. Terms familiar to every Christian—"salvation," "the Holy Land," "the Lamb of God,"—had no applicability or comparability to the Indian's knowledge of life. Neither did the Semitic terms of the Old Testament evoke any associations. It was easier, then, for him to be a Catholic; the priests made the decisions for him, and for a time it seemed to work.

Whereas the Indian was willing and in many cases anxious to augment his own ideas to to learn something of the white man's religion,[7] the Christian not only refused to accept any values other than his own but he failed to demonstrate even the basic concepts of the religion he demanded that the Indian accept. It is not necessary to recite many of the white man's failures; a few instances give the attitudes the Indian experienced as he had to reconcile himself with the teachings of the Christian church. Where was Christian understanding in a directive issued by the agent of the Blackfeet reservation[8] that ordered all Sun Dance structures to be torn down and the poles used for building corrals?

---

[7] The four excursions made by the Flathead-Salish Indians of Montana to St. Louis beginning in 1831 and ending in 1840 have long been considered the "Macedonian Cry," for here were "pagans" coming out of the wilderness seeking Christianity. Perhaps DeVoto has given the best interpretation of the missions when he said, "They (the Flatheads) wanted to acquire an advanced economy by means of the thaumaturgy which they thought made it work. They were altogether uninterested in Christian spirituality, morality, or salvation: they were satisfied with what they had." Bernard DeVoto, *Across the Wide Missouri* (Boston: Houghton Mifflin Co., 1947), p. 13.

[8] *Report of the Commissioner of Indian Affairs, 1894* (Washington: Government Printing Office), p. 159.

Or in the incident that Goddard[9] reports of the nuns from a nearby mission going out to an abandoned Sun Dance grounds and appropriating the yard goods that the Indians had left hanging on the rafters of the Sacred Lodge so that they could make dresses for their Indian charges? Or where is the Christian doctrine of the brotherhood of man revealed in the contempt the practicing Christian displays toward the Indian? And especially in the churches? Why, in two very small towns in Montana, does segregation exist? (Why are two Presbyterian Churches serving a populace of approximately one-thousand people in Poplar, Montana, and two Baptist Churches serving four-hundred people in Lodge Grass, Montana, with the lines of racial distinction rigorously observed?) These are but a few of the tensions the Indian has had to live with as he has watched the members of the dominant group reverse themselves and their religious teachings. Few of them, perhaps, are as vocal or as understanding as was Plenty Coups, one of the last great chieftains of the Crow tribe, who commented to his biographer about the situation:[10]

We made up our minds to be friendly with them, in spite of all the changes they were bringing. But we found this difficult because the white men too often promised to do one thing and then, when they acted at all, did another.

They spoke very loudly when they said their laws were made for everybody; but we soon learned that although they expected us to keep them, they thought nothing of breaking them themselves. They told us not to drink whiskey, yet they made it themselves and traded it to us for furs and robes until both were nearly gone. Their Wise ones said we might have their religion, but when we tried to understand it we found that there were too many kinds of religion among white men for us to understand, and that scarcely any two white men agreed which was the right one to learn. This bothered us a good deal until we saw that the white man did not take his religion any more seriously than he did his laws, and that he kept both of them just behind him, like Helpers, to use when they might do him good in his dealings with strangers. These were not our ways. We kept the laws we made and lived our religion. We have never been able to understand the white man, who fools nobody but himself. However, even with all our differences, we kept our friendship for him. . . .

But where have all of these experiences left the Indian? As the generations have succeeded generations, various attitudes have weakened, both toward the primitive belief and toward the Christian doctrines. At the present time, one finds Indians who are still attempting to follow

---

[9] Pliny Earle Goddard, *The Sun Dance of the Cree in Alberta,* Anthropological Papers of the American Museum of Natural History (New York, 1919), Vol. XVI, Part IV, p. 306.

[10] Frank B. Linderman, *The American* (New York: John Day Company, 1929), pp. 227–228.

Christianity—in some instances with a fair degree of success. Among other groups, Indians will turn toward any new form that is presented to them in an attempt to find some outlet for their religious needs. The success of the Pentecostal churches on the western reservations today gives an indication of the attempt some of the Indians are making.[11] Others are divorcing themselves from all Christian practices and are turning toward new movements—the emergence of the Native American Church provides a good illustration. Revivalistic movements or nativism also is occurring on many reservations; in Montana, the Crow Indians are excellent examples. Many Indians seem to be living in a religious vacuum, yet on closer scrutiny, one notices that they are forever seeking for some answer. And there are still others who have held tenaciously to the past.

To determine why the great divergence among the Indians concerning their attitudes toward religion, perhaps one should assess some of the theories about religion in general. Most of the theories concerning primitive religion support its integrative function. Durkheim[12] interpreted the group's experience of their collective power as something so meaningful that it provides the necessary basis for cohesion in society. Malinowski[13] stressed the same idea when he wrote:

... religious belief and ritual, by making the critical acts and the social contracts of human life public, traditionally standardized, and subject to supernatural sanctions, strengthen the bonds of human cohesion.

Firth emphasized the importance of religious belief and ritual to social organization:[14]

Religious rites unite the members of the society in common assembly, under an aegis which cannot be easily disputed, and so reaffirm their solidarity and enforce social interaction. Religious beliefs can supply not merely a theory for this social interaction, but also wider principles of order in the whole social universe.... They also give a frame of reference for attitudes towards nature. The position of man vis-à-vis other living things and the manner in which he proceeds to exploit natural phenomena are to be defined in their most general

[11] For a more complete coverage of the effect of the Pentecostals among the Montana Indians, see Verne Dusenberry, "Montana Indians and the Pentecostals," *The Christian Century*, Vol. LXXV, No. 30 (1958), pp. 850–852.

[12] Emile Durkheim, *The Elementary Forms of Religious Life* (London: Allen and Unwin, Ltd., 1915).

[13] B. Malinowski, *Magic, Science, and Religion* (New York: Doubleday Anchor Books, 1955), p. 24.

[14] Raymond Firth, *Elements of Social Organization* (London: Watts & Co., 1951), pp. 215–250.

terms, in regard to some religious principles. Religion, then, prompts the establishment and maintenance of social patterns outside its own immediate field.

And, finally, Radin,[15] who explains religion "as one of the most important and distinctive means for maintaining life-values," adds:

> As these (values) vary, so will the religious unit vary. Religion is thus not a phenomenon apart and distinct from mundane life nor is it a philosophical inquiry into the nature of being and becoming. It only emphasizes and preserves those values accepted by the majority of a group at a given time. It is this close connexion with the whole life of man that we find so characteristically developed among all primitive cultures and in the early phases of our own civilization. . . .
>
> In the midst of the multiplicity of life-values three stand out most prominently and tenaciously—the desire for success, for happiness, and for long life. Similarly, from among the heterogeneous mass of beliefs, the one which stands out most definitely is the belief in spirits who bestow on man success, happiness and long life. At the basis of primitive religion there thus lies a specific problem: the nature of the relation of these spirits to the life-values of man.

The unity of belief and the cohesive quality that such belief exercises upon the individuals concerned is obvious. Furthermore, it is my acceptance of these theories that provides the background for this study.

Thus it was that with religion functioning as it did in primitive times with the American Indians, the disruptive effect of the Caucasoid Christian is manifested in varying ways today. The Plains Indians now living in the state of Montana are illustrative of what has happened elsewhere. Among the Northern Cheyenne, particularly, the social organization was closely tied to the tribe's religious beliefs. Their Council of Forty-four, heralded by many as the finest and most democratic of all Plains social structure, was quasi-religious. The four high chiefs were also custodians of the sacred holies of the tribe. When the organization was destroyed, the cohesiveness of the tribe was broken. Today the Northern Cheyenne continue halfheartedly at their religious ceremonies, but the symbols of unity in the tribe—the Sacred Hat and the Medicine Arrows—are but empty tokens of something once significant.

The reservation system imposed upon the Indians by the United States Government assisted in the disintegration of their religious values. As the government forbade the great religious rites that had been the unifying force, the people were left without a sustenance of values that

---

[15] Paul Radin, *Primitive Religion: Its Nature and Origin* (New York: Dover Publications, Inc., 1957), pp. 5–14.

24

were meaningful. The economic situation, paralleling the social and religious loss, contributed to the weakening of the bonds of unity. No longer dependent upon their own resources, the Indians were forced to accept the charity of the government. And, as has been pointed out earlier, they soon learned that if they were to survive physically, it was necessary for them to pay some sort of obeisance to their superiors, particularly in religion. Yet, at the same time, they did achieve some form of security—they had their land (even though they did not know how to use it nor did they care), they had some rations, they had a hollow existence without a focus for any specific values of their own.

Without a set of religious values that were operative, most of the Indians on the reservations of western America and particularly in Montana were lost. This situation is but a further example of peoples of a dominant culture destroying the values of another group without giving them anything to replace those values. Whenever that has happened, those people of the submissive culture experience anxiety; they grasp for anything they can, indiscriminately, that presents itself to them. Outwardly, they accept and conform—for that is the easiest way to exist. Inwardly, the tensions are there. So it is with many of the once-proud Plains Indians. Indian belief has all but disappeared although Christianity has not supplanted it.

But with one small group, those on the Rocky Boy reservation, primitive religion is not only persisting, it is functioning. But the Indians on that reservation have evolved from many blood lines and numerous tribes. And they have been persecuted and have been forced to wander homeless in comparatively recent times. The force of religion—that cohesiveness of Durkheim and Malinowski and others that have been mentioned—has sustained them during their wanderings. They have reacted, as Freud says,[16] in a way that indicates that they have sought a remedy against their sense of "man's insignificance and impotence in the face of the universe".

Driven away and rejected for thirty years by the dominant culture with which they were in contact, living in a sort of sufferance for forty-five years more, they have welded themselves into a new tribe. The binding force that seems to have kept them together and caused them to evolve as a new tribe is their religious core. While they too had their anxieties, they reacted by borrowing traits from other Indian tribes to reinforce their own interpretation of the supernatural world. As can be

---

[16] Sigmund Freud, *The Future of an Illusion* (New York: Doubleday Anchor Books, 1957), p. 57.

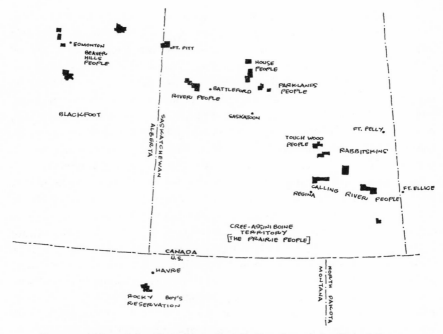

FIGURE 1. Map of the Cree reservations in Canada and the United States.

seen in the pages that follow, these people have borrowed items from many sources—from the neighboring Plains Indians, from other Woodland tribes, perhaps even from Christianity—but basically they have oriented themselves to the religion of the Cree. As a result, they have emerged as "Cree Indians," have thus formed a new tribe, and have developed a religion that not only is helpful to them, but one that has served as a binding force, a cohesiveness that has held them together in times of strife.

This study, then, is one of the Cree Indians of Montana. It is not, strictly speaking, an historical reconstruction of former Cree practices nor an ethnographic account of what is being done now, although one finds examples of both in the chapters that follow. Through these chapters I have attempted to point out how the religion is functioning today in various forms and how the practices that are being followed correlate in general with Cree beliefs elsewhere as observed by other ethnographers. I have drawn heavily for examples and contrasts from the Assiniboine Indians because the Cree have been allied with the Assiniboine for over three-hundred and fifty years, because the historical movement of this particular band of Cree has been so closely allied with the Assiniboine that the group has often been referred to as the "Cree-Assiniboine," because the nearest reservation in Montana to the Rocky Boy is the Fort Belknap where Assiniboine live, and finally, because I have spent many years doing field work with the Assiniboine on the Fort Belknap reservation.

My concern is with religion as a functioning and persevering force in the life of the Indians. Where or when they received their ideas is unimportant now; it is the belief that is important. For I believe that here on a small reservation in a lonely area of Montana, one can see how these Indians have gained recognition and cohesion through the adoption of a set of values that were meaningful to them. And, as one can see from the material that follows, the life-values that stand out most prominently are those that Radin mentioned, "the desire for success, for happiness, and for long life."

It is in this frame of reference, then, that we examine the religion of the Cree Indians of the Rocky Boy Reservation in Montana—those whom I have chosen to designate as the "Montana Cree." It is a study of a religion that is existing and persisting in the latter half of the twentieth century, for it gives to its members the sustaining quality of recognition that has been destroyed among many of the other Indian groups. And, finally, I believe this study provides an example that a people transplanted and persecuted can maintain and develop a tribal identity and unity through the continuance of their religious values.

CHAPTER I

HISTORICAL BACKGROUND

The only Cree Indians recognized by the Bureau of Indian Affairs in the United States live on the Rocky Boy reservation in northern Montana. These Cree are in Montana as a result of the Riel Rebellion in Canada in 1885; their vicissitudes in finding a home in the United States cover a period of over thirty years. Wandering homeless from one reservation to another, from one city dump to another, they finally secured a home on an abandoned military reservation where by Act of Congress they were allowed to live, only after a bitter fight on the part of the white citizenry of the area, however. For the charge was ever present—these are Canadian Indians with no claim to protection from the United States government.

In truth, they were at one time Canadian Indians. Canadian, that is, according to the fact that the Cree inhabited much of western Canada. Bands of them crossed the International Boundary between the United States and Canada at will as they followed the buffalo. But the Cree, ignorant of an imaginary line across the wide prairie, were recognized as Canadians. That many of them were born on the American side of the line seemed unimportant. Too long had their residence been associated with eastern Canada for any one to give them recognition as being Americans simply because some groups of them preferred in later years to live along the Milk River in America.

Scarcely any tribe is better known among historical references than the Cree. The first record of them is that given by the Jesuit priest, Father Barthelemy Vimont, who in 1640 mentions[1] that the Indians known as the "Kiristinon,... live on the shores of the North Seas...." The following year, 1641, Father Le Jeune wrote[2] "...our Nepisiriniens,

---

[1] Reuben Gold Thwaites (editor), *The Jesuit Relations and Allied Documents. Travels and Explorations of the Jesuit Missionaries in New France. 1610–1791* (Cleveland: Burrows Brothers Co., 1896–1901), Vol. XVIII, p. 239.

[2] *Ibid.,* Vol. XXI, p. 125.

returning not long since from the Kyristinouns[3] who trade on the Northern sea. . . ." Jesuit work began among them in 1661 when Fathers Claude Dablon and Gabriel Druilletes established a mission among them. Father Dablon mentions[4] that "Upon this bay (Hudson's) are found, at certain seasons of the year, many surrounding nations embraced under the general name of Kilistinons." Ten years later the same priest stated[5] that ". . . the Kilistinons are dispersed through the whole region to the North of this Lake Superior—possessing neither corn, nor fields, nor any fixed abode, but forever wandering through those vast forests and seeking a livelihood there by hunting."

That they had a religion of a type recognized by the priests is indicated in Father Marest's report in 1702.[6] "As for the Religion they profess . . . I cannot say in what their idolatry consists. I know they have some sort of sacrifices and they are great jugglers. . . . They use a pipe, they also smoke in honor of the sun, and also in honor of absent persons. They have smoked in honor of our Fort and our vessel."

In the same report, Father Marest indicates[7] that the Cree have moved westward and southward: "The Kriqs are numerous and their country more vast, they are spread as far as Lake Superior where many go to trade. I have seen some of them who have been at the Sault Sainte Marie and at Michilimokinak, and some who have gone as far as Montreal." Thirty-four years later, Father Aulneau indicates[8] that the Cree have moved still farther west when in his report he writes: ". . . Lake of the Woods. It is on the shores of this lake, that I purpose passing part of the summer with the Assinipoils who occupy all the land to the south of it. The lands on the remaining sides are taken up by the Krisinaux who occupy not only the northern part as far as the sea, but all the vast stretch of country beginning at the lake of the woods."

It is not necessary to trace the complete westward movement of the Cree. Mandelbaum[9] has done an excellent job of reporting the movement and has utilized the early source material well. Suffice to say that

---

[3] Many variations in spelling and usage will be found for these terms for the Cree. The Chippewa word for the Cree is *Knistenou*, a word signifying "more than one." Personal interview, Four Souls, March 10, 1960.

[4] Thwaites, *op. cit.*, Vol. XL, p. 249.

[5] *Ibid.*, Vol. LV, p. 99.

[6] *Ibid.*, Vol. LXI, pp. 109–111.

[7] *Ibid.*, p. 107.

[8] *Ibid.*, Vol. LXVIII, pp. 291–293.

[9] David Mandelbaum, *The Plains Cree*, Anthropological Papers of the American Museum of Natural History (New York, 1940), Vol. XXXVII, Part II, pp. 172–187.

the Cree early allied themselves with the English at Hudson's Bay. From that source they received guns and so armed, pushed other tribes out of their way. Also as the beaver decreased in the Woodland areas because of the ruthless trapping, the Cree pushed westward until eventually one group of them ended on the Plains where they quickly dislodged the Indians whom they found there—especially the Gros Ventre (Atsina) and the Blackfeet—and with the advent of horses, became well established in Plains culture. It should be emphasized, however, that in the movement not all the Cree came west. Those who remained behind were, in time, designated as the "Woods Cree" and the "Swampy Cree." While the material culture of the Plains Cree changed from that of their eastern brothers, other elements of their culture remained much the same.

The Plains Cree roamed over Manitoba, Saskatchewan, and Alberta. Sources indicate that they moved northward and pushed back some of the Athabaskan tribes.[10] Southward they travelled into Montana, at least as far south as the Missouri River.[11] The Milk River seems to have been a favorite rendezvous of the Cree, especially where the Milk makes its big bend north of the present city of Malta, Montana.[12] But as the encroachments began when the white settler moved west, the Plains Cree had to submit to government authority, and at Forts Carlton and Pitt, in 1876, they signed their first treaty with the representatives of the Crown.[13]

By the last part of the nineteenth century, the Cree had divided into eight loosely knit bands. Mandelbaum[14] identifies these bands as the Calling River People, the Rabbit Skin People, the Cree-Assiniboine, the Touchwood Hills People, the House People, the Parklands People (or Willow Indians), the River People, and the Upstream People (or Beaver Hills People). He states also that the Cree-Assiniboine, who were so called because of the close association and frequent intermarriage with the Assiniboine, lived farthest south and "was deepest into the true

---

[10] *Ibid.,* p. 183.

[11] *Ibid.,* p. 185.

[12] Many early accounts mention the Cree having camped frequently on the Milk River. In the vicinity of the Big Bend I have travelled for miles and found archaeological evidences of buffalo traps, so numerous that they defy counting. Both Assiniboine and white friends who have been with me in this region identify the traps as having been made by the Cree.

[13] Mandelbaum, *op. cit.,* p. 185.

[14] *Ibid.,* pp. 166–167.

plains."[15] He also says that they were sometimes called *paskwa wiyini-wak,* Prairie People.[16] These are the people who eventually moved into Montana, for the Cree living on the Rocky Boy reservation today state that they are *paskwa wiyiniwak,* Prairie People.[17]

In the years following the signing of the treaty at Fort Carlton and Fort Pitt, unrest followed. One band, the Cree-Assiniboine, is reputed not to have signed the agreement, and thus were unassigned to any reservation. This group, under the leadership of Big Bear, had spent much of its time in Montana, and after its chief's refusal to accept a reservation they wandered, especially in Montana, looking for the nearly extinct buffalo.[18] Trouble was in store not only for the non-signers of the treaty but for all the Cree during the decade following the signing of the treaty. From being proud, independent people who lived luxuriously, they were now reduced to beggary. Thus the mental outlook was right when the half breeds under the direction of Louis Riel staged a rebellion in 1885. Riel, who earlier had been the half-breed or Metis leader and who had established a provisional government in Manitoba in 1869, had left Canada and had come to the United States where in 1879 he had become a citizen. As the grievances of the Metis multiplied, a delegation headed by Gabriel Dumont came from Saskatchewan to St. Peter's Mission, near present-day Cascade, Montana, in the spring of 1884 to induce Riel to return to Canada and lead the Metis in an organized opposition to the encroachments of the Crown. When the case for the mixed bloods and the Cree was explained to Riel, he reluctantly agreed to leave his teaching position at St. Peter's and return to Canada.[19]

When war came in the spring of 1885 between the Metis and the Dominion soldiers, two bands of Plains Cree openly joined the Half Breeds—Poundmaker leading a group of the River People and Big Bear with his Cree-Assiniboine or Prairie People. Big Bear and his group were camped at Frog Lake in Saskatchewan. Hearing of the attacks

---

[15] *Ibid.,* p. 166.

[16] *Ibid.,* p. 166.

[17] Four Souls, Raining Bird, and Windy Boy, all well-informed residents of the Rocky Boy reservation, have given me this information separately and at different times over the years.

[18] Raymond Gray, "History of the Cree Nation," a W.P.A. Writer's Project, January 16, 1942. Unpublished typewritten manuscript.

[19] For a complete account of this event, as well as an extensive coverage of the Metis troubles, see Joseph Kinsey Howard, *Strange Empire* (New York: W. Morrow Co., 1952).

elsewhere, the young men of the band—especially Big Bear's son, Iman-sees (later to be known in Montana as Little Bear)—urged that they attack the white settlement nearby and destroy it.

On Maundy Thursday, April 2, 1885, two Oblate priests at Frog Lake were saying Mass when into the church strode a group of young Cree Indians from Big Bear's band. Especially noticeable was Wandering Spirit, war chief of the group, who stood defiantly and scornfully in the center aisle. Near him was Imansees. Before the Mass ended, Big Bear appeared, agitated and worried. The priests continued the Mass. A handful of white residents were in attendance and felt the tension, but the priests continued until the end of the service. At the conclusion, the Indians walked out of the church and stood waiting. Big Bear urged them to leave. Instead, Wandering Spirit deliberately waited for a trader named Quinn to come out of the church. When he did, Wandering Spirit aimed his gun and shot him. Three other white men likewise were killed. The two priests rushed out and met the same fate despite Big Bear's attempt to stop the murders. Wandering Spirit, Imansees, and the young men went into the village and killed all of the white men there with the exception of a boy named Cameron.[20] With two white women, Cameron became a prisoner of the Cree and for two months travelled over much of Saskatchewan and Alberta as the Indians eluded the army. When it became evident that they could no longer completely resist the army, Imansees and several members of Big Bear's band including Little Poplar made their way into the United States. Wandering Spirit refused to accompany them. Later he was caught and hanged. Big Bear received a three-year prison sentence.

The presence of the Cree in Montana was first noticed in the *Fort Benton* (Montana) *River Press,* December 30, 1885, in an item that reported that Lt. Robertson of the First Cavalry had turned over to the Commanding Officer at Fort Assinniboine[21] (the Army spelled the name of the fort differently from the accepted spelling of the name of the tribe) 137 Cree Indians, "62 bucks, 50 squaws, 25 children." Included in this group were Little Bear and Little Poplar. "Little Poplar, the chief proved refractory and was deposed, disarmed and tied to the wagon,"

---

[20] A good account of this incident is found in Wm. Blaisdel Cameron, *Blood Red the Sun* (Calgary: Kenway Publishing Co., 1950). The author relates his experiences as a prisoner of the Cree in a story that he wrote in his older years.

[21] A United States military post established in 1879 located sixty miles north of Fort Benton and approximately forty miles south of the Canadian border.

reads the account.[22] The correspondent also mentioned that the capture raises an "interesting point of international law," for once delivered to Fort Assinniboine, the Indians were released on orders received from Washington by wire. President Cleveland had granted them political amnesty.

Now came the years of trouble. For the next two years, Little Bear and his band spent most of their time in the vicinity of Fort Assinniboine. The men cut wood for the fort and did other jobs as required by the military force. That they were well liked appears in a statement from the Commanding Officer, Col. E. S. Otis of the 10th Infantry, who in February, 1888, wrote: "These Indians are workers, are eager to have land assigned them for cultivation and have some knowledge of soil tillage." During the severe winter of 1886 and 1887, however, most of the band camped on the south fork of the Sun River in Montana where in temperatures ranging from 35 to 40 degrees below zero and with 15 inches of snow on the ground, the *River Press* for January 19, 1887, reported that they "are in destitute condition."

Evidence is available, however, that during these first years in Montana, this band of Cree made attempts to find a place to settle and to live. In August, 1887, one of them, Pierre Busha, appeared before a council of chiefs and representatives of the Flathead, Pend d'Oreille, and Kutenai tribes and asked for homes for sixty families on the Flathead reservation. "The Indians listened attentively to the pathetic story of Riel's lieutenant who depicted the suffering, privations, and hardships of these exiles of a lost cause in their escape upon American soil where they sought refuge after the execution of their leader."[23] Michelle, chief of the Pend d'Oreille, spoke for the confederated tribes, expressed his sympathy, but could not offer the Cree a home since the government planned to move Chief Charlo's band of Salish to the reservation from the Bitter Root valley; such move would utilize all the land. Busha stayed on the Flathead reservation until that fall, however, for in late October he visited Peter Ronan, agent for the Flathead, and begged him to wire the Indian department. Ronan complied with Busha's wishes and on October 28, sent the following wire to the Commissioner of Indian Affairs:[24]

---

[22] Little Poplar was killed near Fort Assinniboine by a halfbreed scout named Ward about a year and a half or two years later over a dispute concerning the ownership of a horse. Legend has it that Little Poplar's head was severed from his body and sent to Canada in the hope of securing a reward.

[23] The *Fort Benton River Press*, August 24, 1887.

[24] The *Anaconda Standard*, January 19, 1896.

Pierre Busha of Cree refugees is now at this agency, will leave for Cree encampment in three days from date. He is desirous to learn if encouragement be given to Crees by government either to settle upon public lands or give them homes on some reservation, the Blackfeet reserve would suit them if they cannot remove to this reservation. He awaits an answer if he can encourage his people to this effect.

On October 31, the Commissioner wired his reply:

Tell Busha that the Indian department can make no promises in regards to land for British Cree refugees.

Busha took the trail to Dupuyer Creek where the Crees were encamped.

The hard winter of 1886–1887 brought trouble to the cattlemen of the northern frontier. Now that it became evident that open grazing could not meet the demands of the cattle herds, owners sought lands for their herds—lands that would produce hay—and they cast envious glances at the choice areas lying north of the Missouri River. This region was Indian land, but in 1887 and 1888 new treaties were effected with the Assiniboine, the Blackfeet, and the Gros Ventre that shrunk their reservations to a fraction of their former size. With these tribes safely on their reserves, and the Army at Fort Assinniboine ready to keep them there, the wandering displaced Cree antagonized everyone. Typical was the experience related by John W. Collins who in 1887 was manager of the Home Land and Cattle Company, an outfit that grazed 7,000 head of cattle between the Missouri and the Milk Rivers—land lying on this new domain. During the winter of 1887 and 1888, nearly forty lodges with about two hundred Cree Indians camped near the home ranch were reported as being on the verge of starvation. "The cowboys poisoned several hundred coyotes and threw the carcasses into the ravines where the Indians found them and devoured them and seemed to grow fat on the poisoned meat."[25] Later Collins reported that he had given the Indians forty head of "snowbound" cattle (that is, cattle that had frozen to death in snow banks), but at his first absence from the ranch, they came to the place, frightened Mrs. Collins, and carried off everything they wanted.

Incidents like these multiplied and grievances poured into the office of the Territorial Governer of Montana and to Washington, D. C. On April 18, 1888, the Commissioner of Indian Affairs wrote to William F. Vilas, Secretary of the Interior: "I am aware that these refugees are not native Indians of the United States, nor that they have rights on

---

[25] The *Anaconda Standard,* January 19, 1896.

any of our Indian reservations, but as a simple act of humanity, I think they should be given a chance to earn their bread when that is all they ask. They have been wandering about from place to place . . . homeless and helpless. . . ."[26]

Montana became a state in 1889, and its first governor, Joseph K. Toole, received letters from several people in Montana complaining about the Cree and stating the "British Cree were flocking into the state." All of the letters, plus a request of his own, went to Washington. Finally, on September 24, 1892, L. A. Grant, Acting Secretary of War, forwarded a report from the Commanding General of the Department of Dakota to the Governor:[27]

Enquiry from all Posts in this Department on the Northern Frontier fails to establish that there have been any recent incursion of Cree Indians who were political refugees who took part in the Riel Rebellion. These have been permitted to remain and have been up to 1887 fed and clothed through the intervention of the Army. At the present time, these Cree men and women in Montana and North Dakota are employed by Citizens in wood chopping and laundry and other works, which shows that they are very useful, are well conducted and would be greatly missed in the industries of the country were they now removed. This information comes from citizens.

Governor Toole left office, and his successor, Governor John Rickards, seems to have intensified his efforts to rid the state of "These Dirty Crees," as the *Anaconda Standard* for January 10, 1896, headlined them. "Silver Bow County would gladly part with the renegades. . . . The renewed efforts by Governor Rickards to solve the Cree difficulty has great hopes in Silver Bow County. . . . The county is practically supporting between fifty and one hundred of these Canadian beggars. . . ." A few days later, Governor Rickards wrote to Richard Olney, Secretary of State:[28]

Sire, this office has had previous correspondence with department of State in relation to the presence of a number of Cree Indians in our state. These Indians are wards of the British government and generally referred to as refuges of the Riel Rebellion. In default of a reservation and the restrictions of the Federal government, they have become an intolerable nuisance constantly violating our game laws, foraging our herds, and not infrequently looting isolated cabins. The patience of our people has been sorely tried.

[26] *Senate Reports,* Vol. 4, No. 821, 54th Congress, 1st Session.

[27] Official Correspondence Relating to Admission of Montana as a State into the Union Including Proclamations and Official Address of Joseph K. Toole (Helena, 1892). Compiled by R. P. Stout, Private Secretary to the Governor.

[28] *Senate Reports,* Vol. 4, No. 821, 54th Congress, 1st Session.

While Governor Rickards was attempting to remove the Cree, some of them—including Little Bear, were already out of the state. Prompted no doubt by the success of Wild West shows some years earlier that had featured Sitting Bull, two Helena entrepreneurs named Davenport and Beveridge conceived the idea of starting their own show and using the Cree Indians as a main attraction. Their show was known as "Montana's Wildest West Show," and it advertised its feature the Cree Indians who had taken part in the Canadian Riel Rebellion—"the only people in the United States without a country."[29]

Travelling in a special train, the show troupe left Helena in April, 1895, stopped at Havre, Montana, where more Cree joined the group, and then moved on to Joliet, Illinois, where it opened its first performance. Later, it played in Chicago, New York, and New Orleans. Reports differ as to its success. Davenport and Beveridge claimed that the Indians were not very good actors and that the excursion was not a success. The Indians maintained that the show did take in a considerable amount of money, but that they did not receive anything more than enough money to buy food. They also said that Beveridge and Davenport left them stranded in Cincinnati Ohio, early in the spring of 1896, and that they had a terrible time getting back to Montana.[30]

Before they had returned to the state, however, Congress had appropriated $5,000.00 "to remove from the State of Montana and to deliver at the International boundary line the refugee Canadian Cree Indians...."[31] Shortly after Little Bear and his stragglers returned to Montana, Major J. M. J. Sanno of the Third Infantry, arrived in Montana from St. Paul, Minnesota, under orders to inquire into the Cree situation. This was June, 1896. The government seemed to be undecided whether deportation should include Cree who had certificates showing that they were Montana born and thus not wards of the Canadian government. Governor Rickards insisted, however, that all Cree must be sent to Canada as "they are caught."[32] Within a week, First Lieutenant J. J. Pershing,[33] commanding a 10th Cavalry unit from Fort Assinniboine, surprised an encampment of Cree near Great Falls, Montana, and arrested them. Telling them that the "Great Mother of

---

[29] Raymond Gray, *op. cit.*

[30] *Ibid.*

[31] *Senate Reports*, Vol. 4, No. 821, 54th Congress, 1st Session.

[32] The *Great Falls Tribune*, June 11, 1896.

[33] Later General of the Army, John J. Pershing, A. E. F. Commander during World War I and a military hero. The *Great Falls Tribune*, June 19, 1896.

Canada" had granted full pardon to them for all acts done in the Riel Rebellion and that no punishment awaited them, Pershing stationed soldiers at intervals around the camp and told the Indians that they were under arrest. John Hoffman, an attorney in Great Falls, promptly appeared in court for the Cree and said that the act of Congress did not authorize the deportation but merely made an appropriation for their deportation; that the law reads "Canadian Cree," and that at least sixty American citizens born in Montana were being deported contrary to the Constitution of the United States.[34] Judge Benton ruled, however, that the state courts had no authority to act and that the deportation should proceed.

At the same time, detachments of soldiers began a systematic state-wide roundup. The *Helena Independent* of June 26, 1896, gleefully announced that a trainload of "Cree and their horses and dogs," had passed through Helena enroute to Coutts, Alberta. The same article stated that the problem was growing more complicated because many of those caught claimed to be Gros Ventre, Assiniboine, or Chippewa. From Fort Assinniboine an officer wrote Governor Rickards to the effect that ". . . about seventy Indians have been turned loose upon the grounds that they were not Cree. Some did belong upon the Belknap reservation, but were caught in the dragnet while troops were sweeping the country. Others were real Chippewas who never have been confined to any reservation but have been camp followers or hangers on about the Assiniboine and Gros Ventre camps since the memory of man runneth not to the contrary."[35]

By July 9, all the money appropriated by the United States Congress was exhausted and there were still approximately 192 Indians yet to be taken to Canada. Since the appropriation was exhausted, there was nothing left to do but to force them to march approximately two-hundred and fifty miles from Helena to the Canadian border. They travelled through a rain storm, with the roads wet and muddy, and every night forced to sleep upon the damp ground. Four persons died on the trip.[36] The Royal Mounted Police of Canada sent two constables to the border to meet the detachment of American soldiers and the 192 Cree. As soon as Little Bear and Lucky Man crossed the border, they were arrested for complicity in the Frog Lake murders. The other Cree dispersed, and many of them were back to the Milk River in Montana before the

---

[34] The *Great Falls Tribune,* June 26, 1896.

[35] The *Helena Independent,* June 26, 1896.

[36] Raymond Gray, *op. cit.*

soldiers who had escorted them to the border had returned to their headquarters at Fort Assinniboine, also near the Milk River. The *Great Falls Tribune* called the arrest of Little Bear and Lucky Man "... an outrageous breach of faith.... As it now stands, Indians have a right to say that the word of a United States Army officer was used to induce them to walk into a trap which had been treacherously laid for them."[37]

One of the best descriptions of what happened to the Cree is found in a letter written by A. M. Hamilton, later secretary of the Saskatchewan Historical Society, to Mrs. Anne McDonnell, for many years librarian of the Montana Historical Society:[38]

The majority of the Cree were taken and distributed on various Canadian reserves and caused no more trouble. Aimiceese (a variant of Imansees, Little Bear's Canadian name) and Lucky Man, however, were well known to have been the prime movers in the Frog Lake Affair, and who by proclamation had been excluded from the terms of amnesty, were at once arrested and charged with the murder of Thomas Quinn and others. Preparations were made to bring them to trial, but eleven years had passed since the Rebellion and it was difficult to obtain witnesses. All the white people had been killed, except for two women and the boy Cameron, and they were in such a state of fear and excitement that the two women at least had no definite recollection of the circumstances. Cameron had been at his store at the time and apparently did not see the actual killing.

It was, therefore, very difficult to get witnesses who could convict these two men. It was decided to send to Fort MacLeod for the Cree woman who was Quinn's widow. ... If she identified Aimiceese (Little Bear) and Lucky Man, they would be committed for trial, otherwise proceedings would be abandoned.

I was present in the office of the Indian Commissioner at Regina when Mrs. Quinn was brought there to identify or repudiate the killers of her husband. It was a dramatic scene and one that I will never forget. Mr. A. E. Forget, the Indian Commissioner, sat behind his big desk, looking as always, very dignified. Beside him sat Major Perry of the Northwest Mounted Police. ... The two prisoners were brought in manacled. Aimiceese sat in a chair facing the Commissioner and the police officer, while Lucky Man sat on the floor shrouded in his blanket. Aimiceese was a striking looking man, and I should judge about forty years old or more. He was much stouter than the Crees usually are and powerfully built. He had a predatory falcon face and he looked around the room with a bold and insolent air. His handcuffs he concealed in the folds of his blanket. Lucky Man was a dreadful looking rascal, thin and emaciated, with his face seamed by a thousand wrinkles. ... Two Red Coats, with side arms and open holsters, stood beside the prisoners as guards. Johnny Pritchard, a young half-breed, the son and brother of the two men who had saved the lives of Mrs. Delaney and Mrs. Gowenlock (the two women who had been

---

[37] The *Great Falls Tribune*, July 4, 1896.

[38] Letter dated January 12, 1942, now in the files of the Historical Society of Montana, Helena.

38

captured by the Cree at the outbreak at Frog Lake in 1885), stood between the prisoners and the Commissioner, in the traditional attitude of an Indian interpreter, with his hat held in both hands across his breast.

When all were in place, Forget said, 'Pritchard, bring in the woman.' Johnny went out and returned with Mrs. Quinn. She was a large and bulky Cree woman of the pure blood and had no English.[39] Mr. Forget said, 'Tell her, Pritchard, to look at these two men and say if she has ever seen them before.' Pritchard rendered this into Cree and Mrs. Quinn, despite her great bulk, walking in moccasined feet as lightly as a cat, walked to the prisoners and gave them careful scrutiny. It was a tense moment. There is no doubt that both men knew that what the woman said meant their freedom or shameful death, but neither gave the slightest sign. Aimiceese continued to boldly stare about the room. ... Lucky Man paid no attention.

There was silence for a moment, broken only by the metallic clink of the handcuffs on Lucky Man's wrists. Then the woman came to a pause and spoke in Cree to the interpreter. 'What does she say, Pritchard?' said Forget. 'She says, Sir,' said Johnny, 'she has never seen either of these two men before.' 'By Gad!' said Mr. Forget, 'I might have known. These are her own people and it was only her husband that they murdered.'

Subsequently, they were both released.

Five years later the Cree were back in Montana and the press in the state was crying for their expulsion. The *Anaconda Standard* recommended that "The Cavalry should cooperate with the agents in driving the Crees off every reservation."[40] The *Montana Daily Record* of Helena reminded its readers that these Cree were the Indians that had been moved by the War Department in 1896, but "...had hurried back to Montana as soon as the soldiers were gone." Also, the correspondent of the same paper in the same issue voiced the fear that the Cree would carry smallpox throughout the state. "...and it will be impossible to prevent epidemic of smallpox along our northern border unless these people... who are continually wandering about like gypsies are removed," he wrote.[41]

Little Bear, still undaunted by the rebuffs he received, used every source open to him during the next few years to try to help his people. In 1908 he and members of his band collected cones from the lodgepole pine and sold the seeds to nurseries in the state. When a few years later, he heard that Franklin K. Lane, Secretary of the Interior, was in Helena, "...he stalked into the lobby of the Placer Hotel at Helena and had a

---

[39] Mrs. Quinn subsequently remarried two times; each of her husbands, like Quinn, was part white. Her sons and daughters and their progeny people the Rocky Boy reservation today.

[40] The *Anaconda Standard*, August 1, 1901.

[41] The *Montana Daily Record*, August 1, 1901.

conference with the representatives of the White Father. 'God was taking care of us all right until the white man came and took the responsibility off His hands. Last winter our wives and our children lived on dogs and the carcasses of frozen horses to keep from starving.' 'God ordained,' said the Secretary, 'that man must work to live and nobody gets the land who does not use it. The white man took the land to raise wheat and corn and oats and cattle. The land produces nothing. It is the man who produces things.' 'That's what we're after,' responded the sober old chief."[42]

As the years passed and Little Bear saw the futility of securing land for his people, he began to relinquish some of his leadership. He knew that he was under the stigma of being a participant and leader of the Canadian murders, even though the courts there had cleared him. He seemed to realize that he could not secure for his people rights on American soil. Hence, as a matter of expediency, he joined forces with another band of Indians who had been wandering over Montana seeking a home, that of Rocky Boy and his band of Chippewa.

Whether it is Rocky Boy's Chippewa who were the "camp followers and hangers on about the Assiniboine and Gros Ventre camps since the memory of man runneth not to the contrary"[43] is a matter of speculation. We know that Rocky Boy was a Chippewa, some say Canadian, most agree that he was American born. His wife and one of Big Bear's wives were cousins.[44] Undoubtedly, the two men had a long acquaintance and the two groups had intermingled and intermarried. We know too that the public had been cognizant of Rocky Boy's presence in Montana for many years since in 1904 a bill was introduced into the United States Senate to provide a home for Rocky Boy and his group of 110 wandering Indians on the Flathead reservation.[45] The bill was killed, however, and it was not until 1909 that any action was again started to secure a place for them.

When the attention of Helena residents was called to the starving condition of the Indians, they immediately acted by sending food, clothes, and blankets. The response was reported in the *Helena Daily Independent*, January 10, 1909, as follows: "With tears streaming down his cheeks while resting in the snow on his knees, and with his hands

---

[42] The *Cut Bank Pioneer Press*, August 8, 1913.

[43] See footnote 35 of this chapter.

[44] The relationship between these men was supplied to me by Four Souls, son of Little Bear.

[45] *Senate Reports,* Vol. 4, No. 1020, 58th Congress, 2nd Session.

lifted in supplication, Chief Rocky Boy . . . offered thanks to the people of Helena . . . saying God would bless them." In Great Falls, William Bole, editor of the *Great Falls Tribune* who had known Rocky Boy for many years, began a crusade in his paper for support. "His (Rocky Boy's) annually starved women and children get kicked around from pillar to post, enmeshed with department red tape, and nothing is done about it."[46] Charles M. Russell, later to become Montana's foremost cowboy artist, started a subscription list in Great Falls to provide assistance to the homeless band of Chippewa. He is quoted[47] as saying, "It doesn't look very good for the people of Montana if they will sit and see a lot of women and children starve to death in this kind of weather. Lots of people seem to think that the Indians are not human beings at all and have no feelings. These kind of people would be the first to yell for help if their grub pile was running short and they didn't have enough clothes to keep out the cold, and yet because it is Rocky Boy and his bunch of Indians they are perfectly willing to let them die of hunger and cold without lifting a hand."

Judge Hunt of Helena was among the sympathetic officials who became interested in the Chippewa. As a result of his wires to Washington, a special investigation was ordered which resulted in the Secretary of Interior directing the General Land Office to set aside certain lands for their use.[48] The Commissioner of Indian Affaire directed T. W. Wheat, a clerk in the allotting service, to proceed to Helena to investigate the condition of the band.

In a letter to the Commissioner written from Browning, Montana, and dated April 20, 1909, Mr. Wheat reports:[49]

I have found Chief Rocky Boy and a portion of his band camped near the slaughter houses about one mile east of Helena. From Rocky Boy I learned that his band of Indians was scattered over the western part of Montana. . . . It may be stated here that there are a great many Canadian Crees roaming over the entire state of Montana, but very few are affiliated with Rocky Boy's band of Chippewas. . . .

I found that the Indians belonging to this band are very poor. Nearly all of them are camped in the neighborhood of slaughter houses near the towns and cities, and their food is limited to bread and refuse that they receive from these slaughter houses. They obtain their flour, clothing, bedding, camp equipage,

[46] The *Great Falls Tribune*, January 8, 1909.

[47] *Ibid.*

[48] *Ibid.*

[49] A copy of this letter is on file at the Rocky Boy Sub-Agency. Permission to use the files and copy the letter was generously given by Robert Crawford, formerly Assistant Superintendent at Rocky Boy.

etc., by selling bead work and polished cow horns made into hatracks. A few of the men work on ranches and at cutting wood. They seem to be willing to work after they receive employment, but they are backward about looking for work. These Indians know no home except ragged filthy tents.

From Helena, it is about 400 miles, as the crow flies, to the lands on which it is proposed to locate these Indians. ... It is impossible for the Indians to make this journey by their own efforts. Their horses are not equal to the task of making the trip, and the Indians have absolutely no means of subsistence on the way. In view of the long journey, the condition of the Indians' horses and the utter lack of any means of subsistence, I would respectfully suggest that the Indians, their horses, wagons, and camp equipage be loaded on freight train and taken to the lands on which they are to be located.

The land set aside for the Chippewa was in the extreme northeastern corner of Montana. Reports vary as to why they were not sent—some hint that J. J. Hill, president of the Great Northern Railway Company and promotor of white settlement in the area, used his influence to open the land for homesteaders. "The *Tribune* made a blunder in trying to fasten public prejudice in the affair by associating it almost exclusively with President Hill of the Great Northern Railway Company and intimating that it was a purely selfish motive that caused him to take the interest he did in the matter (the opening of the land for white occupancy) that resulted so happily for eastern Valley county," editorialized the *Havre* (Montana) *Plaindealer,* November 6, 1909.

On the same date, the editor of the *Great Falls Tribune* reminded his readers of the public subscription that had been made by Great Falls residents for the benefit of Rocky Boy and his people the preceding winter. He also stated that a check for the amount of the subscription had been forwarded to Helena where the group was living. The editor wrote:

... it (the check) was returned with the information that the government was at last awake to its responsibility and ... that Rocky Boy and his band would be fed and cared for and located on land in the spring. Then the government went to sleep again and more red tape was wound around Rocky Boy and his band. Winter was approaching and the lean hunger wolf grinned at the lodge doors. An urgent appeal was sent to Washington for relief of these Indians. The *Tribune* was creditably informed that about $65 was spent in telegraphing back and forth to all sorts of absent officials and after 17 days of this sort of monkey business, the princely sum of $100 was forwarded to relieve the necessities of about 125 people during the winter. Then Rocky Boy's band scattered again. They deemed it safer to trust to the tender mercies of a Montana winter than to the Great White Father which had so often proved a broken reed to pierce their hand.

Public pressure to provide a home for this band of Indians continued to mount, however, during the summer of 1910. That autumn the

Indians were shipped to Browning and the Blackfeet reservation from Helena in boxcars. According to Malcolm Mitchell,[50] a Chippewa who was with the group and who now lives on the Rocky Boy reservation, most of the people who went to the Blackfeet reservation were Chippewa although he remembers that there were a few Cree including Little Bear. Mitchell stated that the Blackfeet each had been allotted 320 acres while the Chippewa and the Cree who were sent there each received 80 acres. Several of the members, Mitchell remembers, stayed on their allotments for three years and during that time Little Bear was the outspoken critic of their location. He was particularly dissatisfied with the small acreage given to the newcomers in contrast to the amount of land that had been allotted to the Blackfeet. Also the Blackfeet made the Chippewa and the Cree feel inferior and unwanted.

The superiority manifested by the Blackfeet further incensed Little Bear. A powerful speaker and dynamic leader, he enlisted Rocky Boy's support and urged that they leave the Blackfeet reservation. This time the canny chief suggested that Rocky Boy, a more kindly and less controversial figure, should agitate for another refuge. One argument that Little Bear used was the location of their lands, an area lying in the extreme northwestern corner of the Blackfeet reservation adjacent to Glacier National Park and the International Boundary. Snow, Little Bear pointed out, was so deep and the winter season so long that no profitable living could be made in that area.[51] About the time that the vocal Little Bear was making these suggestions, talk was beginning to be heard about the plans the army had for abandoning the military reservation surrounding Fort Assinniboine.

The impending closing of Fort Assinniboine and the notice that the lands would be open for homesteading in another year brought a gleeful notice in the *Havre Plaindealer,* December 9, 1911. Two hundred thousand acres would soon open adjacent to Havre. Havre residents were loud in their attempts to keep any of the former military reservation out of the hands of the Indians, for one suggestion was made early that the buildings at the Fort, valued at $2,000,000, be given to Rocky Boy and his band. While the newspapers in the area carried on the fight against such action, Congress gave the buildings and one section of the

---

[50] Personal interview, March 24, 1953.

[51] Even with mechanized equipment, the present-day Blackfeet as well as the white residents of that region are frequently marooned there during the winter months. Such a situation occurred as late as the winter of 1957, when supplies had to be dropped by air to them.

land to the State of Montana.[52] In the meantime, the newspaper row continued.

An editorial in the January 11, 1913, issue of the *Havre Plaindealer* was directed against "Rocky Boy and his band of trifling, lazy, renegade Chippewa Indians. . . . Located near Havre, they would inevitably become a charge upon the bounty and charity of local people. There is no earthly reason why these people should be sluffed off by the government on Havre." Finally a state senator from Havre presented a resolution to the Montana Senate asking Congress not to place the Indians on the Fort Assinniboine reservation.[53]

William Bole, the crusading editor from Great Falls who was always alert to the Indians' problems, came to the defense of the Chippewa and attacked the memorial in his editorial in the *Great Falls Tribune*, January 19, 1913. After reviewing the sufferings of the Indians, he wrote:

> The government of the United States owes them a debt. It is a debt of honor. The fact that the Havre folk or the Great Falls folk, or any other people in the State do not like to have them around makes no difference. . . . While we agree with the people of Havre that they should not be located near that city or any other city, it is because we are sure that it would be bad for the Indians rather than the people living in these cities. Rocky Boy and his band have the prior claim in Washington.
>
> These Indians have no powerful friend, they have no money, they have no property. They have nothing to commend themselves to the favor of any white man, but a claim that has justice and equity back of it. We hope they will get a reserve of land assigned to them . . . and with this land we hope they will get houses and stock and tools and food and everything they need to give them independence and self-support. And when they do get this they will get nothing more than long delayed justice. . . . The condition of Rocky Boy and his band is dark with dishonor to every member of the white race. That memorial to Congress needs radical amendment in order to express the truth.

Frank B. Linderman, later to become an outstanding writer about Indians of the West, visited the Rocky Boy camp near Helena on March 9, 1913. A few days later he was in Great Falls and the *Great Falls Leader* for March 13, 1913, printed an interview with him. "Jealous boomers who look forward to the complete settling of the West stand in the way of giving land to the Indians. . . . Each hour the task of aiding them becomes greater and the condition worse because the game is going and the farmer is coming. . . . Assinniboine is an abandoned military reserva-

---

[52] The *Havre Plaindealer*, December 21, 1912.
[53] The *Havre Plaindealer*, January 25, 1913.

44

tion and belongs to the national government. ... Land boomers have their eyes on it and the politicians will listen to them." To which the *Havre Plaindealer* retorted two days later: "Frank Linderman who has gained his knowledge of the noble redman from a too faithful reading of Leatherstocking Tales in which Pathfinder and Deerslayer, Indian heroes, had been exalted for their fidelity to principle and to whom faculties of reasoning almost superhuman were given by the author has become interested in Chief Rocky Boy and his tribe of human scavengers and has determined to find for them a haven upon the Assinniboine military reservation."

Late in November of 1913, Editor Bole went to Washington, D. C. to enlist the support of the Department of Interior in securing a place for the Indians on the Assinniboine reserve. He found hope that such action could be accomplished and that rations would be provided during the coming winter.[54] Promptly a delegation of three Havre citizens went to Washington bent on protesting against putting Rocky Boy and his Indians on the old military reserve. In an interview with Cato Sells, Commissioner of Indian Affairs, the Havre trio brought out:[55] (1) that most of these Indians were Canadian Cree; (2) that the Indians had no claims to Assinniboine lands; (3) that the lands are most valuable and desirable for white settlers; (4) that the Indians are notoriously improvident.

Some months after their visit to Washington, the Havre residents received a letter from Montana's senator, Henry L. Myers, who informed them that Commissioner Sells had agreed to move the Indians back to the Blackfeet Indian reservation. That they were not moved is evidenced in the Cut Bank *Press,* July 3, 1914, which reported:

The Havre papers are very peevish over the efforts being made to set aside the Assinniboine reservation as a home for Rocky Boy. The editors of the Havre papers are holding up their lily-white hands in horror at the prospect of having these nomads at their front doors, occupying the choicest tract of the land in the Bear Paw settlement and are scolding everybody concerned because they were not permanently placed upon the Blackfeet reservation, which according to their myopic view seems fit only for the homeless and unfortunate band. ... It is a ridiculous assumption and a brazen affront to the residents of the Blackfeet to assert in one breath that the Assinniboine is too good for the Rocky Crees and that the proper place for them is on the Blackfeet reservation. ...

[54] The *Great Falls Tribune,* December 1, 1913.
[55] The *Havre Plaindealer,* December 27, 1913.

Throughout the rest of 1914 and during all of 1915, the battle raged over the settlement of Rocky Boy and his people. Finally, fearing presidential veto from President Wilson unless some lands were set aside for Rocky Boy,[56] Senator Myers introduced a bill in April, 1916, setting aside 30,900 acres of Fort Assinniboine as a permanent reservation for Rocky Boy's band of Chippewa and for other homeless Indians in Montana. The bill passed and the Indians were given 56,035 acres of lands.[57]

Thirty-one years after they had left Canada, Little Bear and his people had a home!

---

[56] The *Havre Plaindealer*, February 13, 1915; April 1, 1916.
[57] *U. S. Statutes 38*, No. 807.

CHAPTER II

THE RESERVATION YEARS

One year after the creation of the reservation named for him, Rocky Boy died. Little Bear lived until 1921. Both men are buried on the reservation, Little Bear in the cemetery near the Agency, while Rocky Boy lies on a little hill top in Parker Canyon about three miles from the agency center. A small house covers his grave. Tobacco and food are frequently left there.

With the setting aside of land for the Indians, problems immediately began to arise as to who was eligible for American citizenship (or, in this case, wardship). Of the 658 names[1] submitted to Washington, 206 were eliminated, and on July 16, 1917, the final roll of 452 Indians who were declared to be entitled to membership and to the benefits of the reservation was announced. In 1935, some of those whose names had been eliminated were adopted into the tribe with the permission of the Bureau of Indian Affairs. Some of those rejected remained in Montana, and they and their progeny constitute some of the unaffiliated group that are known as the Landless Indians of Montana. Members of that organization claim that those adopted by the Rocky Boy tribe in the 1930's were principally Canadian-born Cree, while they, the American-born Chippewa, have been denied the privileges accorded the Canadians.[2]

Trouble was not over, the Cree soon found, even though they now had a reservation. In the first place, the region was small and mountainous, for the least desired area of the old military reservation had been given the Indians. Problems of authority arose, for these two bands, Little Bear's and Rocky Boy's, had wandered for years at will and were not ready to accept the responsibility of permanency. Housing and land utilization posed more difficulties. Schools to the ever-wander-

---

[1] Tentative roll of Rocky Boy Indians, May 30, 1917. Photostatic copy on file in the office of the sub-agent, Rocky Boy Agency, Montana. Files made available to me by Robert Crawford, formerly sub-agent at that reservation.

[2] Joe Dussome, president of the Landless Indians of Montana, so believes.

ing Cree were an anathema. "Civilization" was not an easy quality to acquire.

John B. Parker was the first superintendent of the reservation. Rocky Boy, Little Bear, and Peter Kenawais formed an executive council while Roger St. Pierre acted as the government-appointed farmer. "Poor Rocky Boy had little better luck than Moses, for he lived to enter the promised land and died soon after."[3]

Among the early actions taken for the residents of the new reservation was the assignment of lands. It seemed to be the intent of the government to provide small homes for the Indians where the families might secure enough income by farming, perhaps with some supplemental earnings, to support themselves. Thus 160 acres were assigned to each member of the tribe who applied. The first assignment was always just for two years; after that, it could be for any length of time. Families have now lived on the same piece of ground for two generations, and a person is able to will his assignment to his heir. Buildings have been considered as personal property and can be moved or willed to the heir also.[4]

Describing the situation that has resulted from the assignments as well as mentioning the trouble encountered, the unknown authors of a document now on file in the tribal office are quite specific. The following paragraphs come from that source:[5]

The lands of the Reservation have been assigned in units of 160 acres to eligible members. Some of the units would be and are capable of supporting a family, but the vast majority of these units are not. Most of the land on the reservation is dry land and range land. In recent years a small acreage of irrigated land has been acquired. The dry land suitable for farming will probably produce wheat on the average of about 10 bushels to the acre. The range land will carry one cow for every 2 acres. Some of the better mountain range will support one cow for every 20 acres during the summer months.

These assignments entitle the member to use and to occupy the land. It does not give him title to the land or allow him to pass it on to a purchaser or an heir at his death. Most of the homes are built from logs, and in the beginning many were roofed with sod. The government established loan funds, but the limit on one loan was around $600 to an individual. With this sum he was to buy cattle, equipment, materials to get started on, and probably eat. The start

---

[3] From a typed coverage of problems on the Rocky Boy reservation entitled "The Promised Land." No date or author is given. The manuscript was loaned to me by George Denny, secretary to the tribal council, September 1, 1960, and is on file at the tribal office.

[4] Personal interview, George Denny, September 1, 1960.

[5] See footnote 3, this chapter.

was too small and the people assigned were not experienced enough at that time to have much of a chance of becoming self supporting.

If a member desired to be a dry land farmer, he would be assigned to 160 acres of dry land. Using good farming practice he would summer fallow one-half of that each year. Thus he would be able to plant only about 80 acres of crop each year. In an average year he would harvest about 800 bushels of wheat. If the cost of working the ground and harvesting the crop is subtracted from the value of that crop, very little is left. In addition there is the initial investment for machinery and improvements which must be repaid. The income from such a unit of land is not sufficient and the assignee soon loses interest in that type of project and looks for greener pastures.

The member who desires to enter the cattle business has had a better chance of success, but he too has had his troubles and handicaps. A cattleman also is entitled to a 160-acre assignment as his home. In addition some of the land on the reservation has been used as a Tribal Grazing Reserve and the cattlemen run their cattle on this during the summer months. However, the winter feeding has in the main been up to the individual cattlemen. Some of the individual assignments are capable of raising feed for 40 or 50 cattle in good years, but most of these assignments cannot produce hay or feed or forage for more than 20 or 30 cattle.

If a cattleman had prospered and saved over a period of years and has built his herd up to 30 head, he can probably count on about 24 calves a year. If he sells these for $75.00 a head, his income for the year would be about $1800. However, out of this sum he must pay a range and bull fee of $7.00 a head, his haying and farming expenses, and make repayments on any loans he may have had. Once again we see that very little is left over for actual living expenses. In addition he has had to remain on his assignment and tend his crops or haying during the summer and feed his cattle during the winter. If the winter is severe he may have to buy some additional hay and some more of his profit is gone. By hard work and by leading a very frugal existence, a cattleman in this class might be able to get along with a minimum of aid.

For a variety of reasons, most of the members have not been as successful in the cattle raising business. Due to loans being made in quite limited amounts, most of the assignees have started out with too few cattle to ever be able to build up a sizeable herd. A man with a start of ten or fifteen cattle is in the position of not being able to stay on his assignment and make a living and not being able to leave his assignment for fear of losing what start he does have in the cattle business. Other reasons for the failure of some of the cattlemen are drouth conditions and lack of feed, low cattle prices, failure to put up all the available hay in the summer time, and poor business practices.

The assignment system has not seemed to foster a sense of permanency among the inhabitants of the Rocky Boy reservation.

Instead of living on the lands assigned or available to be assigned, the Indians at first chose to reside in a central camp at the agency. Their frequent absences from the reservation and the difficulties involved in getting their children to school were most frequently heard as reasons for the lack of interest in moving away from the camp. In May, 1930,[6] the government issued an ultimatum to disband the central camp and remove to farms within thirty days. Accordingly, fifty or more families are reported to have moved to farms and started some form of agriculture.[7]

Another indication that trouble had arisen during the first decade of reservation life was disclosed when a special investigation was conducted in 1929 before a subcommittee of the Senate Committee on Indian Affairs. The chairman was Senator Burton K. Wheeler of Montana who returned to his home state to conduct the meetings. It was disclosed[8] that the autocratic superintendent then in charge of Rocky Boy's reservation required the Indians to work their land, raise a garden, and perform other jobs as specified or else be placed in jail. The Committee reported that schools were overcrowded and incompetent and that hospital facilities were non-existent. A doctor from Havre came one day a month, a distance of twenty-five miles, to check their health. (It has always seemed rather ironic that this doctor, who was so employed by the Indian Service, was one of the three men from Havre who in 1913 had gone to Washington to protest the granting of a reservation to these Indians.)

Following the visit of the investigating committee, the health program seemed to be expanded, for two years later we find reported[9] that a field nurse visited each of the families at least once a week. In addition to the nurse, the contract doctor received visitors in his Havre office as well as making semi-monthly visits to the reservation. Schools also were provided; in the next two years, Haystack, Sangrey, and Parker day schools were built as well as a new one at the Agency. Schools, however, were not restricted to academic training, for some of them maintained herds of milk cows and flocks of chickens. The products, milk and eggs, were used to provide noon meals at the schools. "In this way, a profitable source of food revenue is established and, not the less valuable, the children are taught fundamentals of poultry raising."[10] The value of such training from the standpoint of permanency may be

---

[6] Margery Burg, "Much Accomplished Among Rocky Boy Indians on Reservation," *Great Falls Tribune,* July 3, 1932.

[7] *Ibid.*

[8] "Survey of Conditions of Indians in the United States," Hearing before a Subcommittee of the Committee on Indian Affairs, U. S. Senate, 72nd Congress, 1st Session. Part 23, Montana.

[9] Burg, *op. cit.*

[10] *Ibid.*

questioned. Nearly thirty years later, neither milk cows nor chickens are to be seen in the farmyards of the inhabitants of the Rocky Boy's reservation.

Events of more lasting nature than chicken raising occurred to the Indians on the reservation in the early 1930's, however. Under the Roosevelt administration in Washington, John Collier, Commissioner of Indian Affairs, began active programs on the reservations of America. Shortly after his appointment, Congress enacted a bill known as the Indian Reorganization Act in 1934. Under the provisions of this act, Indians had the right to organize themselves under the corporate laws of the various states and transact business themselves. "The Indian functions best as an integrated member of a group, clan, or tribe. Identification of his individuality with the clan or tribe is with him a spiritual necessity," wrote John Collier in his report for 1935.[11] And basically this thinking permeates the material in the act. Much of the Reorganization Act dealt with land, directly or indirectly. Its first section repealed the General Allotment Act of 1887. But other significant principles appear. One was the establishment of a revolving credit fund to supply long- and short-term requirements. Another section dealt with the reorganization of the tribes to develop leadership through tribal organizations and corporations. Special elections were necessary on each reservation in order for the Act to function.

On November 2, 1935, the Indians on the Rocky Boy reservation voted to accept the constitution and charter that had previously been worked out and to operate under the provisions of the Indian Reorganization Act. The Preamble to the Constitution and Bylaws[12] carries an interesting statement:

Preamble

We, the original and adopted member of the Rocky Boy's Band of Chippewas enrolled upon the Rocky Boy's Reservation in the State of Montana, in order to exercise our rights to self-government, to administer all tribal affairs to the best advantage of the individual members, and to preserve and increase our tribal resources, do ordain and establish this Constitution of the Chippewa Cree Tribe of the Rocky Boy's Reservation, Montana.

Subsequently throughout the Constitution, the group is always referred to as "the Chippewa Cree Tribe." For instance, Article III, Sec-

---

[11] *Report of the Commissioner of Indian Affairs for 1935* (Washington: Government Printing Office).

[12] *Constitution and Bylaws of the Chippewa Cree Indians of the Rocky Boy's Reservation* (Washington: Government Printing Office, 1936).

tion 1 reads: "The governing body of the Chippewa Cree Tribe shall be known as the 'Business Committee.'" No mention is made in the Constitution of Little Bear or of the Cree Indians, who in number exceeded the Chippewa at the time of the founding of the reservation. Yet the name "Cree" persisted in all other references to the tribe except in the original sentence that opens the preamble.

If the Indians were unsure as to what to call themselves, they were not alone in their doubt as attested by communications between Earl Woolridge, Superintendent of the Agency during the early 1930's, and the Bureau of Indian Affairs in Washington.[13] Late in 1932, the Bureau requested all superintendents to prepare a census roll in 1933 and to include in that roll the blood quantum, according to recognized tribes in the United States, of each person enrolled. In a letter dated January 19, 1933, Woolridge wrote to the Commissioner of Indian Affairs:

> It is noted that the Office still believes it would be possible and practicable to divide this small band of Indians into various tribes, though these people have never been affiliated with or enrolled with, any definite tribe of Indians. If this method of listing these people is to be made mandatory, it will be necessary for the Office to give us specific instructions as to how the families are to be divided.
>
> Shall we take for example the family of Chief Stick. (No. 85 to 88 on 1932 roll.) The father is shown as Assiniboine-Blackfeet; the mother as Cree-Chippewa. We have absolutely no means of determining which is the predominating blood in either case. . . .
>
> As we have advised the Office repeatedly, there are no separate tribes here in the sense that is the case on many other reservations. These people had wandered together, and intermarried to such an extent before they were ever listed anywhere, the majority of them do now know themselves how much Indian blood they have or exactly what tribe. It is not uncommon to hear one say, 'My mother lived near the old fort, so she must have been Assiniboine.' Or, 'My father came from Canada, so I suppose he was a Cree. . . .'
>
> It must be remembered that these people have never been enrolled elsewhere, so that in the majority of cases there was no record of them at all until they were adult, or even middle-aged people. They have become one people in every sense of the word and it promises to cause a great deal of confusion if we attempt to separate them into several tribes.

The Commissioner relented and simply instructed the superintendent to secure the amount of Indian blood if possible, but to designate them as "Chippewa-Cree." Consequently, whether the Indians had Assiniboine

---

[13] Correspondence on file at the Agency office. Permission to see the material came from former Assistant Superintendent Robert Crawford, to whom I am indebted.

or Blackfoot or Crow or Flathead or Sarsee blood as well as Cree or Chippewa they became "Cippewa-Cree." Nevertheless, the framers of the Constitution indicate that they thought of themselves as Chippewa. As the years went on, though, the members have been called "Rocky Boy Indians" by both Indians of other reservations and neighboring whites.[14]

As the years passed, the "Rocky Boy Indians" survived the depression of the 1930's and the vicissitudes of World War II. About ten percent of their members served in the armed forces.[15] Several of the other tribal members left the reservation to secure jobs in the booming war-time labor market. Several of these people have not returned to the reservation. The population figure, as of 1960, is 1409 with about half of that number living off the reservation.[16] The non-resident families live in the larger cities of Montana and in the western states. For those living on the reservation, however, many of the families continue doing just what they had done before the establishment of the reservation—work as transient help for white ranchers in Montana and now also in Idaho, for most of them have some kind of old car that gives them mobility.

The pattern in general has remained unchanged. Many of the families load their possessions in their cars in April, take their children out of school, and leave the reservation. They usually find their first employment picking rocks from large-scale farmers' fields. They then follow the seasonal work on the ranches—fixing fences, cutting hay, and preparing for the harvest. Usually they return to the reservation late in June or early in July for the annual Sun Dance, and leave again for more seasonal work. By October, they end their work picking potatoes for southern Montana and Idaho farmers, and by early November they are back on the reservation. During these months they earn enough money to live on as well as to buy gas to get back to the reservation. It is impossible for them to save sufficiently from their meager earnings (which may range from $150 to $1800 for the season) to live during the winter months. From November until April, many of them are recipients of relief administered by the Federal Government.

Relief figures prominently in the economy of the Rocky Boy Indians. From a resident population of about 150 families, Wilbur Barnett,

---

[14] This designation is heard frequently on other reservations as well as in the town of Havre, principal shopping center of the tribal members.

[15] "The Promised Land," op. cit. Author and date unknown.

[16] Figure supplied by George Denny, Tribal Secretary, September 1, 1960..

Social Worker on the reservation, gives the approximate breakdown as follows:[17]

For the Period, November 1 to May 1 (For any year)

General Assistance	40% of the families
Categorical Assistance	30% of the families
(includes:	
Old Age Assistance	
Aid to the Needy Blind	
Aid to Dependent Children	
Aid to the Permanently and	
Totally Disabled)	
Other Income	30% of the families
(This income may come from	
Unemployment Insurance, farming,	
ranching, or fulltime employment)	

According to Barnett, the demand for assistance is growing. For example, May, 1960, was cold and rainy and a difficult month for the people to get jobs away from the reservation. As a result, the government made an additional general assistance payment. In late June, another application was made, but in this case it was denied. In mid-July, 1960, about thirty-five women came to Barnett's office and said that they did not have anything to eat. Barnett claimed that food was available, particularly since the government had distributed surplus commodities to these Indians. However, many of the people are growing more and more resistant to leaving the reservation during the summer months, since they say that they want to get out logs and add additional rooms to their cabins. Such statements have not been accepted, and relief during the summer months has been denied.

For those who live off the reservation, economic problems must be met also. Most of the men work as unskilled laborers. Some of them have jobs that last during the entire year, and these people usually try to take their vacations to coincide with the annual Sun Dance. On their small wages, they generally are able to exist and maintain a home unless a strike occurs or a recession causes them to be unemployed. The latter was the case during the winter of 1957. Local welfare refused to assist these Indians because they are enrolled on a reservation. To exist then, they were forced to return to the reservation where they are eligible for government relief. Their returning causes other social problems, however, since housing in particular is always at a premium. Conse-

---

[17] Personal interview, August 29, 1960.

quently, they have to move into already crowded cabin with some of their relatives. When work opportunities open again in the cities, some of them leave. Others remain on the reservation, beaten in spirit to a certain degree, accept what odd jobs are available during the summer season and live on relief again during the winter. They all agree that their greatest need is a source of employment near home.

Not all of the residents of the reservation live in this fashion, however, for a few of them are quite successful farmers and ranchers. The land area was enlarged during the 1930's by several additional purchases. Today, the Bureau of Indian Affairs lists the following breakdown of the resources of Rocky Boy's Reservation:[18]

Resources — Rocky Boy's Reservation.

Type	Tribal	Ownership Reserves	Total
Agricultural Land:			
Dry Farm	5,937		
Irrigated (present)	993		
Irrigable (probable)	1,507		
Sub-Total			8,437
Grazing	70,409		
Timber	27,000 *		
Waste	187		
Mineral (undetermined)			
Sub-Total			97,596
Administrative Site		800	
School Sites		60	
School Pastures		160	
Sub-Total			1,020
Grand Total			107,053

* 9,000 Acres predominantly forest.
  18,000 Acres partial forested.
  27,000 Acres included in grazing permits.

The resources, however, are insufficient to support the entire population of the tribe. Robert Roush, Associate County Agent for Hill County who is in charge of the Indian services, states[19] that approximately twenty-

---

[18] "Brief on the Rocky Boy's Reservation," a duplicated report prepared by the Bureau of Indian Affairs for planning purposes only, October, 1956.

[19] Personal interview, March 21, 1956.

five families can maintain an adequate economic status from the resources of the reservation. In 1959, a committee from the Tribal Council studied the situation and made a similar statement. This study resulted in considerable friction among the enrolled members as the older ones became worried about their future. Some of them believed that they would be shunted off to one small area of the reservation while the "breeds would get all the land."[20]

The squabble over land usage is reflected in the social division of the tribe. A small number of members now utilizes the land by stock raising and by farming. These people, often referred to as "breeds" by the so-called full-blood population, are energetic, have embraced the competitive spirit of the white man, and are quite successful. They number, however, but a fraction of the tribe. Sociologically, their influence is more pronounced in that they represent the advanced group—those who "are trying to live like white men."[21] Opposed to them are about eighty percent of the tribe—members who embrace the older Indian philosophy and who practice many of the primitive beliefs. The distinction is cultural and not physical. Among the so-called "breeds" may be found men who look distinctively Indian while among the "full bloods" it is not uncommon to find men with blue eyes, Nordic features, and brown hair worn in long braids.

Another cause of friction among the members of the tribe during the last several years has been the school situation. The buildings erected in the 1930's have deteriorated and have become too small for the present school population. Beginning in 1953, the high school students who formerly went to one of the government-operated boarding schools in South Dakota began attending the Box Elder high school, about 14 miles away. There at first they were welcomed because they came in such numbers that the accrediting official permitted the school to remain open. However, discrimination began, and in 1957, no Indian boy was allowed to play on the school basketball team. Since the Indian boys are usually exceptionally good at basketball and many attend school only to participate in that sport, and more especially since only about five or six white boys attended the school that year, the Indians knew that the town resented their presence. Because of that attitude, they began to agitate for their own high school.

The Bureau of Indian Affairs and some of the progressive tribal

---

[20] Personal interview, Big Knife, January 1, 1960.

[21] A common expression frequently heard on the reservation especially among the older members.

members thought that the education system should be transferred to a local school district. Such instances have worked satisfactorily in many regions of Montana. In fact, government schools have been operating in recent years only on the Rocky Boy and the Northern Cheyenne reservations. Money is now available from Public Law 840 to construct new buildings. The Bureau of Indian Affairs is able to transfer money to the district for the education of each Indian child enrolled and to supply funds for hot lunches for the children as well. The majority of the Rocky Boy Indians seemed to resent the program, however, and it was not until 1959 that an agreement was reached. The school system of the town of Havre agreed to take over the administration of the school, to build a new and modern plant for the students in the elementary grades, and to transport by bus the high school students to Havre.

Despite the opposition of many of the parents, the plan went into effect. The most frequently voiced criticism was the fear that their children would not be dressed sufficiently well to attend the Havre high school. Nonetheless, construction of the school plant began during the summer of 1959, and the first group of twenty-five students started high school in Havre. By September, 1960, the new elementary school operated by the Havre Public Schools opened. In general, the new system seems to be operating to the satisfaction of most of the parents. One obstructionist seems to be the Lutheran missionary at the Agency who has made his mission bus available for transportation to Box Elder; thus about fourteen high school children have elected to remain in school at Box Elder.

While the operation of the school bus by the Lutheran missionary is one aspect of missionary work on the reservation, such work in general has not been too effective. Nominally, all the Indians on the Rocky Boy reservation are either Roman Catholic or Lutheran. Each denomination has a church building. The Lutheran mission has been established since 1918 and has a spotted history. Some of the accounts indicate that an active institution flourished for several years. Recently, however, under the direction of a well-meaning but not too understanding pastor, the influence of the church has been negligible. Each Thursday, many of the women gather at the church hall to sew, since facilities and materials are made available to them. Sunday services are attended by but a few, chiefly members of one family. During the Christmas season, the mission sponsors a party where candy and nuts and other holiday foods are distributed to the children and where the pastor cannot refrain from speaking about the large attendance there and the small attendance at church services.[22]

According to Paul Mitchell, an active member of the Lutheran church, a clerk for the tribal office, and a particularly well-informed tribesman, the majority of the tribal members are professed members of the Roman Catholic Church.[23] No resident priest serves the community, however, but one comes every two weeks from Big Sandy, a town about twenty-five miles away. During recent years, however, a particularly active priest has been in charge and as a result of his influence, a large frame church building—abandoned by a white community about sixty miles away—has been moved to the agency center. Tribal members donated labor in erecting the foundation and in helping move the building. The priest hopes to establish a youth center and to maintain some sort of activity for the younger people on the reservation in the basement of the church.

No other established denomination has ever attempted to hold meetings or to gain any following on the reservation. Occasionally the Salvation Army from Havre comes to the reservation on Sunday afternoons and conducts Sunday school in some of the homes. Since these people usually bring something to eat or to wear, attendance at these meetings is fairly good. As one young mother, herself not a professed Christian, said,[24] "It don't hurt none to let the kids know something about Jesus." In addition, some of the members have been interested in a healing sect, known locally as the "Oral Roberts bunch." Some of these people have travelled to the larger cities of Montana and have participated in the services of the well-known American evangelist, Oral Roberts, and have been impressed by his ability to heal the afflicted. In an attempt to keep his teaching alive, this small group under the leadership of a local woman holds occasional meetings. The Native American Church is also functioning rather effectively on the reservation and draws its membership from Indians who are Catholic, Lutheran, or primitive in belief.

No substantial evidence exists to indicate that families are united in following the precepts of one particular denomination. Again from the information supplied by Paul Mitchell, one can see that in many households, parents are divided. Perhaps the father is nominally a Catholic while his wife is a Lutheran. The children attend neither church re-

---

[22] So reported to me by personages, both Indian and white, who have attended the gatherings.

[23] Personal interview, August 29, 1960.

[24] Personally reported. The name of the informant is purposely withheld.

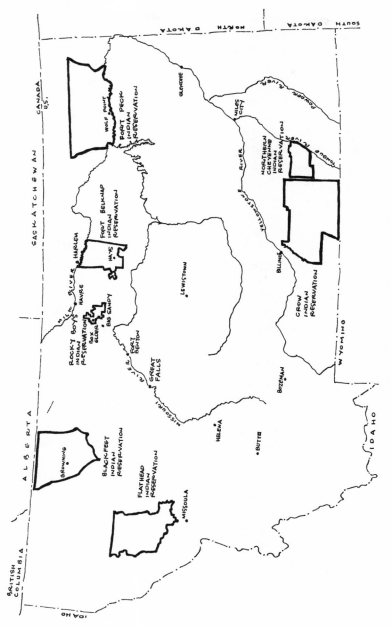

FIGURE 2. Map of Montana showing the Indian Reservations.

59

gularly and grow up in an atmosphere where Christian teachings are not stressed. As they become older, some of them—especially the boys—often are attracted to the services of the Native American Church or become interested in the Sun Dance or some other aspect of primitive religion. Consequently one sees many more young people among the Rocky Boy Indians participating in the rituals of the past than among other Indians in the state. Christianity has never been an integral part of the life of the Rocky Boy Indians.

Quite opposite to their seeming diffidence to the white man's religion is the ready acceptance of some of the material culture of their neighbors. To the white stranger, the Indians of the Rocky Boy reservation present an acculturated appearance both in their homes and in their visits to the neighboring towns. The men dress like the white men of the vicinity, complete with levis, sport shirts and jackets, cowboy boots and hats. Not a trace of their Indian past can be seen in their outward appearance. They are a good-looking people, and when dressed for an occasion, make handsome appearances in western clothers. The younger women dress also as do their white contemporaries, either in tailored slacks or dresses. Most of the older women wear a shawl or blanket over their store-purchased dresses and cover their feet with knee-length moccasins.

All but the very old speak English fluently. Unlike many of the other Indians of the West, the Rocky Boy Indians are very friendly and approachable to strangers and will visit with a white person at the slightest provocation. They drive cars exclusively—seldom does one even see children riding horseback on the reservation—have their cabins wired for electricity, have radios and in some instances TV, and look and act much as do their white counterparts.. They shop in the supermarkets in Havre, and the women bring their clothes to be washed in the self-service laundries also in Havre. They usually bring their children with them when shopping or doing their laundry; and they seem to indulge the youngsters with ice cream, pop, Coca Cola, and other sweets to a greater degree than do the white parents. The general impression, then, is one of an acculturated people, who look, dress, and act like their white neighbors.[25]

But it seems as if another transformation, aside from the outward semblances of acculturation, has taken place on the Rocky Boy reservation. As was noted earlier in this chapter, the tribe incorporated them-

---

[25] Impressions are those of the writer who has spent many months during a period of eight years on the Rocky Boy reservation.

selves as "Rocky Boy's Chippewa." Then the term "Chippewa-Cree" occurs in the constitution and charter. But in the twenty-five years that have passed since the granting of the charter, another generation has developed. And the members of that generation seem to regard themselves as "Cree." Young men of that tribe now are "Cree" when they are asked to state their tribal affiliation. "They're going to make a Cree Indian out of you," they say to a white participant in the sweat lodge ceremony, the Sun Dance, or any other tribal function that a white man may share. Older men too refer to themselves as "Cree" even though they may tell one of the Blackfoot ancestor or Assiniboine heritage. Likewise, men and women will point out areas where Chippewa ceremonies such as the Great Medicine Lodge once took place. "It's all gone now," they will say. "We're all Crees here." There are also visitations with the Canadian Cree, for renewal of acquaintanceship with the northern relatives has developed. Members of the Rocky Boy reservation travel north into Canada at the slightest provocation, for they go not only to attend the Sun Dance or other ritual but to visit their friends on the Canadian reserves. It seems that it is information pertinent to religion which they are most interested in securing from their Canadian-Cree friends, for they quote material learned from the Canadians. My own informants frequently express their regret that I am unable to meet and visit with the Cree residents in Canada, for on small points of religious belief they will refer to some one in Canada who would know. Once when an elderly Cree from Rocky Mountain House in Canada visited the Rocky Boy reservation, my informants introduced me to him and arranged for me to have an interview with him.

Consequently, it appears that from among all the various tribes whose blood has mingled in the Rocky Boy Indians, a new tribe has emerged. Proud of their difficulties in the recent past, unified by a religion that has kept functioning during the years, and more or less secure on a little reservation in a remote corner of Montana, these people are now Cree. Despite the varying amounts of Indian blood as well as the sprinkling of French that is found in many of them, their values are oriented toward those of the Cree. They have been unified by their common suffering and sustained by their religion—a religion that is Woodland related but Cree rooted.

In all references then to these Indians, they will be referred to as Cree, a designation they have developed for themselves out of their checkered and wandering past.

CHAPTER III

THE HIGH GOD AND CREATION

In every discussion about their religion, in every plea for tolerance, in every association with the supernatural, the Cree refer constantly to the fact that there is but one God. "We are all children of one God," they say as they ask for understanding from their white neighbors. "The same God created the Indian that created the white man," they will explain patiently to an investigator. "The Creator just intended for the Indians to live differently," they will add.

The Cree know the Creator as Kitchi Manitou, but it is a term they never use when speaking about him or to him. In this context "kitchi" carries the connotation of the "main thing," or "that which is most important." Present day informants say that Kitchi Manitou is the old Cree term for the Creator and is one that is no longer in use. Because of the great respect for their High God, He is referred to as *Ki-sei-men'-to*. (The Cree pronounce this term very rapidly; the *k* is almost silent. To the untrained ear the sound is almost *tse-mun'-to*. Originally, the term may have been a contraction of Kitchi Manitou.) "You say *Ki-sei-men'-to*, like the leader or the main one. You say that instead of the holy name Kitchi Manitou," explains Raining Bird.[1] The Cree also speak of their Creator as *outa-wi-mau,* which can be translated as "like the father," or the "father of everyone." Sometimes they use another term, *ka-kai-jo-ki-ig-otshi,* "the God who made everything." Currently, the Christian term, "father," is used by almost all of the people as they pray to their God.[2]

The Cree idea fits well with the general Northern Algonquian belief in a Supreme Being. For, like the other Algonquians,[3] the Cree conceive of His abode as somewhere above; thus whenever He is addressed or offered the pipe, it is always upward. Yet in the majority of cases, no hint of any relationship exists between the Supreme Being and the sun

---

[1] Personal interview, Raining Bird, August 27, 1960.

[2] Information supplied to me by Raining Bird and Windy Boy.

[3] J. M. Cooper, "The Northern Algonquian Supreme Being," Catholic University of American Anthropological Series, No. 2 (1934), pp. 37–39.

or any other heavenly bodies. The apparent exception to this concept seems to be the Blackfeet who do have ceremonies directed to the Sun and to the Moon and to the Morning Star. In fact, the Sun is married to the Moon and their one son is the Morning Star. The Sun is the principal god of the Blackfeet. When they pray, they speak to Him first. It was He also who made the earth, mountains, prairies, rivers, forests, as well as animals and people. All good things come from Him, including the power that animals possess and which may be transmitted to humans.[4] Father Schmidt states[5] that these ideas are the result of a strong Siouan influence. That assumption is a rather broad one, though, for historical references do not show much chance for diffusion between these two traditional enemies of the Plains.

The general Algonquian belief, however, is that the Supreme Being belongs to another time and has never been seen by anyone. The Cree visualize Him as "glowing something like the sun."[6] As evidence that the concept of the High God was pre-Christian, Cooper points out[7] certain non-Christian elements such as the High God's ability to send dreams to the individual, various taboos about wasting meat lest He be offended, and the first-fruits offering to strengthen the cause of the belief being pre-white in origin. Several of these beliefs remain; consequently, one can see in the active relationship which the present-day Cree have maintained certain ideas that would be hard to reconcile to Christianity. As further evidence, Cooper quotes from an early explorer, H. A. Ellis, who spent the winter of 1746–47 with the Cree of York Factory. Ellis wrote:[8] "They (the Cree) acknowledge a Being of infinite Goodness, whom they stile *Ukkewma* which in their Language signifies the Great Chief; they look upon him as the Author of all Benefits they enjoy and speak of him with Reverence. They likewise sing a kind of Hymn in his Praise, and this is a grave solemn tone, not altogether disagreeable."

Later authorities such as Mandelbaum state:[9] "The concept of a single all powerful creator was dominant in Plains Cree religious ideology

---

[4] George Bird Grinnell, *Blackfoot Lodge Tales* (New York: Charles Scribner's Sons, 1920), pp. 167–168.

[5] W. Schmidt, *High Gods in North America* (Oxford: Clarendon Press, 1933), p. 64.

[6] Personal interview, Raining Bird, March 23, 1959.

[7] Cooper, *op. cit.*, p. 71.

[8] *Ibid.*, pp. 55–55. See H. A. Ellis, *A Voyage to Hudson's Bay* (London, 1748), pp. 193–194.

[9] David Mandelbaum, *The Plains Cree*, Anthropological Papers of the American Museum of Natural History (New York, 1940), Vol. XXXVII, Part II, p. 251.

and ceremonialism." Father Rossignol,[10] who likewise knew the Plains Cree intimately, stated about them:

Religion seems to have revolved largely around the Supreme Being and the Guardian Spirits. God was believed to have supreme domination over the world and was reverenced. The homage paid to Him was mostly internal without elaborate external cult. It is seemingly this lack of external cult that has deceived passing visitors and investigators with limited time and opportunity for getting at the underlying facts. There appears to be no indication of a supreme evil being.

Only in one instance do the accounts give a definite statement that the Crees did not recognize a Supreme Being. Skinner writes:[11] "Certain it is that they (the Cree) were, as is so universal in North America, polytheistic, and that the idea of a single Great Spirit (Kitchi-Manitou) is entirely a European importation, and none are more positive of this than the Cree themselves."

Another rather widely disputed concept held by the Montana Cree is that of an evil spirit. All evil, according to the Rocky Boy Cree, that happens to man comes from the Evil Spirit. Death, sickness, witchcraft all come from him or are his fault.[12] In the beginning man and animals lived forever. The Evil Spirit changed all that and gave everyone only twenty years to live. Later, he made another change and arranged it so that humans could live longer. Since he did not make any change pertinent to the animals, their life expectancy seldom exceeds twenty years.

The Evil Spirit is known as Matchi Manitou. Again, just as with the Great Spirit, Kitchi Manitou, euphemisms are used when speaking of him. Sometimes he is called *ma-tasa-is,* the Evil Man. Generally, he is referred to as *he-ka-ka-mi-o-sit-men'-to,* the "not good spirit."

Raining Bird gives an explanation of the origin of Matchi Manitou when he says:[13]

When everything was coming along all right, one creation helper who had been good somehow thought he had as much power and strength as did *Ki-sei-men'-to.* He wanted to know if his powers really existed, so he challenged *Ki-sei-men'-to* in order to test the strength of the two. For a while he seemed to succeed, but then *Ki-sei-men'-to* came to life and created another helper called

---

[10] M. Rossignol, "The Religion of the Saskatchewan and Western Manitoba Cree." *Primitive Man* (1939), Vol. XI, pp. 67–71.

[11] Alanson Skinner, *Notes on the Eastern Cree and Northern Salteaux,* Anthropological Papers of the American Museum of Natural History (New York, 1911), Vol. IX, Part I, p. 59.

[12] Personal interview, Raining Bird, August 31, 1960.

[13] Personal interview, Raining Bird, March 25, 1959.

ki-cha-tchak[14] who is something like the Christian's Holy Ghost. This helper's job was to track down the spirit who had challenged *Ki-sei-men'-to*. He did, for he chased him over the oceans, the land, and the world. He chased him down into the earth, and presently everyone heard a great noise. The good spirit had caught the evil one under the earth and made this evil one promise that he would not work on this earth again. However, the bad things had already been done.

As can be seen, certain Christian influences could account for the presence of the Evil Spirit, Matchi Manitou. Nonetheless, he is an active functioning agent in the mythology of the contemporary Cree Indians of Montana.

In other phases of the creation story, the Cree follow more closely the beliefs of other Algonquians. Father Cooper states that in general the Algonquians differ in their interpretation of the role the Supreme Being played and do not all agree if He is both the maker and creator.[15] He believes that the majority of the Indians conceive of Him as "the master rather than the maker." The Montana Cree do not subscribe to this idea, for to them He is both. Their story of creation is explicit and definite:[16]

Before any soul existed, there was Fog and it was very dark. Somehow, out of this Fog, which contained the spirits of Day and Night, these spirits became bound together and formed the soul that is Manitou. That was the beginning. Day was made first and then Night. Manitou then created the Sun and the twelve Moons and then the world. He created the four seasons. Then He gave Mother Earth a companion to raise the things that would be created and would be needed to live and to survive.

When Mother Earth knew and heard that she had been called upon to do this job, she went to the Creator and asked Him what to do.

'I have given part of my life, the water, to make things live. What shall I do now?'

'Help me raise my children. That is what I ask of you,' replied the Creator, for He referred to the grass, the animals, and everything as His children.

'My father, *Ki-sei-men'-to,* you have given me hard work to do if I am to raise your children right. I will have to call upon the Thunderbirds that you have created and ask them for help.' And right off she sent for the Thunderbirds.

'What do you want us to do, Mother Earth?' asked the Thunderbirds as soon as they had landed on the earth.

'I want you to help me raise these children of the Creator here. I want you

---

[14] This name, though sounding somewhat similar, must not be confused with *Wi-sak-a-chak,* the Trickster.

[15] Cooper, *op. cit.,* pp. 39–40.

[16] Personal interview, Raining Bird, December 30, 1959.

to have the power to carry the water, part of my body, up in the air. In the springtime, you will take care of things so we can raise everything that is necessary here on earth.'

Now that it had been arranged for all things to live, Manitou drew a sketch of a man on the ground. He spoke to the drawing and told it to move. It did. Finally, He took a rib from the lower left side of man and from that rib He created woman. That is why woman has less strength than man. After He had done this job, He spoke to the man and woman.

'My children,' he said. 'I am going far away. I am going up where nobody will ever see me. However, I am leaving you certain things—main things that are very important. There will be four of them. Fire, Pipe (and the rock from which the pipe is made), Pipe stem (and the tree from which the stem is made), and sweetgrass. The tobacco is already in the pipe.'

'If, in the future, you wish to make any connection with me, these are the things to be used. And they must be used in this order: First, upward, in memory of your Creator; next, to the spirits of the four directions; and lastly, down to Mother Earth.'

'My children,' he continued. 'I don't eat. Neither do I smoke, but when you remember me, you must do these things. My children, be sure. Regardless of any hardships, never let any of these things go. If you do, that is the time that I will have to change the world.'

'Try to be kind to each other. Do not fight. Do not say bad things. Do not steal. If you do these things you will be happy. But there will be another kind of person in this world, and they will be in great numbers and will come here. They will try to teach you how to live and how to pray. They will claim that they are smarter than you. But if they overcome you, they will destroy themselves. Those of you who follow my rules and live as I tell you will survive. These people who are coming have white skins and you will call them *wap-i-ski-as*.'

'For those of you who will not listen or who do not want to listen, I will leave these things as punishment—fire and wind and earthquakes. These will happen to all men who do not listen to my teachings, whether they are Indian or white. But those of you who live up to my rules and my teachings will find everlasting happiness and the good life. Whenever you want anything, then, you must use these things—pipe, stem, sweetgrass, and fire. Then through smoking these I will know that you are asking from me. Do not quit doing this. Keep on.'

During this conference with the First Man, the Creator had with him the Four Souls who assist him, and Mother Earth and the Four Souls who help her. All of them joined in the instruction and told him how to believe and how to worship through the use of certain ceremonials, which were also given to man at that time. The Creator has four main offices stationed at each of the four directions; therefore, He has four souls working for Him all of the time. Mother Earth has the same. She has four souls of her own, one at each of the four directions. This meeting with man was the last time that anyone ever saw the Creator. He is too great and too powerful to be seen any more.[17]

From this evidence, it seems quite evident that the Cree believe that their Supreme Being is both Maker and Master of the Universe. Cooper says[18] that some question has existed whether originally the Algonquians might have considered that there were three phases or parts of the Supreme Being—the Master of Food, the Master of Life, and the Master of Death. According to Raining Bird[19] these three master spirits do exist. The Master of Life is the Creator, the Master of Food is the buffalo, while the Master of Death is the Evil Spirit—Matchi Manitou.

Here again, however, we may have an example of adaptation and diffusion. Certain it is that the early Cree knew little or nothing about the buffalo. Until they left the woods of eastern Canada and became located on the Plains, through the aid of European metal goods and the horse, they may have had another interpretation of the Master of Food—the moose, perhaps. Since the taboo still exists about referring to their High God by name, the terms Master of Life and Master of Food may simply have been translations of some of the euphemisms used by the Cree to designate their Supreme Being.

Be that as it may, a close relationship does exist between the story of Creation as told by the present-day Cree and the one Father Schmidt attributes to the Algonquians. He writes:[20]

The creation of man is the creation of the first pair; the body is formed out of earth, and the soul is breathed into it by the Creator. The form of the immediate creation of the earth, where the earth proceeds directly from the creative power of God, is to be found in old myths of the north-east Algonquians. But a wider diffusion is the form of mediate creation: namely, at the bidding of the Creator a little earth is brought up from the ocean by the turtle and water birds diving into it.

This mediate creation of the earth just described ... must be rigorously distinguished from a secondary creation of it, executed not by the Supreme Being, but by the culture hero ... when saved from a great flood raised against him by evil water spirits, thereupon forms a boat or raft in which he saves different land animals and makes them dive to bring up a little mud. This legend comes from the matrilineal and lunar mythology of the Iroquois religion.

Now Father Schmidt's interpretation is worth considering. Other western Algonquians have the story of the mediate creation done by diving

---

[17] Personal interview, Raining Bird, August 31, 1960.

[18] Cooper, *op. cit.*, p. 38.

[19] Personal interview, Raining Bird, September 1, 1960.

[20] Schmidt, *op. cit.*, p. 66.

—the Cheyenne send down the duck, the Gros Ventre (Atsina) send the turtle, while the Arapaho has the Creator change himself into a duck and go down with the turtle. In each case, nothing but water and the First Person exist until the First Person decides to form the earth. And in each case, a bit of mud taken from the feet of the bird or animal forms the basis for the earth. This account is not found in Cree mythology at all, but the story of the secondary creation is present. The instrument through which the Cree explain the secondary creation is their trickster, who now is in the role of a Transformer.

The Cree trickster is Wi-sak-a-chak. Translated literally, his name means "hypocrite," or "two faced."[21] His father was the Big Dipper (*o-tse-ka-tak*) while his mother was the three stars that form the belt of Orion (*o-ki-na-nisk*). He was a human being who looked and acted just exactly as did everyone else. He was always travelling, and once he received a message from *Ki-sei-men'-to*.

It seems that people were living and doing the wrong things. They were hating and killing each other and in general living lives far removed from the teachings of the Creator. The Spirits became worried about the situation and wanted the world created again so that it could be as pure and good as it had been in the beginning. Some of the Spirits went to *Ki-sei-men'-to* and asked Him if People could not be born again on a land as good as the one that had first been created. *Ki-sei-men'-to* replied that He would do what they had asked, for He had the power to make the change, and He stated that in time, people would be on earth again.

The trickster, Wi-sak-a-chak, was the chosen instrument. He was travelling with some of his younger brothers, the wolves, when *Ki-sei-men'-to* came to him and explained the mission He wished to have accomplished. Once he learned of the task required of him, Wi-sak-a-chak turned to one of the younger wolves.

"My young brother," he said, "I have a difficult task ahead of me and you must help me. Will you go out among all the animals and birds as well as the men and women and tell every one you see that I want one pair of each animal to come to me? You understand. I want one male and one female. I also want one man and one woman. Tell them to come to me on that mountain top over there, for I will be camped there."

The young wolf did his bidding. It was not long until a pair of all of the animals and a man and a woman came to the mountain where

---

21 Personal interview, Four Souls, October 31, 1959.

68

Wi-sak-a-chak now had his camp. At first, they were quite restless, for they could not understand why they had been thus summoned. It was not long, however, until they noticed that a lake had begun to form in the valley below them. Day by day the water increased, day by day Wi-sak-a-chak kept working on a raft that he was building, yet still he refused to explain why he had called them or what he was doing. At last the day came when the water had reached nearly to the top of the mountain. Just as the animals and the man and the woman had become very agitated about the proximity of the water, Wi-sak-a-chak turned from his labors, and announced that all of them should get on his raft. When the last pair of animals had walked on to the raft, the water reached a new height and the raft pushed out into the sea. Not until then did Wi-sak-a-chak tell the animals and the humans that *Ki-sei-men'-to* intended to destroy the world by water in order that a new one could be created.

For several days, they floated around on the water. As their food supplies began to diminish, the animals and the people worried lest they starve to death amidst all the water. At last a spokesman for the group came to Wi-sak-a-chak and asked him if he would not make the Earth again so that they could all live on land.

"Not yet," replied Wi-sak-a-chak. "You will have a place to live again once I have carried out *Ki-sei-men'to's* instructions. He wants us to have a place again, but we must be re-born. He has decided to have us do it through this water. And from this water we will get mud to form the new earth. Some of you will help me do this. But remember, in helping me some of you will also lose your lives. Are you ready to help me?"

No one replied. The days passed and hunger began to assail the group. Finally, We-sak-a-chak asked again if someone would come forward and help him create the new world—one that would be free from the bad things of the old one. At first, no one came forward. All the animals looked about at one another, but no one moved. Finally, Muskrat volunteered. He admitted to Wi-sak-a-chak that he was frightened and that he would probably drown, but Wi-sak-a-chak assured him that if he did drown he would bring him back to life.

"I just wanted to see who the bravest person was," said Wi-sak-a-chak. "I will not let you die."

Muskrat, thus assured, dived, but presently he came back to the surface and was dead. True to his promise, Wi-sak-a-chak revived him and when Muskrat was conscious again, asked him what he had seen.

"I could see nothing," replied Muskrat. "Absolutely nothing. No bodies, no earth, nothing." And so poor Muskrat lay down to rest again. When he seemed to be revived, Wi-sak-a-chak insisted that he go down again. He was under water a longer period of time on this second adventure, and when he came up he was again dead. Once more Wi-sak-a-chak revived him and asked him what he had discovered.

"I reached the ground this time. That is all I know," he answered. So after he had rested, Wi-sak-a-chak insisted that he go down again. When he came back the third time, although he was dead, he did have bits of dirt in his mouth and in his claws. Wi-sak-a-chak hurriedly revived him, and even before Muskrat was ready to go, Wi-sak-a-chak hurried him off. When he finally came back from this fourth try, not only was he alive, but he had brought enough dirt in his mouth and on his feet for Wi-sak-a-chak to make a little ball out of it.

As Wi-sak-a-chak rolled the ball around in his hands, he blew on it, and as he blew the ball became bigger and bigger and bigger. Finally, it became so big that it seemed to be large enough for people to live upon. Since he could not tell just exactly how big it had become, Wi-sak-a-chak asked if one of the birds would volunteer to go out and see how big the earth had become. A beautiful white bird with a particularly pleasing voice (one that was known as the crow) volunteered. He went out, but when he returned he stated that he did not believe that the earth was big enough for all of the animals and the people. Wi-sak-a-chak continued with his labors and when he had enlarged the ball to a much bigger size, he asked Crow if he would go out again. This time Crow gladly went, but he did not return. As the days went by and Crow had not returned, those on board the raft became restless and pressed Wi-sak-a-chak to let some of them go out on the newly-formed land. When he refused, some of them left without his permission and swam toward the shore. But none of these ever came back. At last, Wi-sak-a-chak decided that he had waited long enough for Crow to return, and worried too about the fate of those who had gone without his permission, he asked Coyote if he would go out to find the others and to see as well if the earth were large enough. Coyote was not gone long. When he returned, he reported that in his opinion, the earth was large enough.

"Did you see anything of Crow out there?" asked Wi-sak-a-chak.

"Yes, I saw him all right," answered Coyote. "He is out there near the water, and as the animals who have left the raft swim to the shore, he catches them and eats them."

"You go out and get him and bring him here," commanded Wi-sak-a-chak.

Coyote did as he was told. It did not take him long; soon Crow stood before Wi-sak-a-chak who lectured him sternly.

"Our Creator, *Ki-sei-men'-to*, has destroyed the world because of the bad things the animals and the people were doing. He has sent this flood and we have floated around on all this water. Poor Muskrat died three times, but I have brought him back to life each time just so that we could have another world—a better one that came out of this water. Now, you, the most beautiful bird of all and the one that has the sweetest voice have tried to destroy all that *Ki-sei-men'-to* wanted to secure in this new world where there would be no hatred and greed. You shall be punished. I will rub your feathers with ashes and make you eat some of them. From now on, you will be black and your voice will be harsh and coarse. When people hear you or see you, they will remember that you disobeyed the instructions of our Creator, *Ki-sei-men'-to*. Go."

And the bird, now black, flapping his wings and croaking miserably, flew out toward the land. The raft had drifted toward the shore now, and in an orderly fashion the animals and birds and the man and the woman stepped from the raft and on to the shore. The world was occupied again.[22]

Although Father Schmidt calls this flood story Iroquoian, or at least expresses the opinion that Iroquoian influence might be present, little evidence seems to support it. Because of the close association the Cree have had with the Assiniboine, there is a greater possibility that the story of the second creation was borrowed from them. A quick survey of the Assiniboine stories of creation does show some similarities.

The Assiniboine creator is Inktomi, a human being in form, who went around carrying an old brown buffalo robe without hair thrown over his shoulder. His long hair was never braided, but rather was left flowing. His clothes were simply a breech cloth and moccasins. Where he came from and where he went, no one knows. In the end, he evaporated into space, yet he is expected to return. While he was here, he was the master of everything; now that he has gone he is recognized only as the maker.[23]

The Assiniboine believe that Inktomi created all things in four stages. They consider four rocks to be representative of these stages of creation

---

[22] Four Souls narrated the entire flood story to me, March 24, 1959.

[23] For this information, as well as other material about the Assiniboine, I acknowledge my indebtedness to Rex Flying, an Assiniboine living on the Fort Belknap reservation in Montana.

which may have taken millions of years to complete. Colors of the rocks are blue, black, white, and spotted. Inktomi created everything first in spirit. Thus the universe was dark, but it had spirits, from which Inktomi separated the spirit of daylight from the spirit of darkness. He continued then in his creation and made everything that we see on both heaven and earth. Once that he had made all these things, he realized that he had created nothing that would rule over all his creation. Consequently, he created man from clay (clay is decomposed vegetation; hence when man becomes ill, he can be cured by an herb preparation— something likewise from vegetation. Inktomi had thus arranged for nature to take care of its own creation.)

When Inktomi had finished with his creation of man and woman, he created the animals. He gave each one of them certain purposes here on earth, purposes the humans have never quite understood. The power quests that individuals endure are nothing more than an attempt to learn from the animal his power so that man can succeed as well in certain instances as does the animal.

The first people whom Inktomi created multiplied and became numerous. They were a large race of people who with their great hands could do anything. As time went on they became cruel and savage and killed each other. Inktomi could not control them. Finally, he selected one of them, a man whom he could trust, and told this person what to do. He asked the man to make a raft and gave him specific instructions how to do it, even to being as specific as telling him to put the middle plume of the eagle on the corners of each log.

When the man had finished constructing the raft, Inktomi told him to wait. Four days later water came and covered everything. All human life and most of the animal life was destroyed. The man floated around alone on his raft. Finally, Inktomi gave him a great power and directed him to float to a certain area which he called *men-ne-wakan,* "mysterious water." (This spot is Lake Winnipeg in Manitoba.) When the man had reached there on his raft, Inktomi came to him and told him that he would now create a new generation of people, so he called all of the fowls of the water together.

"Brothers and sisters," Inktomi said to the fowl, "I am going to select seven[24] from among you. Those that I select must dive to the bottom of this water and bring me some mud. And you must not come back unless you bring me the mud."

---

[24] Since the Assiniboine are an offshoot of the Dakota, the number seven may have some relationship to the seven council fires of the Dakota.

All seven fowl that Inktomi had selected went down into the water. For seven days and nights, Inktomi and the man waited and watched for their return. Finally, on the seventh night the birds that had gone down began to appear floating dead on the surface of the water. Inktomi examined the claws or webs of each bird but found no mud.

"We made a mistake," he said, "and so we must try again. This time I am going to select the muskrat, the mink, the beaver, and the fisher. Now each of you dive down and don't come back unless you can bring some mud."

Down they went. At the end of the fourth day, they began to float to the surface of the water, just as the fowl had done before. The muskrat came first, next the mink, then the beaver, and lastly the fisher. All of them, like the birds before them, were dead. But Inktomi looked over their little feet and to his amazement and joy found tiny specks of mud clinging to each one. Carefully he took the mud from each of the animals, and from this mud he made the land that we are now living upon for his people. For now he had decided to create a partner for the man whom he had saved. When he had finished creating the woman, he created six more men and six more women. These fourteen people, divided evenly in seven couples became the ancestors of the seven council fires of the Dakota.

The similarities between the stories of creation, both primary and secondary, are obvious, for both the Cree and the Assiniboine consider that Night and Day were created first. Then Man comes from earth. Because Man has erred, all creation is destroyed and a rejuvenation through water occurs. Man has been given a second chance to live in a world wrought from dirt brought by small animals. One can only conjecture the amount of diffusion that has occurred between the two tribes. Historical evidence shows that they have lived closely for at least three and a half centuries.

Although the Cree attribute the creation to another time and place, they feel definitely that *Ki-sei-men'-to* has an abode of his own. They conceive of the universe as consisting of four levels. The highest place is the home of the Creator and is spoken of as the "Creator's Place." A spirit stays with *Ki-sei-men'-to* all of the time, and since it is next to the Creator at all times, it is prayed to whenever anything special is desired. The name for this spirit is *We-kas-kwi-nju*, "Sweetgrass Man." Prayers wafted to this spirit through the medium of sweetgrass incense are easily interpreted to the Creator. The next highest level is the place where another particularly good spirit resides. It is not as holy as *We-kas-kwi-*

nju, but one that intercedes for man in many difficulties. On the third level resides the First Man, the one *Ki-sei-men'-to* made, and who is spoken of as "a kindly old man." Here also live the dead, ruled over by this same old man who was the handiwork of the Creator. And finally, on the fourth level is Mother Earth. Each place is more beautiful than the preceding one. The higher three places can only be reached through fasting and prayer so that in dreams one's soul can go and see the beauty and wonder of these particular places.[25]

Yet, despite the fact that the Cree recognize the Supreme Being, their High God *Ki-sei-men'-to,* and acknowledge the power and assistance of other gods, there does not seem to be any hierarchy of gods established in their minds. Each one of the great powers has certain well-defined duties; at one time, a Cree will call upon one, at another time, he will direct his prayers to others. For example, at the Sun Dance, it is *Ki-sei-men'-to,* Mother Earth, the Master Spirit of the Buffalo, Sun, and the Thunderbirds to whom the participant directs his main prayers. At the Smoke Lodge ceremony, however, the Master Spirit of the Bear is the one who rules it, while at the Ghost Dance, it is to the holy old man, the First Person, who rules over the land of the dead, that offerings are made. The concept of a hierarchy of goods then, as Western civilization has interpreted it since the time of the Greeks, seems to be missing in the thoughts of the Cree people.

The Cree Indians living on the Rocky Boy reservation in Montana firmly believe the story of their creation by *Ki-sei-men'-to,* and they think that We-sak-a-chak brought them a new world after the first one had been destroyed. They listen politely to the story of creation and destruction as told them by the missionaries. It is nothing new to them, they say, for their forefathers had told the same story before the white man ever came to the North American continent. To them, that is proof that there is but one God, and that they came, as did the white man, from the same Creator. That is why in their ceremonies, which are conducted to "put one's heart into God's,"[26] they pray for all men, Indian and white.

---

[25] Personal interview, Raining Bird, August 30, 1960.

[26] Personal interview, Pete Favel, December 29, 1959.

CHAPTER IV

POPULAR RELIGIOUS BELIEFS AND PRACTICES

Like the Hebrews of old, the wandering of the homeless Indians over the face of Montana served to strengthen the faith of the Cree. In their subsequent years on the reservation—years in which they still have remained outcasts—they have developed and unified their belief until they have emerged, as has been mentioned earlier, as a new tribe, one in which the center of their life is their religion. They cling to it tenaciously, for it functions in every aspect of their life, just as it did in the lives of their buffalo-hunting ancestors.[1] The core of their lives, that which makes them Cree, will be the subject of this chapter.

Theoretically, Cree religion should be a good study in nativism. Linton says[2] that causes of nativistic movements lie "in situations of inequality between the societies in contact." Certainly the Cree have been placed in situations of inequality during the last seventy-five years. While wandering homeless, they were placed not only in an inferior position to the dominant white society; they were also placed in an unequal basis with other Indian tribes in the region. The other tribes had secured their reservations by treaty rights; the Cree had none. One of their main reasons for wanting to leave the Blackfeet reservation, as has been mentioned before, was the attitude of the Blackfeet. To a certain extent, the superiority of other Indian tribes is still manifested toward them. The Crees are laughed at, joked about, and ridiculed by their Indian neighbors.[3] With the Cree in double jeopardy, from both

---

[1] Compare, for instance, beliefs and practices reported by Skinner who worked with the Eastern Cree and the unpublished notes of F. E. Peeso who recorded information gained from the progenitors of these Rocky Boy Indians in 1905. In general, the reports are very similar.

[2] Ralph Linton, "Nativistic Movements," *American Anthropologist*, Vol. XLV (1943), p. 243.

[3] I draw much of my information from personal acquaintanceship with Indians living on other reservations in Montana. For instance, one friend living on the Blackfeet reservation reported an incident that occurred in a ladies dress shop in Browning. Two Blackfeet women were shopping and one had tried on a dress. Her friend looked at her, laughed at her, and said, "You look like a Cree."

whites and Indians, one would assume that theirs would be a ripe field for nativistic movements.

Yet an examination of Cree religious practices today shows but few elements that are distinctly nativistic if we follow Linton's definition of it as "Any conscious, organized attempt on the part of a society's members to revive or perpetuate selected aspects of its culture."[4] Instead, in the 1960's, we find a healthy, strong belief in a functioning religion that is drawn primarily from the religious beliefs of old.

Voget[5] would probably classify the Cree as "native-modified." Such people, he says, are "nativist in orientation. Their formal education within the dominant society plus a limited participation in segments of American culture have led them to support modifications of native institutions and to inject new meanings into native ceremonial forms." In part, this statement describes the religion of the Montana Cree. They may well have injected new meanings or modified some of the old beliefs, but changes do not seem to have been made deliberately. Instead, the Cree are following the inherited beliefs which they regard mainly as truth. Some of them they have discarded; others perhaps have been modified to some extent by the association with Christianity as well as with other Indian beliefs. Some practices no doubt are nativistic. But in general, the Montana Cree persist in following the teachings of their ancestors. An examination of those beliefs follows.

In the first place, an Indian does not find his religion or see or hear his spirits just by sitting and waiting for them. He must seek his spiritual help by fasting and praying. "Christ fasted for forty days. Just in the same way, Indians must fast and not drink water in order to have our messages heard."[6] Watetch, a Canadian Cree, expands on the explanation of fasting when he says:[7]

Fasting from food and drink plays a considerable part in all Cree religious functions. But when an Indian for any reason ... determines to drink no water for a specified time, he precedes the fast by addressing the spirit of water by explaining that he is not repudiating the use of this good manifestation of the Great Spirit but that he is making a sacrifice in refraining from its use. If he fasts from food he also explains the sacrifice he is making. To him, food and water are conscious of him and it is courtesy to explain his action.

---

[4] Linton, *op. cit.*, p. 230.

[5] Fred Voget, "Acculturation at Caughnawaga: A Note on the Native and Modified Group," *American Anthropologist*, Vol. LIII (1951), p. 226.

[6] Personal interview, Raining Bird, March 10, 1960.

[7] Abel Watetch, *Payepot and His People* (as told to Blodman Davies), Saskatchewan History and Folklore Society (n. d.), p. 38.

Furthermore, the Cree do not believe that it is necessary for one to be a medicine man to pray. Any individual may beseech help from *Ki-sei-men'-to* if he knows the teachings of the Creator and asks properly. In prayer, people ask *Ki-sei-men'-to* for good luck, for health, for better homes, and for better things for their children. They also ask Him to show them how to find the way to get these things. And in these prayers, they do not just ask for help for the Indian people, they beseech if for the whites as well. Raining Bird gave the following prayer as one that is typical:[8]

> Our Father, I pray to you this time.
> I want to ask blessings for everything.
> I ask you to help me have good health,
> And the health of all the people.
> I ask for a good mind.
> I ask for good homes, something to eat and something to use.
>
> Mother Earth, I ask that you give us something to raise,
> That crops will grow and Life be supplied.
>
> All the Spirits, I ask that you see that we have peace,
> That America and the world be blessed.

While the Cree recognize all of the forces of nature, certain elements stand out in their minds as being particularly important. The Sun is a spirit that gives out life and heat. The Creator gave the Sun a job to do every day. One of its tasks is to listen to the prayers, for every day the Sun goes toward the Creator in the south. The Sun takes care of many things also, for it watches everything on earth so that it can grow. Children, grass, wild berries, and all living things thrive because of the favor of the Sun. Likewise, it makes people feel good.[9] While the Sun is thus given particular recognition, no special observances or tales are told about it as they are among the Crow and other Siouian tribes. Neither is it regarded as a principal deity as among the Blackfeet, who, as Father Schmidt constantly states, have lost most of their true Algonquian religion.[10]

The earth is a stationary force, but it is an extremely important one. It is called *no-tu-ke-o,* a term often used to refer to an old lady or to a home. It is also used to designate a crowded home where lots of children and grandchildren live.[11] If the Indians follow the regulations as set

---

[8] Dictated to me personally, August 27, 1960.

[9] Personal interview, Raining Bird, August 27, 1960.

[10] W. Schmidt, *High Gods in North America* (London: Clarendon Press, 1933), Chapters IV, V, VI.

[11] Personal interview, Raining Bird, December 30, 1959.

forth by *Ki-sei-men'-to,* they will have many children and will live to enjoy many grandchildren; consequently, this term includes Mother Earth. For Earth is a spirit that is alive. It breathes and hears things all the time. As long as it lives, it will continue to yield things that grow upon it. That is the test of its life. And to the Cree, the Earth is their social security. The white man can have a number written on a piece of paper, they say,[12] but the Indian has the Earth. When he lets go of the Earth he has nothing left. That is why he wants to hold on to his small reservation and keep it intact from white settlement. The Cree point out that they are the only Indians in Montana as well as in Canada who never signed a treaty with the United States or the Canadian government.[13] "In Indian history," Joe Stanley—one of the Rocky Boy Cree—wrote,[14] "it has never been found where a Cree Indian has sold his land." In their thinking, the Earth is something the Creator gave them and thus something that cannot be sold.

Other astronomical phenomena that are especially recognized are the stars which are lights suspended from the sky; the North Star, called the "Stationary Star," and the Milky Way, often referred to as "The Chief's Road."[15] The Cree are especially careful and cognizant of the Aurora Borealis, or Northern Lights. These colorful phenomena are frequently seen on the reservation and are considered a reflection of the land where the dead are living. The dead realize how the Indians live today, and they want *Ki-sei-men'-to* to hurry up and bring the Indians to the place of the dead—hence the Northern Lights appear as a two-way communication. The dead tell *Ki-sei-men'-to* and He is telling the Indians here. The Northern Lights are powerful and have a strong whistling sound. Therefore people do not whistle when they are playing for fear of them.[16]

---

[12] Personal interview, Pete Favel, December 30, 1959.

[13] See chapter on historical movements of these people (Chapter I). Big Bear, chief of the forebears of the Cree population, refused to sign a treaty with the Canadian government.

[14] Joe Stanley in company with three other Cree men came to my room on the night of December 30, 1959, and brought with them a document Stanley had prepared written in the Cree alphabet. He read it in Cree. Pat Chief Stick interpreted it to me who wrote it in English. The men wanted me to rewrite the material so that it could be presented, along with a formal request for betterment of conditions on the reservation, to the Bureau of Indian Affairs.

[15] F. E. Peeso, Unpublished manuscript, typewritten copy, p. 45.

[16] Personal interview, Raining Bird, March 25, 1959. See also discussion of ghosts and whistling in Chapter VI.

Vital to the life of the Cree are the Thunder Birds. Conscious always of their environment, the people recognize the association of the thunder storms and rain—especially the storms that come to the oftentimes parched plains in the spring of the year. The Thunder Birds drop the water on the land and start life growing again. The grass and the flowers spring up again; the young trees come into bloom. The Indians know that there will be wild berries to eat and to preserve for winter use; there will also be grass for the wild animals to eat so that they will be plump and tender when the time comes to kill them and prepare them for winter use.

Responsible for the rains are the four Thunder Birds, for each direction has one. The main one is in the south; in the west is the half Eagle and half Thunderbird. A white Thunder Bird, one that has a black head, lives in the North; it is he who sends the snow and the winds of winter. In the east is the black Thunderbird, yet at no time is the color black ever associated with him; instead orange symbolic of the Sun, is used. It is this Thunderbird who is particularly associated with the Sun Dance. With each of the birds having a definite function, each is called upon at various times. Each is important, then, in its own right. Together, they help man; they provide for his food through the beneficent rains they send. To the Montana Cree, they are an integral part of one's environment—another element to be recognized and appreciated.

In many small ways too the Cree are conscious of the supernatural forces around them. Their sole musical instrument, the drum, can talk. It represents the voice of the person who is beating it and carries his voice directly to *Ki-sei-men'-to*. The owner of the drum should keep the instrument clean and hang it outside if necessary, so that it will be away from the odor of human beings. It should also be painted—half of it blue to represent the day, and half of it red to represent the night.[17] Drums have other powers for the individuals, too. For example, another of my informants,[18] related an experience that had happened to him while he was serving in the South Pacific during World War II. One night he had gone to bed and during his sleep he became conscious of the sound of an Indian drum. The next thing he knew, he was in the air, heading for home, for the drum seemed to be directing his movements and bringing him home. When he reached home, he saw that a tipi was standing near his own cabin. The drum deposited him on top of the poles of the tipi where he could look down on his relatives who were all

---

[17] Personal interview, Tom Gardipee, November 4, 1959.

[18] Name is purposely withheld.

assembled. They had the pipe and were praying, singing, and beating the drum as they begged *Ki-sei-men'-to* to return all of the Cree boys safely home from war. He could recognize the people individually as he sat there on the forks of the poles at the top of the tipi. Later, when he returned to full consciousness again, he was back in his bunk in the South Pacific, but he knew that which he had experienced was more than a dream.[19] The drum, he is sure, had been powerful enough to carry him home and then return him to his company, thousands of miles away. Sometimes, when drums are difficult to handle or to carry, an individual can use a rattle. To the Cree, a rattle is a substitute for a drum. *Ki-sei-men'-to* hears the rattle immediately and recognizes it as the voice of the person who is using it.[20]

Animals are looked upon with reverence. The Rocky Boy Cree, like their Canadian brothers, have a very definite set of ideas developed around the bear. "A bear is not a bear," said Tom Gardipee, "it's a spirit."[21] Pete Favel, Tom's father-in-law, added,[22] "The bear is one of the greatest spirits that there is. He has lots of power. The Cree call him the four-legged person, *neo-koteo-n-shin."* A person who kills a bear has to make a feast of berries and give it to the bear spirit. Usually service berries (*Amelanchier alnifolia*) are used. Before the animal is cut up, though, the hunter lights the pipe and smokes. He has to perform that ceremony or else the bear spirit would become very angry. In general, this practice is very similar to that reported by Skinner,[23] who says that "Among all the animals with which they are familiar, there is none more impressive to the minds of the Eastern Cree than the black bear. Its courage, sagacity, and above all, its habit of walking manlike, upon its hind legs, have convinced the Indians of its supernatural propensities."[24] My informant[25] says that among the old people, the bear

---

[19] Along with the beliefs of other tribes, this experience might be interpreted as an example of the free soul and its ability to travel. For a discussion of the Cree belief in souls, see Chapter VI.

[20] Personal interview, Tom Gardipee, November 4, 1959.

[21] Personal interview, November 4, 1959.

[22] Personal interview, December 29, 1959.

[23] Alanson Skinner, "Bear Customs of the Cree and Other Algonkin Indians of Northern Ontario," *Papers and Records,* Ontario Historical Society, Vol. XII, (1914), pp. 203–204. See also Skinner, "Political Organization, Cults, and Ceremonies of the Plains-Ojibway and Plains-Cree Indians." Anthropological Papers of the American Museum of Natural History (New York, 1914), Vol. XI, Part VI, pp. 541–542.

[24] Skinner, "Bear Customs of the Cree and Other Algonkin Indians of Northern Ontario," *op. cit.,* p. 203.

[25] Personal interview, Pete Favel, December 29, 1959.

was one of their greatest friends or partners. Some of the bears even lived with the Indians in their tipis in the old days. Certain men had powers sufficiently strong to get along with the bear spirit very well and thus could have the bear in the tipi with them. Such bears always became very tame and played with the children "just like one of them." Later in the summer, when the women in the camp needed to know just where the berries were growing in the greatest profusion so that they could get them to harvest and dry for winter use, these pet bears would lead the people to the choicest spots because in their wisdom, they always knew just where to get them.

This former practice of the Cree in keeping a pet bear is reminiscent of ones found both among the Ainu and the Gilyaks. The Ainu of northern Japan caught a bear cub toward the end of the winter and brought it into the village. If it were very small, it was suckled by an Ainu woman. As the cub grew, it played around the hut with the children and was treated with great affection. When the cub grew large enough to hurt people, it was shut up in a cage and kept for two or three years, fed on fish and millet porridge until it was killed and eaten. The bear was not kept merely to furnish a good meal, but rather because it was regarded and honored as a fetish or even as a sort of higher being.[26] The Gilyaks, a Tungrizian people living in eastern Siberia, brought a bear into the village and kept it in a cage where all the village took turns feeding it. Feeding the bear was a mark of honor as one would manifest it toward a welcome guest.[27]

When a Rocky Boy Cree kills a bear, he stuffs the skull with sage and arranges the sage so that it protrudes from the cavities in the skull that had once held the eyes and the nose. Usually, too, the bones are put back together again.[28] This care of the skeleton is a trait that Skinner did not find among the Plains Cree, for he reports[29] that he observed that the skull of the bear was not preserved and that the bones were cast about promiscuously and allowed to fall a prey to the dogs, "something the Eastern Cree would not tolerate."[30] The Eastern Cree, Skin-

---

[26] Sir James Frazer, *The Golden Bough*, Abrid. ed. (London: Macmillan Co., 1948), p. 506.

[27] *Ibid.*, p. 511.

[28] Personal interview, Pete Favel, December 29, 1959.

[29] Skinner, "Political Organizations, Cults, and Ceremonies of the Plains-Ojibway and Plains-Cree Indians," *op. cit.*, p. 541.

[30] *Ibid.*, p. 542.

ner says,[31] carefully clean the bones and hang them on a scaffold where dogs cannot reach them. They clean the skull and paint it with vermillion and place it in a safe place; later they take it to the forest and hang it on a tree. In a way, the Rocky Boy Cree seem to follow more the practice of the Eastern Cree than they do their close relatives on the Plains.

All of Skinner's reports mention the fact that a bit of the meat of the bear or bits of its heart or of its intestines are eaten ceremoniously. The Rocky Boy Cree distribute bits of the fat so that everyone present may get a taste of the bear.[32] Again, this practice of eating some of the meat or fat is similar to one found both among the Ainu and the Gilyak. By partaking of the flesh, blood, or broth of the bear, they feel that they are able to acquire some portion of the animal's mighty powers, or its great courage or tremendous strength.[33]

As was mentioned before, the bears always knew where the best berries were growing. The Cree believe that the bear spirits sometimes feed upon berries. These spirits are able to extract the juice of the berry and leave the shell remaining. "It is just like tobacco," my informant explained,[34] "for when we smoke tobacco, we have just ashes left." Because of the affinity that bears have for berries, they are frequently used in ceremonials and offerings.

Another religious item that is considered efficacious by the contemporary Montana Cree is the bundle. Technically, a bundle is a fetish, something that is built by an individual during his lifetime and that contains items that are significant to him. Bundles are built up and added to during the lifetime of an individual; hence, they may be passed on to succeeding generations. Stones with potent results, pipes, sweetgrass, miniatures of different objects all may be found within a bundle, each wrapped in successive layers of cloth or hide. "A long time ago, when people had no sin, the spirits gave the bundles to people to take care," said Raining Bird.[35] "They are kept from one generation to another and then passed along. Many songs go with the bundles," he added. Another informant, Four Souls, explains bundles by drawing an

---

[31] Skinner, "Bear Customs of the Cree and Other Algonkin Indians of Northern Ontario," *op. cit.*, p. 204.

[32] Personal interview, Pete Favel, December 29, 1959.

[33] Frazer, *op. cit.*, pp. 514–515.

[34] Personal interview, Pete Favel, December 29, 1959.

[35] Personal interview, December 30, 1959.

analogy to certain Christian practices:[36] "A medicine bundle is like the Christian cross," he said. "In a dream a spirit shows an individual how to make something, and so the person gets an eagle feather or a coyote pelt or whatever the spirit has told him. This article is put into a bundle and when the owner needs it, he can use it. In sickness, you can use it to survive. In war, bundles protect the fighters. Catholics have St. Christopher medals to protect them. Bundles protect the Indians in the same way." Four Souls explained further that bundles may be purchased or can be inherited. About half of the bundles are good and helpful to the owners; the other half are bad and can cause damage to other individuals. Little of that practice continues on the reservation today, he says.

All of the Cree informants agree that it is Matchi Manitou or one of the bad spirits who puts the evil power in the bundles. To get this power, a person goes to some old man who is good at handling bad medicine and talks to him. He agrees to work for the individual only for a specific price, usually one that is quite high. Aside from money, he might ask for blankets or some expensive item. If a woman is making the request, he might demand the right to have sexual relations with her before he promises to do the work.

Medicine bags of this type can be used for many different purposes. They can be used effectively in gambling or in playing the hand game. A very special use that medicine bundles can be employed for is to paralyze a horse that is considered an excellent runner. In the hands of a medicine man who can carefully manipulate the power in a bundle, a horse can be made to flounder and fall down in a race. One elderly man on the reservation who was always a good worker and generous to all the people became blind because someone was jealous of him. It is also reported that through the use of an evil medicine bundle, on the part of others less prominent on the reservation, Rocky Boy met his death just as the reservation was opening—a time when his advice was most needed.

By far the most common use of medicine bundles, however, is to cause a person to fall in love. The person who desires another may cut two small dolls out of buckskin. These figures are male and female. The person then takes the dolls to an old man with special powers who ties them up in a hide and puts some special medicine with them. Although not much of this kind of thing is done on the Rocky Boy reservation today, it is practiced extensively in Canada. A practice that is used considerably in Montana, though, is one which a man performs when

---

[36] Personal interview, March 10, 1960.

his wife leaves him. He gets a log, hollows it out, and covers each end with rawhide. Inside the hollowed log he puts some of his wife's clothes or hair or something that was hers along with some medicine that is known to be effective. Then with a crooked stick he hits one end of the log. No matter where she is, a woman will hear the drum that is thus made from the hollowed log and will come running back to her husband.

The Cree have long had a reputation for making effective medicines and in former times capitalized upon their ability, even to the point of selling some of their love bundles to other tribesmen, both friends and enemies. The Blackfeet, for instance, did not have a love medicine of their own but made much use of those they purchased from the Cree. Wissler[37] says that Cree medicine could be used both externally and internally and was also effective if conducted properly in absentia. The power of the medicine was very specific in that each particular type had power only over one definite thing. "The Blackfoot regard them (Cree medicines) with fear and consider them very dangerous to handle or use," he writes.[38] Wissler also says that love medicines are the most popular kind. "When a man wishes to win a girl's heart he first tries to secure some of her hair, and when he gets it, he places a lock in the small bag with the medicine. Then as the medicine takes effect, the girl suddenly finds her whole mind occupied by the man who made the medicine and eventually becomes so affected that she is only satisfied by his side."[39]

Love potency was not the only thing to be achieved in using the Cree medicine bundles the Blackfeet discovered. A person could always win in gambling, especially in the stick games, if he concealed a small Cree medicine bag in his clothing. Runners could put it around their legs just before starting a race and would win. Material from the bags could be put on dogs to silence them and to keep them from arousing the camp when intruders came in to kill or to steal horses. Rifle balls were sometimes dipped in Cree medicine before they were placed in the gun. When on the warpath, the Cree rubbed some of their medicine on their legs to prevent fatigue and to retard the speed of the enemy.[40] It was no wonder that when the Blackfeet visited the Cree they were very careful lest they come under the influence of someone's medicine. All

---

[37] Clark Wissler, "Ceremonial Bundles of the Blackfoot Indians," Anthropological Papers of the American Museum of Natural History (New York, 1912), Vol. VII, Part II, p. 88.

[38] Ibid., p. 88.

[39] Ibid., p. 88.

[40] Ibid., p. 89.

visiting Cree were also very nicely treated because should one become insulted he could wreak all kinds of havoc upon the Blackfeet. A few Blackfeet, unknown to their own tribal members, bought Cree bundles and loaned or transferred them to others for a good-sized fee. "The Cree usually demanded high prices for their medicine, even as much as a horse and other property for a single small bag."[41] Even today, the Cree talk about their superiority over the Blackfeet and how much they were able to accomplish in the old days through the medium of their bundles.

As a rite, however, the bundle is not as significant among the Cree as it is with the Blackfeet who have built their Sun Dance around this element. While bundles may be seen supported on a tripod behind several houses on the reservation, many of the informants seem reluctant to talk about the bundle. Today, it seems to have gained a poor reputation and is considered a means of doing evil rather than good which it once was able to accomplish.

Bundles are not the only thing the Cree fear, however. Some people can use witch talk. Talk is powerful, explain Ruth and Tom Gardipee. "It is not just words. It is meaning. For example, a person wants to get a job. He goes out and looks for work. Someone else is saying he won't get it. That is witch talk, for then he won't. There is no special language a person uses. It can be done by any one regardless of race, creed or color. That is why one must be careful what he says. Maybe he is just joking, but his talk can hurt someone else."[42] Raining Bird takes a different view. "Some people think they know more than *Ki-sei-men'-to*," he says.[43] "People have misunderstood the teachings of the Supreme Being. Nowadays, most of these people try to get their witch talk through the spirit lodge.[44] One way that witchcraft is performed today is for a person to carve another's image on a piece of wood or make a drawing of him on the ground. Then the person who has made the drawing can put some bad medicine on the image and can cause the person to go blind or become crazy or have heart disease or any other kind of trouble.[45]

Peculiar to the Cree on the Rocky Boy reservation is their attitude toward owls. In common with other Indians, however, they feel that the owl is an evil bird that brings bad luck. When they hear it, they know

---

[41] *Ibid.*, p. 90.

[42] Personal interview, September 2, 1960.

[43] Personal interview, December 30, 1959.

[44] For a more complete description of the Spirit Lodge, See Chapter XII.

[45] Informant's name withheld. Information secured March 10, 1960.

that whatever its message may be, it will not be a good one. These Cree, nevertheless, have a specialized interpretation and use for the owl. By stuffing a dead one with paper or leaves or something dry, they can fix the owl so that it can fly and find out what the sender wants to know. It can also kill the person to whom it is sent. If this flying stuffed owl is captured, though, one may be able to kill its sender. Informants state that the Canadian Cree are now using the owl in the same manner if they wish to "do bad things such as causing people to go crazy, or maybe to have them grow a big nose or big ears."

It is interesting to speculate upon the concept of the stuffed owl. Other ethnographers have not reported upon it, but its influence could possibly come from two sources. The first similarity is with the Hideous Flying Heads of the Iroquois. These demons were capable of wrecking individuals whom they could attack. The early Cree along James Bay and southward might conceivably have heard of these malevolent demons and have adapted them to the common bird of evil, the owl. Another source, though possibly far-fetched, might have been the French fur traders and trappers with whom the Cree lived and intermarried. These Frenchmen came as early as the beginning of the 1600's and had left a native land steeped in witchcraft. Witches, as we know, were prevalent in western Europe and England during the fifteenth and sixteenth centuries.[46] That the belief was still prevalent in the seventeenth century is attested by the spread of the idea among the colonists in America. Witches in England and Europe all had familiars—usually a cat or a dog but occasionally a bird—and the role of the stuffed owl seems reminiscent of the familiar employed by the witches. Again it seems possible that the idea of the stuffed owl being sent by an individual to wrong another person might possibly have stemmed from a concept introduced by the French.

Besides these larger concepts which the Cree believe and practice, there are countless little things each of which has a supernatural impact upon the Cree. The tipi, for instance, represents Mother Earth. The ears of the tipi represent the sleeves of Mother Earth, while the people inside the tipi are her children.[47] Water equals life. Thus it must be respected, for the earth uses it just as do humans and animals.[48] Bats are the agents

---

[46] For a more complete coverage of the subject, see Margaret Murray, *Witchcult in Western Europe* (Oxford: University Press, 1921).

[47] Personal interview, Raining Bird, August 24, 1960.

[48] Personal interview, Paul Big Child, August 29, 1959.

of the Evil Spirit, Matchi Manitou.[49] Long hair is the natural way that the Creator wanted hair worn in both men and women. When parents cut a boy's hair, they know that they are shortening his life, yet they must do it to conform to the white influence around them. Several youngsters on the reservation do have long hair, however. Once the hair is cut, it must either be burned or put away very carefully else snakes will get into it.[50]

Occasional Christian influences seem to permeate some of the beliefs. For instance, the Cree say that when *Ki-sei-men'-to* created woman He told her not to eat certain foods. She disobeyed His orders and that act accounts for the fact that she has "blood in her that has to be discharged regularly."[51] Because of the blood, she cannot enter a Sun Dance lodge or be near any of the sacred paraphernalia. If she did, the spirits would become frightened and would leave.

Thus it is that the acculturated-appearing Cree on the Rocky Boy reservation lead their daily lives in an active framework of religious values that were inherited from their fathers. That it is persisting and flourishing is significant. That persistance and growth, however, seem to correlate with the emergence of the "Cree Indians" on this particular reservation, as was outlined earlier. Just as religion permeated every aspect of life among their buffalo-hunting ancestors, regardless of the tribe to which they belonged, so it seems safe to generalize now that primitive belief correlates itself with the daily life of the contemporary Cree Indians on the Rocky Boy reservation in Montana.

---

[49] Raining Bird, August 24, 1960. As we were visiting one evening, a bat flew into the room where we were sitting. He said, "See, here we are sitting here talking about something good and that devil came in and interrupted us."

[50] Personal interview, Ruth Gardipee, November 4, 1959.

[51] Personal interview, Raining Bird, December 31, 1959.

CHAPTER V

RELIGION AND THE LIFE CYCLE

As has been pointed out repeatedly, the outward manifestations of the life cycle of Indians living on the Rocky Boy reservation parallel very closely the life of the average Montana citizen of the same income bracket. Most of the women go to the Fort Belknap hospital, operated by the Bureau of Public Health and located about sixty-five miles away, to have their babies. These children are given a Christian name, and in the majority of instances, they are baptized into either the Roman Catholic or Lutheran churches. They grow up, attend school; some of them are confirmed into the church, and when the time comes for them to marry, the ceremony is usually a civil one performed by a justice of the peace in one of the neighboring towns. As they grow older they continue receiving medical care from a resident nurse on the reservation or from physicians at the Fort Belknap hospital. If their condition warrants hospitalization, an ambulance is available to take them to the hospital. When they grow old and infirm, many of them go to the hospital; frequently, they die there. Their bodies are cared for by an undertaker who is under contract with the Bureau of Indian Affairs to supply such services. Funerals are held in the churches. Burial is in the unkept cemetery located on a hill above the agency center. Occasionally in the winter months, deep snow keeps the hearse from reaching the grave. Men struggle through the snow carrying the casket to the grave which has been dug by friends who have volunteered to do it.

Yet despite the obvious similarity to the dominant culture, many of the Indians reject the white man's principles, inwardly at least, and follow the values of the past. Religion or religious practices occur in every aspect of man's life—carefully hidden, however, from the eyes of the white neighbor, teacher, or government employee. While the material in this chapter comes primarily from members of one family,[1] that group

---

[1] Members of this one family, whom I shall not name, are the maternal grandparents, the mother and father, and five children. The grandfather is in his seventies and is considered a mystic by other conservative members of the tribe. The grandmother, who died while this study was being made, was somewhat younger than her

can be considered representative, particularly in view of the ages of the individuals concerned.

When a woman knows that she is pregnant, she begins praying. Every day throughout her pregnancy, she prays to *Ki-sei-men'-to*. She asks for good luck in the delivery of her baby. She petitions also that the baby will be born sound and healthy and will grow up to be a good man or woman. Because she has such great faith in *Ki-sei-men'-to*, she never misses a single morning in making these requests.

During her pregnancy, a woman knows that her life must follow a different pattern. For instance, certain foods must be avoided. She cannot eat anything that comes from the inside of an animal. In the diet of the contemporary Indian woman, the popular sausage known as wieners or frankfurters cannot be eaten. Neither can chickens, especially wild ones, for if she ate those birds that dust their feathers in the dirt, she would have difficulty in delivering her child. "It would be a dry birth," explained a young mother. The flesh of a badger is likewise tabu, for if a woman should even by accident taste that flesh, the feet of the baby will come first and cause a very difficult birth. When a pregnant woman turns around in her sleep, she does not just twist or flop herself over; she must turn her bottom over first and do it easily so that the cord will not twist around the baby's neck. Also she is careful where she sits either in her own home or in the residence of one of her neighbors. She must never be too close to a hot stove or to heat of any kind, for if she is, the heat will cause the afterbirth to grow to her stomach and give her great trouble.

When the baby is born, the people are grateful and thankful for a successful delivery. Prayers are repeated again, similar to those that have

husband. She was born in Canada after the end of the buffalo-hunting days. Their daughter, who with her husband has given the bulk of the information in this chapter, is in her mid-thirties, has never been baptized in any Christian church, has never gone to the hospital to have any of her children, and looks to primitive religion for the source of her strength. Her husband, about forty, a World War II veteran, is a member of the Native American Church. To these people, and especially to the old grandmother now deceased am I especially grateful for the information herein noted. The fact that the woman informant in this chapter has not been baptized does not make her any less representative. Her husband, as perhaps with the majority of the younger Montana Cree, has been baptized but does not adhere to the precepts of the Christian faith. In this connection, it might be well to point out that the Montana Cree do not particularly venerate Christ nor have they added Him to their divine beings. As will be noted frequently throughout this work, the Indians know about Christ and compare some of their beliefs to Christian doctrines. But I have been unable to find evidence of any particular reverence or veneration.

been offered during the mother's pregnancy. This time, however, they are expressions of gratitude to *Ki-sei-men'-to* for making the birth an easy one for the mother. Prayers are also said for the luck and health of the child as it grows up. Water is an accompaniment of these prayers. The water, which has previously been boiled with sage (*Artemisia ludoviciana*) and has been used to bathe the baby when it is first born, is symbolic. As the parents pray to *Ki-sei-men'-to*, they say, "You gave us this water. It is Mother Earth's milk. We want this child to grow up healthy. We need to have your help to make the child grow up so it will be well and have lots of luck." Today, the Cree say that the washing and cleansing of the baby—cleaning its body and its soul together in the sage and water solution—can be compared to baptism in a Christian church except, of course, that it is done immediately after the birth of the child. And it is done "Indian way," a term so frequently heard in their explanation of their own practices.

The afterbirth comes very easily if the woman has observed the proper tabus and has eaten of the right kind of plants which have an effect upon the blood and cause it to circulate properly. After the delivery, the women take the afterbirth, wrap it up, and put it away in trees or on high rocks where the dogs will not bother it. The women who attend the mother cut the cord and allow part of it to remain on the child. When that portion dries, the mother keeps it so that the child will not become a thief when he becomes older. Also so that the child may become a good and an industrious worker, the mother frequently places the cord in a small bag and puts the bag near an antpile or a pile of cord wood. Later the parents may use the bag as a means of prayer as they are communing with the spirits. It is frequently placed on a trail or in the hills where one can kneel beside it and pray.

When the child is quite young, he is given a pet name. Occasionally, these names are endearments; sometimes they are drawn from some characteristic of the child. These names are usually never intended to be permanent ones, for the child himself or his parents may later wish to change them. The ceremony in giving the second name is a serious and sacred one. It is the mother's responsibility to select the second name and to make the arrangements for the naming ceremony. She calls the old men of the locality together and announces that at a certain designated time she will give a feast in honor of her child and that she wishes them to attend. When the appointed day arrives and the guests are gathered, she offers the child to one of them. The man who volunteers to be the sponsor of the child takes him in his arms and sits and beats time with a rattle. After he has shaken the rattle, he begins singing one of his sacred songs and directs the song to whatever spirit may be involved. It may be sung to any spirit and depends entirely upon the one that the old man knows. The decision concerning the spirit rests solely with the old man. During this time, he may sing several songs, frequently assisted by the other old men present. Such songs are known by the Cree as *We-tas-kah-tak*.[2]

When the singing has been completed, the old man takes the pipe, and after offering it to the spirits, prays that the child will grow up and be lucky and will have a long and happy life. Then the mother comes forward and announces the name she wishes the child to have. When the name has been announced, the people present are ready to bless the child with their prayers. The old man hands the child to the person sitting to his left. This person prays for him, says his name over and over, kisses him and passes the baby to the person at his left. The baby is thus given to each person present, each repeating exactly the same procedure. When the child has been blessed by everyone who is there, the mother announces that the feast is ready. It is not necessary to serve any particular food except that before the regular meal is served, the people all partake of berries, the favorite being service berries.

After a child has been given a sacred name in this manner, no one is ever supposed to hit the youngster on the head. The spirit lives in the back of the neck; if one hits the child, the spirit may be driven out. Also people with great power—those people whom the spirits have given the power or who have met the spirits in their visions or dreams—should not touch the child on the back of the neck. Again, the spirit within the child might be frightened away.

These Indian names given to the children are not the ones by which they are enrolled at the agency nor the ones by which they are called by their parents or siblings when speaking to the child in the presence of a white person. Thus each child has an Indian name, one that was bestowed upon him in traditional Cree fashion, plus one or two names drawn from the Anglo-American tradition. On the Rocky Boy reservation, very few of the older men have followed the latter practice and are known only by their Indian names.

While the child is still small, certain restrictions are placed upon the mother although the father seems to be relatively free. When the mother

---

[2] Peeso, in his unpublished manuscript, elaborates upon the same ceremony as given me by my informants and supplies the Cree names for the songs.

nurses her child, she takes a drink of water—water which she or some of her family has prayed over first. She knows that she must not drink too much water else the child will have an upset stomach. Other tabus that she must follow while she is nursing the child refer principally to the youngster: he can never be kept in a swing at night; his diapers cannot be hung outside at night; and he can never be left alone in a tipi or a house because of the Evil Spirit (Matchi Manitou). Children, however, are not frightened by the threat of Matchi Manitou. Rather, it is one of his agents to whom the parents may turn. For instance, parents may say, "If you're not good, the owl will come and get you." Couples are taught that they should not separate when they have children, for if they do Ki-sei-men'-to will think that the children are not wanted and that they have been thrown away.

Of all the changes that have taken place, the practices at the time of puberty have perhaps altered the most. And this is particularly true with the boys, for there seems to be no opportunity to conduct any kind of ceremony for them or to make any substitutions for it in the present-day culture. Although the parents and grandparents continue praying for the child until he reaches manhood and by the same token have tried to teach him good habits, there comes a time, especially in a boy's life, when the older people can no longer exercise the kind of supervision over the young person that the elders desire. Since it is impossible now to have any kind of formal ceremony at puberty, the older people pray with him and relate to him what once was done.

In telling the boy the practices of the past, the old people relate also how much better it was then for everyone concerned. While they attribute much of the juvenile delinquency to the passing of the rites at the time of puberty, they also realize that the change in the material culture has made this element obsolete. Consequently, the elders tell how when the boy in the old days killed his first animal, his family gave a feast. They gathered the old people together and all of them prayed for the boy so that he would have good luck in all of his future expeditions. They taught him how to be kind and how to share his food with others. As presents were distributed to the older friends who were attending the function, the parents thanked Ki-sei-men'-to for allowing the boy to kill an animal and bring back the food and asked that he always be as generous and thoughtful to the people in the camp.

Special ceremonies occurred when the boy killed his first buffalo or bear. Here the Master Spirit of these animals was implored. For example, at the time of the killing of the first buffalo, the family gave the Master

Buffalo Spirit a wand that had been made from a curved willow stick decorated with eagle down and shells. This Master Spirit, which is also synonomous with the Spirit of Food, had sustained the boy during his childhood; hence a special recognition had to be made in appreciation. A similar situation was followed when the boy killed his first bear. The family gave an offering of red cloth and June berries (if they were in season—otherwise any kind of berries) and prayed to the Master Spirit of the Bear and said that they were sorry that their boy had to kill a bear. Now, they said, their boy was a man and must provide food for his family and relatives. He had killed the greatest of the animals and had thus proved himself to be a man. The Master Spirit of the Bear was thus invoked so that he would recognize the necessity of the boy's action and not be vengeful upon the family for the boy's having killed a bear.

People could usually tell when a boy became a man by the change in his voice. Shortly after the physiological change occurred, the boy went out into the hills or trees or near water and fasted and waited for a spirit to come to him. He sought his power, however, only after much preaching had been directed toward him and many prayers said in his behalf. The preaching and the prayers continue; the big difference is that now the boy does not listen as he once did.[3] Here in this situation religion does not function as it once did for the younger people. To the older person, however, it is but another manifestation of the white man's intrusion and subsequently the disturbance of the way of life. The Cree do not think it is their fault, nor the fault of *Ki-sei-men'-to.*

While some changes have come into the puberty rites concerning the girls, more of the primitive pattern continues. At the time of her first menses, the girl is separated from the family. In contemporary culture, the girl may go to live with her grandmother, live in a tent some distance from the house ("but not too far so the girls won't run around"), or if the house should have one, stay in the cellar. The distance away from the family is not measured; the idea is that the girl must be far enough away so that she will not see a man. She has great power at this particular time, power so strong that if she looked at a man his face would break into pimples. During this time also a girl must use just one cup and spoon. These implements must be hers exclusively for a long time after her return to the family; if anyone else touched them he would become sick because of the poison on them. Likewise, one could contract tuberculosis of the stomach if he were to touch the cup. While the girl

---

[3] Boys no longer seek visions. For a fuller coverage, see Chapter X.

is away from the family, she fasts during the daytime but is allowed to eat during the night. In the old days, girls sewed, tanned hides, chopped wood, and did other work pertinent to the needs of the family. Today, the girls usually gather and stockpile wood for later consumption in the cabins of the families. Frequently, an old lady or a grandmother stays with her instructing her in the beliefs of the group as well as teaching her how to do beadwork. During this time, also, a girl must be extremely careful about eating berries. It is acceptable for a girl to gather berries, should they be in season, provided she promises to give a feast and to invite all of the old women in the neighborhood. She knows that if she should eat any of the berries without thus making the promise of a feast, not only would her own hair come out, but from that time forward there would be no berries.

When the girl returns from isolation, some old lady acts as her sponsor and supervises the feast that is given for the old women. The girl or her parents give a present to the old woman who is sponsor of the feast, for it is this old lady who offers the prayers to *Ki-sei-men'-to*. The old lady prays and thanks *Ki-sei-men'-to* for allowing the girl to mature and expresses as well a wish that the girl be allowed to continue having good luck until her marriage.

Today, as in primitive times, a girl learns that her difficulties are not over with her return to society following her first menses. She learns that there are certain tabus to be observed with every returning period. She must never go into anyone else's home during such a time because of the fact that she is unaware of the kind of medicine her neighbor or friend might have in the house. It could be that the medicine in some one else's house might be so powerful that it would cause the girl to hemorrhage and not recover. Likewise, she should not pick up a baby during the time of her period, for if she does, the baby might die.

Of all the tabus the girls must follow, those relating to the Sun Dance and other observances are the most stringent. A girl does not go near the Sun Dance until a year has passed after her first menstruation. After the first year, a girl may go into the Sun Dance Lodge and participate in the ceremony providing that her period has been over for at least four nights. The same situation holds true for any of the other ceremonies such as the sweat lodge, the Smoke Lodge, the Give Away, or any place where the elders use the pipe and sweetgrass. The "respect for the pipe," a term so frequently heard among the Montana Cree, includes a goodly number of tabus on all the people present. For instance, while someone is smoking, no individual is allowed to pass in front of the pipe. Or if a

94

person is sitting and holds the pipe upward, no one is permitted to pass in front of it or to speak. The pipe and the sweetgrass, according to the teaching of *Ki-sei-men'-to*, carry messages to Him. Consequently, one must be very circumspect in everything he does while the pipe is in evidence. A menstruating girl would simply have so much power that she would interfere with the ceremony were she to be present.

While the Cree are able to teach their daughters the proper behavior during their puberty, they realize that white influence has changed the pattern of marriage and that there is little they can do about it. In the old days, they fondly recall, a boy who liked a girl especially well went to her father with gifts. (Occasionally, the practice might be reversed: a girl could initiate the procedure by bringing a gift to the boy, usually a pair of nicely beaded moccasins. Once a girl made a breech clout for a boy with whom she was enamored. The story has been enjoyed by all of the old women, who tell it with great glee and with a Gallic sense of frankness.) If the boy were a good and an industrious worker, the father accepted him as a potential son-in-law even though the lad might not have been particularly wealthy.

When the time came to marry, the girl had prepared her tipi and had it standing beside the tipi of her parents. The boy brought more presents to the girl's father and then moved into the newly-decorated and prepared tipi. To all intents and purposes then the couple were married. Friends and relatives often came, bringing presents with them, to visit the new couple and always offered prayers for them. They asked *Ki-sei-men'-to* to watch the young couple and allow them to live together for a long time and to have many good healthy children. Shortly after marriage, the father usually sent some elderly man to live with the couple and to pray for their successful marriage as he taught them some of the arts necessary for getting along well together.

Occasionally, the young married couple on the reservation today receives the instruction and prayers of an elderly man. Practically all else is lost because of the necessary conformity to the white culture. Here and there some relics of the past thinking exist, however. For instance, one elderly man is rearing his family definitely in the pattern of the past. He permits his daughters to marry only when the boy has brought suitable presents to him. After the marriage, he insists that the boy move into his home and work for him during the first year of married life. Throughout that time, the father-in-law dictates the conduct of the boy and regulates the social as well as the economic life of the young man. Consequently, only two of the older man's daughters have been married and neither marriage has been successful. One former son-in-law admitted that he went into the marriage because of fear since the older man is known to have considerable power, and thus the boy did not know what would happen to him should he have refused the marriage offer. The marriage occurred just as the young man was preparing to leave for the army. He felt that enough improbables existed without antagonizing this older man, so he agreed to the marriage, which, however, did not last. Currently, there is a saying on the reservation, "You do not marry one of the So-and-So girls; you become old So-and-So's slave." With the substitution of civil law for religious observances, the Cree have followed or are following but little of their past teachings regarding marriage.

At the time of menopause, many women "go kind of crazy." While no special prayers exist for them, many women are assisted through purification ceremonies conducted by the men who bring the pipe into use and pray for the speedy recovery of the woman. Sometimes too she is censed with sweetgrass as prayers are said for her. Once a woman has gone through the menopause, she becomes like a man and can participate in any of the ceremonies that men do and from which other women are barred.

While some changes have taken place in the rites at the time of death, much of the thinking of the past pervades the actions of the Montana Cree. Just as in primitive times, a man is dressed in his best outfit, now a suit of store-bought clothes rather than the buckskins of old. The prayers are the same. The people, survivors and friends of the deceased, pray that the man who has died will go straight south and not look back else he might take someone else along with him. The prayer, roughly translated, goes something like this:[4]

> Go. Go straight ahead
> Do not take anyone with you.
> Do not look back.
> When you reach your destination, talk for us.
> Tell them not to trouble us.
> Or not to come here and take anyone else away.

Although, as has been mentioned before, the body is now prepared by an undertaker and placed in a wooden casket, it is returned to the home and stays there the night before the burial is scheduled to take place. Some close friend or relative puts a pipe and some sweetgrass,

---

[4] F. E. Peeso, unpublished manuscript, typewritten copy, p. 54.

which are wrapped together, in the casket. Sometimes food is also placed there. Before the body is buried, the elders give the children some little willow switches and tell them to hit the dead so that they will go away and not bother the living. Frequently, the parents of the children tie a piece of buckskin about the legs and wrists of the youngsters the night before the burial of the deceased so that its soul will not lure the souls of the young children away.

Now, as has also been stated, most of the dead are buried in the cemetery near the agency. In the old days it was different. As soon as a person died, his relatives took his body out the back or the side of the lodge—never through the front door. Usually, the Cree buried their dead on scaffolds. The knees of the dead person were drawn up and the body placed in a reclining position, well wrapped with blankets and robes.

During the years that the Cree were wandering in Montana, a change occurred in their method of burying the dead. To conform to practices required by the Federal Government of the United States, they were no longer allowed to use the scaffold as a means of burying. Allegedly because of sanitary necessity, all Indians were required to bury their dead under-ground, something particularly offensive to the ideas of the Plains' Indians. By some means, most of the Indian tribes on the Plains were able to circumvent this ruling and still abide in general with the regulations of the United States government. The Cree dug a shallow grave which they lined with boughs from quaking aspen or fir trees, and placed the body there along with food and tobacco and the weapons and utensils of the deceased. They then covered the grave with rocks to protect it from coyotes and other animals and birds.[5]

The Cheyenne Indians followed much the same practice, although they built mounds of rocks over their dead who had been placed in high mountainous areas. The Gros Ventre and the Assiniboine compromised, when the United States government ordered them to put their dead in the ground, by carrying their dead to the tops of high hills and there under sand rocks they would place the pipe and household equipment along with the body. Later, they put the dead in wooden boxes and carried them to the hills. More recently, the boxes have had silver-plated handles on them.[6]

As soon as possible after a person dies, some near relative of the

---

[5] *Ibid.*

[6] I have seen many such instances in the hills of the Fort Belknap reservation.

deceased gives away all of his property, including his clothes and all of his personal belongings. The property is given away for two reasons: one, so that those who are left, the relatives, will not look at it and grieve, and two, so that those who are dead will not come back to look at their belongings and bother the living. In the old days, the relatives gave away the tipi, too. Their tribesmen, however, contributed to the needs of the survivors—one giving a lodge, another a blanket, and so on until the bereaved family was as comfortably fixed as before.[7]

A few other tabus related to death are still with the Cree. No one should cry at night after a death in the family else the soul of the dead will be summoned. A person should not look back after he is returning from a burial or he might see the soul of the dead person. Men working as grave diggers should not get too tired as they dig the grave or else they always will be tired.

Religion, Cree religion, functions in the life cycle of the Montana Cree Indians. While it is more operative at some periods of an individual's life than at others, it is still a meaningful experience that has persisted throughout the years.

---

[7] Peeso, *op. cit.*

CHAPTER VI

GHOSTS AND THE SOUL

When a person dies, his soul leaves the body and goes south. Some say[1] that it travels over three humps and when it reaches the fourth one, it has reached the place of the dead. Another informant, Windy Boy, relates[2] that the souls of those who are good and honest go south and travel the Heaven Road. During one's lifetime, a person cannot see this road, but it is a good broad and even road that goes to the land of the dead. When one reaches the place at the end of the road, the place that the white man calls heaven, he will find buffalo and tipis and the Indian way of life continuing. Windy Boy believes that Indians and whites go to separate heavens. He maintains that there is the same God, but that there are different heavens. "It's like the United States and Europe," he adds. "Two different areas."

Raining Bird says[3] that the place where the dead go is called *i-dei'-kam-me-ju-sik,* "where it is good," or perhaps just "a good place." Sometimes, the Cree refer to the land of the dead as *ka-pit-shak-uski,* a faraway land. "The place of the dead is in the south," Raining Bird adds. "It is a good place where the ground is good and everything smells nice. The people sing and dance. They have the buffalo there to eat. They live in tipis and have everything they want. It is the old way of life." The First Person, the one whom the Creator made first, rules the land of the dead, for he is the owner of the human souls that were made like him. (In some respects, this idea parallels the Master Spirit idea which will be covered in a later chapter.)

My informants explain that the souls of those who are evil go to a different place from the "place that is good." The Evil Spirit, Matchi Manitou, presides over this place and it is called for him simply by adding a suffix, *nak,* the Cree syllable indicating "place" or "location." It is deep down into the earth where everything is dark and where snakes, bats, and others of Matchi Manitou's agents reside. Many sharp

---

[1] Personal interview, Mrs. Ruth Gardipee, October 31, 1959.

[2] Personal interview, December 21, 1959.

[3] Personal interview, August 31, 1960.

things are there also. While this idea of a hell may have its origin in Christian doctrine, the concept has been developed by the Cree to its present meaning.

Then the Cree also consider those who have not followed their Creator's teachings here on earth and hence their souls must suffer. In fact, they have to remain here on earth until the world is remade.[4] Although this idea lacks the specific detail that the Cheyenne Indians have, certain parallels exist which point to the concept's being Algonquian rather than Christian. According to Cheyenne informants[5] the souls of the Cheyenne dead follow the Milky Way across the sky to reach Se-yan', the land of the departed. About mid-heaven, where the Milky Way branches, the Cheyenne say the good separate from the bad. The good souls keep on the bright and shining pathway to the left whereas the bad ones are stranded on the path at the right which sort of dissolves into nothingness. The same idea is found among the Maidu, according to Father Schmidt[6] who reports: ". . . it is by the Milky Way that the soul passes to heaven. Where that divides, there the souls separate themselves from each other: to the left is an easy and good way . . . leading to the land above."

Soul leaving is like going to another country, reported the late Mrs. Mary Favel.[7] But, she explained, the soul of the dead does not leave the body for four days after the death of the individual. During those days, the relatives know that they should not cry too much for if they refrain from shedding tears, the soul will be all right. Also the people know that they are all heading in the same direction so they should not be too distressed by the death of their relative. On the fourth day, the relatives prepare a feast. On that day, the survivors know that the door opens to the place of the dead.[8] Thus the people at the feast realize that they are eating and smoking with the soul that is now departing. To help purify the departing soul, the pipe is used ceremoniously. Smoking precedes and concludes the feast. If Northern Lights appear on the fifth night after the death of an individual, the survivors know that the soul of the

---

[4] Personal interview, Raining Bird, March 25, 1959.

[5] Personal interview, Del Seminole, a well-informed member of the Northern Cheyenne tribe, September 15, 1959.

[6] W. Schmidt, *High Gods in North America* (Oxford: Clarendon Press, 1933), p. 34. R. B. Dixon reports more fully on this concept in *The Northern Maidu*. Bulletins of American Museum of Natural History (New York, 1905), Vol. XVII, Part III.

[7] Personal interview, December 23, 1959.

[8] Personal interview, Raining Bird, December 30, 1959.

deceased has gone straight to the good place. During the four nights after a person dies, a soul may roam about, however. For example, a Cree tribesman died in Great Falls, Montana, one hundred miles away from the reservation, on December 27, 1959, at a time when I was visiting the Cree. Two nights later, one of the elderly men on the Rocky Boy felt the presence of the soul of his deceased friend.[9]

A certain amount of confusion seems to exist in making the distinction between a soul and a ghost. "A ghost is a soul and a soul is a ghost," said one of my informants.[10] The Cree terms can be used interchangeably. The word for ghost is *tchi-pay* and the word for soul is *at'-tshak*. Ghosts, however, do not like to be referred to as *tchi-pay* and if so called, they are more likely to bother the individual who used that term. In general, the Cree believe that when a soul remains here on earth it is a ghost, but when it goes to the place of the dead it is a soul. Apparently, the ghost is one who is not bad enough to go to *Matchi-manitou-nak,* but instead the ghost is the representative of the individual who did not follow the Creator's teachings here on earth. Their purpose seems merely to be to "hang around and scare people."[11] Some of the informants maintain that they can see ghosts while others say that they can merely feel their presence. All agree, however, that ghosts frighten people.

In general, ghosts are similar to the living. They are dressed just exactly as they were when they died. Since they want to be human again and do the things humans do, they "hang around people all the time."[12] At the social dances, especially those held near the holiday times, the Indians know that the ghosts are present and are dancing too—again simply because they want to be human. Because the ghosts are there, some one always announces at the conclusion of the dance, "This is the end. We're going home."[13] Parents tell their children the same thing when they awaken them after the dance to take them home. Should they not do so, the ghost might take away the soul of the child.

In other ways, ghosts are quite different from the living. For example, they cannot touch the earth when they are walking or dancing because

---

[9] Personally related to me by the daughter of the man who saw the soul of his deceased friend.

[10] Personal interview, Tom Gardipee, September 2, 1960.

[11] Personal interview, Windy Boy, December 21, 1959.

[12] Personal interview, Ruth and Tom Gardipee, September 2, 1960.

[13] Personally related to me on December 29, 1959, by a sincere informant whose name I am purposely withholding.

they are dead, so they stay about twelve inches above ground. Since they are capable of walking through the logs or the walls of a house, they do not need to use a door. Sometimes, but not always, a person can hear a ghost but cannot see it. If one talks to it without seeing or hearing it, the individual so doing will have bad luck.

Since ghosts are known to exist in the community, members of the Rocky Boy tribe practice certain definite tabus concerning them. For instance, they never leave any food uncovered after it becomes dark. Fats such as grease or lard or butter must always be covered at night. Water also must be covered. Ghosts like to play in open buckets of water and to sprinkle it on the fire or on the stove. A little charcoal in the water will repel the ghosts, however. A person cannot take lard outside the cabin at night because if he does, ghosts will come and whistle at the person. Whistling is ghost language anyway, so one never whistles when he is outdoors at night. If he does, the ghosts will come and cause him to become mentally deranged.

There are always a few skeptical people who doubt the existence of ghosts. The Rocky Boy Cree like to relate the story of a young man who did not believe all of the stories that the people told concerning the presence of ghosts. Once when the people were camped together in their tipis away from the white settlements, this young man went outside at night and walked a considerable distance away from the camp. He heard nothing, so rather scornfully he started sauntering back to the encampment, whistling as he came. Suddenly a ghost appeared and untied his moccasins. Frightened now, he ran for home as rapidly as he could. As he ran, other ghosts started taking off his clothing, first one piece and then another until he was completely naked when he reached his lodge and stumbled against the poles of his tipi. His parents heard the noise and coming out, found him nearly unconscious lying near the flap of the entrance. The next day, his relatives went with him along the trail he had taken the night before and found his clothes scattered along the way. Young people still listen to this story and do not venture any tricks that might annoy the ghosts on the Rocky Boy reservation today.

Despite the fact that the Cree are quite clear in their distinction between the souls of the dead who in life had lived a good and pure life and the souls of the dead whose living habits had caused them to remain on this earth, a certain amount of confusion seems to characterize their attitude toward a plurality of souls. Mandelbaum[14] reports that "during

[14] David Mandelbaum, *The Plains Cree,* Anthropological Papers of the American Museum of Natural History (New York, 1940), Vol. XXXVII, Part II, p. 251.

a vision the soul could leave the body and travel with the spirit helper." Skinner thinks that he found evidence of two souls, one the *"tcipai,* which stays behind with the corpse in the grave and another, the *niukaneo,* which goes to the hereafter."[15] (While the first term agrees in general with my informants and with my knowledge of the Cree language, the second term does not. Not only is it not known among the Montana Cree, but it does not compare with other words that might possibly be synonyms. For instance, I asked definitely the terms for the following: breath which is *ye-ye-win',* heart, *mdte',* and mind, *ma-mi-tu-ne* or *i-tshi-kun.*) Paul Big Child, an elderly Cree from the Rocky Mountain House in Canada, told me that while the Cree name for themselves was *na-wi-a-wak,* which literally means four bodies, there was only one soul.[16] Yet among the Montana Cree one finds suggestions of the belief in the plurality of souls from the stories they tell.

An adventure related to me by the late Mrs. Mary Favel[17] gives some indication of a belief in the ability of the soul to travel. At the time the incident occurred, Mrs. Favel said it was customary for people to sit up quite late each evening and visit. A group of her friends, following this custom, would come to her tipi to talk and gossip almost every night, usually staying quite late. One night, they heard an owl talking. As they all stopped their chatting to listen to it, they realized that it sounded quite different from the regular call of the owl, so they came to the conclusion that this one must be a stuffed owl.[18] Thus some witchcraft must be afoot. Consequently, her guests left immediately for their own camps. Since nothing happened that night nor the next day, the people came back to visit her the next evening as usual. As they sat there talking, they heard the owl hooting again. Once more the pleasant gossip and small talk was interrupted and the people went home. The third evening the sound came again, and once more the visitors scurried home. They did not come the fourth night because of certain apprehensions. Consequently, Mrs. Favel was alone in her tipi. Sometime during the night she awoke to nurse her small daughter. Before she awakened her baby, however, she stirred the fire and made it relatively light and warm

[15] Alanson Skinner, "Notes on the Plains Cree," *American Anthropologist,* Vol. XVI (1914), p. 76.

[16] Personal interview, August 29, 1959. Big Child speaks no English but is considered an authority on religious matters by the Montana Cree. Tom Gardipee interpreted for me.

[17] Mrs. Favel, with her daughter Mrs. Gardipee interpreting, told me this story November 3, 1959.

[18] See explanation of stuffed owls in Chapter IV.

within the tipi. Then when all was pleasant, she picked up her baby and suckled it. As she sat there, nursing her child, a little girl opened the flap of the tipi and said, "You're wanted." She did not recognize the child, but thinking her to be one of the children of the camp, wrapped her baby up warmly and taking the child with her, accompanied the little girl outside.

Once outdoors, they seemed to disappear into space and travelled for a long time. Finally, they came to a place where several other tipis were standing. The little girl took her inside one of them. An old man sat at the place of honor behind the fire at the back of the tipi. Other men and women sat along the side. The little girl took her to the old man who motioned her to sit down. She sat there resting, for no one said anything to her and she recognized none of them. Finally, the old man said, "Here she is."

Shortly after the old man had made that statement, a woman entered the lodge. Mrs. Favel had known this woman well but was very surprised to see her, for the woman had been dead for over a year. She was more startled yet when the woman came up to her and said, "The horse you sold me is lost. Have you taken it back? I want to know, for I want that horse." When Mrs. Favel said that she had not taken the horse back nor had she even seen it since the time she had sold it to this woman, the woman became quite angry. "Don't take her back," she said to the old man. "Let her go back by herself."

With that outburst, the woman vanished. So seemingly did all the others who were sitting in the lodge. Mrs. Favel walked out of the tipi, which she now noticed had been set on a spot where the grass and dirt had all been scraped away and where the pipe rested as it should on a little altar behind the fire. It was getting light when she lifted the tipi flap and walked out. She did not know where she was although she was sure she must be in Canada. No one was in sight. She sat down and prayed that she would reach home safely. She had with her a little medicine bundle, a rattle, and some sweetgrass, all of which she now used to pray that she might reach home. When she had finished her prayers, she started walking south. After she had walked for a long time, she began to recognize landmarks, and presently she knew that she was near the Cypress Hills (in Canada). There she stopped to rest, and as she lifted her blanket, she became conscious for the first time that her little daughter was with her. She remembered picking the child up and carrying her out of her own tipi, but from then until the present, she had no memory of the child's being with her on the trip to the tipi nor when she was within the strange tipi. She sat down, nursed the child, and then started walking again toward the south. At last she saw Long George Butte, a distinguishing feature of the terrain of the Rocky Boy reservation, and realized that she was nearing home. She can give but little explanation for this phenomenon, but she insisted that it was not a dream. It seems plausible that this experience is perhaps some small evidence of a former belief in the duality or plurality of souls.

Raining Bird, philosopher that he is, is not as definite about the plurality of souls as he is about many of the religious beliefs. He knows that the soul is located near the base of the skull just above the back of the neck.[19] This location agrees with the findings of Mandelbaum who wrote, "It (the soul) resided at the nape of the neck. Only when danger threatened did a man feel the presence of his soul along the back of the neck."[20] Raining Bird goes on to say that ordinarily a person has just one soul, but if he follows *Ki-sei-men'-to's* instructions and teachings a person can earn a total of four souls.

Since the soul is a person's guardian, one can become much more intelligent and also have the power to divine the future if he is able to secure these four souls. All of them cannot, however, be secured at one time. A person has one when he is born. If an individual follows *Ki-sei-men'-to's* instructions and laws, he can earn two more souls. Now, counting the one he has had since birth, he has three souls. This is the point where most individuals stop, but if one continues doing all of the good things *Ki-sei-men'-to* requires, he can eventually earn the fourth soul. Because of the difficulty involved, few people ever do all of the things that are required. Consequently, only a very limited number of individuals ever earn them. What the gradations in souls are like, or whether they are free souls or life souls, I have never been able to ascertain. Since this fogginess on Raining Bird's part is so completely different from his usual definite alertness, it indicates to me that he is not clear in his own mind about the multiplicity of souls. It seems then that it is impossible to generalize about the Cree belief in the plurality of souls.

It would be much easier if the Cree had as concise and definite a knowledge of souls as the Assiniboine, their long-time friends and allies. The Assiniboine have four souls:[21] two of them are for the living, one

---

[19] Personal interview, December 30, 1959.

[20] Mandelbaum, *op. cit.*, p. 251.

[21] Rex Flying, custodian of the secrets of the Assiniboine on the Fort Belknap reservation, gave me this information, September 5, 1958.

for daylight and one for the night; two of them are for the dead, one that wanders out in the blue and one that remains here on earth. These four souls, however, are all part of the living person, even though two of them are not used while the individual is living. A child has all of these souls also. So do animals. For that matter, anything that moves has a soul. A tree has life and moves; hence it has a soul. A shadow does not have a soul because it does not move except as the living object moves. A shadow is simply the light from above, either the sun or the moon. Hence it cannot have a soul.

The Assiniboine equate soul and spirit. In fact, they use the same word, *na'-qhi,* to designate both soul and spirit. Thus when a person becomes very ill and sinks into a coma, the soul vibrates "like electricity." As it vibrates farther and farther away from the body, there is nothing anyone can do to help bring it back, for there is nothing left for it to come back to. The souls of Death triumph over the souls of Life.

With information as precise and definite as the Assiniboine give, one can see how little they have influenced the thinking of the Cree, despite the fact that they have been friends and allies for over three hundred and fifty years. For centuries they were friends in Canada; in the United States, their reservations are separated by approximately forty miles, and no intervening tribes live between them. The Montana Cree have followed the old Cree pattern. In attaining identification, whatever little there is, they are Cree in their thinking, uninfluenced by their friendly neighbors and friends, the Assiniboine, in their concepts of the soul.

CHAPTER VII

SPIRITS

Of all the aspects of Indian religion, the concept of the spirits is perhaps the most difficult to comprehend. This inability to understand Indian thinking about the unseen forces in the universe may stem from confusion about names. Some writers term it "animatism," while others use the term "animism." And these terms themselves have led to speculation and endless discussion that have in general confused rather than enlightened the product of Western thinking. Radin[1] did not think that the matter belonged in the sphere of religion at all, for he wrote: ". . . animism is not a religion at all; it is a philosophy. The belief in the general animation of nature has nothing to do with the supernatural. An object, animate or inanimate, derives its supernatural quality from its association with a number of distinct elements and from the transference to it of certain ideas, concepts, and activities."

But to the Montana Cree, the belief in spirits is definitely part of their religious experience. That it is misunderstood by the whites no doubt stems from the fact that here again is an illustration or an example of a concept that appears completely illogical to the white man. Here is something entirely outside his own experience, therefore it is illogical to him; it becomes something that is false and untrue. But the Cree have another explanation.

"*Ki-sei-men'-to* has power over this earth. He is the law. But the Spirits (*ot-tchak*) take care of this world," says Raining Bird.[2] "In prayer, one prays to *Ki-sei-men'-to* first and then to the Spirits. The unseen Spirits are the messengers of God." He goes on to point out that the Indians themselves were different a long time ago. In those days, when the people followed the instructions of their Supreme Being, they lived close to the Spirits and could see them. They could tell how each one of them looked and what his background or history was. The Spirits, in turn, would sing songs to them and talk to them and do other things

---

[1] Paul Radin, *Primitive Religion: Its Nature and Origin* (New York: Dover Publications, 1957), p. 198.

[2] Personal interview, December 30, 1959.

that were pleasing to the individual. Today only a very few Indians are left who can do these things.

Among the commoner spirits is Daylight. It was created first. Then there was not enough light, so the Creator made the Sun and gave to it the bright light.[3] Hence, two spirits are responsible for lighting the universe—Sun and Daylight. Since these are spirits, they hear all that is said. As an example, once toward the end of a November day—one in which I had spent nearly eight hours interviewing my informant—she looked out the window and said, "I hate to see it get dark."

"Yes," I replied, thinking that the reference was made to the waning hours of daylignt now that autumn had really started and snow was falling. "It's getting dark early these days," I added.

"That is not what I meant," said my informant. "Daylight is a spirit. I hate to see Daylight go today because it has heard everything I have told you. Maybe I have told you too much or things it doesn't like. That's why I don't like to see it leave today."[4]

Another spirit that controls light is the Moon. In fact, twelve spirits exist, one for each of the twelve moons. Each of these spirits protects a person for at least a month during the year.

Fire provides another example of the spirit. Long ago, a spirit came from the south and talked for a long time with the old people. It said that it would stay with them always, for it was the fire spirit.

"I will be with you," it said.[5] "I am half man and half woman. I will take care of your homes. I will take care of the children. But I must ask something in return from you. You must take care of me always. When you move, you must take a little piece of live charcoal with you. Then I can always help you." Thus it was that in the old days, when people lived in tipis and moved from place to place hunting the buffalo, they would take a few charcoals and some ashes with them. They carried these in a buckskin bag to the new camping place. When they had started a new fire and it was hurning well, they put the ashes they had carried with them into the new blaze. Thus they had taken the Fire Spirit from the old place and had put it into the new.

Fire spirit is a good illustration of the task that each spirit has, for at the time of the creation, *Ki-sei-men'-to* gave different jobs to various spirits. For instance, as has been pointed out before, Sun Spirit lights

---

[3] Personal interview, Raining Bird, August 30, 1960.

[4] Actual conversation. The name of the informant is purposely withheld. November 4, 1959.

[5] Personal interview, Raining Bird, September 2, 1960.

the world by day while Moon Spirit lights the world by night. Wind Spirit takes care of our breathing and supplies the oxygen necessary to life. Thunder Spirit sends rain and makes things grow so that the people will have plenty to eat.[6] Snow is not a spirit, for it comes from the White Thunderbird Spirit, the one that controls the North Wind. White Thunderbird Spirit covers the sickness in the winter time. It puts the sickness under the snow. (That is why people are much less likely to become ill in the winter when the snow is deep than they are when the winter has no snow.)

The Montana Cree know but a few of the spirits and admit that there are thousands that they do not know.[7] Many of these unknown spirits are good ones that come to a person through fasting or through the individual's experience at the Sun Dance. Fasting may last for only four days and four nights or it can extend into weeks, months, or years. If the fast is extensive, the spirits feed the individual. For instance, the Montana Cree tell about one elderly man who once lived on the reservation and who fasted for four years. He knew the spirits who were very good to him. Not only did they feed him but they enabled him to forecast or divine the future as well. Because of the songs they had taught him, he could commune with the spirits whenever he wanted to do so and thus learn the events of the future. For example, he knew all about the power of uranium and told the people about it long before anyone knew anything about the atomic bomb.[8]

Good spirits often take pity on people who are asleep and "will take a person around."[9] This practice of allowing a person to move into other and more pleasant regions while the body sleeps is not done much anymore. In fact, it seems increasingly more difficult to get in touch with all the good spirits because they are moving upward and leaving in their place the evil spirits. That is why there are so many bad things done on earth now, for the evil spirits seem to be gaining supremacy here.

Many of the unseen spirits are evil. For instance, during the springtime the Tiger Spirit tries to lure women and get them to look into water and then go under the earth. If a woman does that, she will see a very attractive looking and handsomely built man. If she succumbs to his charms and has intercourse with him, her children will die and she

---

[6] Personal interview, Raining Bird, August 27, 1960.
[7] Personal interview, Raining Bird, August 29, 1960.
[8] Personal interview, Raining Bird, August 28, 1960.
[9] Personal interview. Ruth and Tom Gardipee, September 2, 1960.

will be unable to bear any more. All the rest of her life she has to feed the spirit of this evil person who is an agent of Matchi Manitou as are all evil things such as owls, bats, snakes, and mosquitoes. All of these things are directed by Matchi Manitou.[10]

Anthropologists may debate over the difference between spirits, that is whether the spirit is in something or whether an object is a spirit. But the Montana Cree are not so involved. They know definitely that objects in nature are spirits. For instance, the Earth is a Spirit. That is why the grass is green. "If you put a spirit in the earth it would not let the grass grow," explains Pete Favel.[11] "So it is with Fire and all the other spirits." Ruth and Tom Gardipee are just as emphatic. "Mother Earth is the Spirit," they say. "There is no spirit in her for she is the spirit. It is the same with wind, or fire, or anything else."[12]

The Spirits send luck to people. Those things that are desired by the people such as happiness, health, good children, and good housing are included in this general category defined as "luck."[13] Some of the areas of the reservation are better than others for getting in touch with the Spirits. For instance, Baldy Mountain is one of the very best places. The good spirits are there, especially the ones that can tell the future. On the southwest side of Baldy Mountain resides the spirit that gets one in touch with the bear.

Other regions are also good but as might be expected, some of them are bad. For example, the Haystack region is inhabited by spirits that can kill people. All one ever learns in that region is something evil.[14] Again, it is an area frequented by owls, snakes and also has many mosquitoes that suck the blood.

Since the Montana Cree believe so definitely that the spirits are the messengers of their Creator, they constantly make offerings to them as they pray. Prayers are said to the spirits because their leader is Sweetgrass Man. He is the spirit who is always with the Creator and the one who takes care of prayers which are offered. When one applies live charcoal to the braided sweetgrass, the smoke that arises goes to the

---

[10] Personal interview, Ruth Gardipee, September 2, 1960. This was undoubtedly Mountain Lion Spirit, for tigers are unknown on the North American continent. Yet, questions remain. Could it have been southern American influence where jaguars are known? Or, why are tigers near springs of water which is their Asiatic habitat?

[11] Personal interview, July 1, 1960.

[12] Personal interview, June 30, 1960.

[13] Personal interview, Raining Bird, August 31, 1960.

[14] Personal interview, Raining Bird, August 27, 1960.

Sweetgrass Man. He is always clean and pure and kindly disposed to the people on this earth.[15]

Along with the prayers, offerings are laid out to the spirits. In many secluded places in the mountainous parts of the reservation, one may find hundreds of pieces of cloth hanging on the branches of the trees. The cloth may be something very new or something that has almost disintegrated with the seasons. During the summer, one sees, hiking in these lonely areas, many bright new pieces of cloth in the primary colors of red, yellow, and blue with an occasional white or orange piece contrasting vividly against the brilliant green of the leaves on the trees. In the autumn and winter months when the trees are denuded, then one becomes conscious of the number of offerings that have been placed on the trees, for now the leaves no longer cover them. In one area, I have seen the stark limbs of the hawthorne, chokecherry, quaking aspen, and cottonwood covered for almost half a mile.

"You take yard goods that are clean and fresh from the store and take them away from people and put them in the hills where it is clean and where no one lives," says Paul Big Child.[16] "You name the spirit to whom you are making the offering, but when you pray, you make a smudge of sweetgrass and put the cloths over that. The smoke interprets what you ask for."

"The spirits will see the words of your prayers just as if they were written on the cloth," adds Raining Bird.[17] "The Spirits will tell the Creator about what you are saying. The cloth will rot but the prayers will be answered. And you can hang the cloth any place that is clean. It does not have to be in just certain places. A lot of them are hung in the draw above the Parker School, where you have seen them, just because that is a convenient place for the people who live there to put them." Raining Bird goes on and draws a parallel with Christianity to explain some of the uses of the cloth. He points out[18] that in the Roman Catholic Church, Lent comes once a year, and during that time people may give up drinking or smoking or some of the other things they usually do. These offerings, he says, are used in much the same spirit, except that they can be used any time one wishes to do so. For instance, if one of the children gets sick, the parents may promise or vow to fast or to do something to themselves if the child recovers. Perhaps they might not

---

[15] Personal interview, Raining Bird, September 3, 1960.

[16] Personal interview, August 29, 1959.

[17] Personal interview, August 30, 1960.

[18] Personal interview, October 31, 1959.

take a drink of water for two days. And during the same time, they will hang a piece of cloth out as a visible and tangible evidence of their prayer.

At other times, people pray to the spirits for better health, better future for the tribe, better education for their children—the "luck" that was mentioned earlier. When one wishes to make these prayers, he does not need to wait for a special celebration such as a Sun Dance or a Sweat Lodge; instead he simply goes to the hills with a piece of cloth and fastens the cloth on the tree. Once the cloths, which the Cree refer to as flags, are placed in the hills or hung on the bushes or put in some clean place, they must be left there. One cannot take them down and put them some place else with a prayer to any other spirit.[19]

Before the white man came, the Cree did not have the colors to dye the skins that they hung out to the spirits or placed on the center pole of the Sun Dance Lodge. Instead, they painted sticks using the colors they wished and tied the nicely-tanned hides to these sticks. Oftentimes the whole thing was very well decorated with feathers before it was hung up.[20] Currently, the material used is cambric or chintz or "print" of some solid color. About two yards of each color is used.

The neigboring Assiniboine follow the same practice but in somewhat different manner. Instead of tying the material to the tree or fastening it to the bushes, they take about a square yard of the material, fasten it on all four sides with a slender piece of wood, and then lay it out in the high places. They put rocks on the edges of it to keep the wind from blowing the cloth away.

Long ago, Rex Flying told me,[21] the Assiniboine took antelope skins, or buffalo calf or fawn skins and decorated them with porcupine quills as elaborately as it would be possible for them to do. In a way, Flying said, these cloths may be compared to a pledge that the white man makes to his church, but with the Assiniboine, these gifts are not given to man but to the Great Power in the universe, the *Wakan' tanka*. The well dressed hides represent the best that the Indian could produce. With these, the remembrance is the significant thing—remembering that man is insignificant beside the great power in the universe. In the spring especially, man remembers his position on the earth and his dependence upon all the great powers in the universe. Thus he makes his sacrifice of something especially good and puts it out in the hills.

---

[19] Personal interview, Ruth Gardipee, December 22, 1959.

[20] Personal interview, Raining Bird, December 30, 1959.

[21] Personal interview, July 6, 1956.

Now plain cloth is used as a substitute for the very fine pieces of hide that were offered. The practice, Mr. Flying explained, increased after the United States Government forbade the Sun Dance. As a result the Assiniboine felt bewildered, for with their most solemn ceremony forbidden them, there was no place left for them to go. Consequently, each spring they took their remembrances and went out beyond the eyes of the white man to the hills, arranged their cloths, and prayed all day.

Since the prayers are entirely different as they are directed to different sources, it is an interesting speculation as to whether one of the tribes might have borrowed the idea of the "flags" from the other. The Cree practice seems very old and it is altogether possible that here is a trait that the Assiniboine took and developed according to their own thinking.

More similar to the Cree concept of the spirits is that of their Algonquian brothers, the Cheyenne. Yet with the Cheyenne, the spirits or *mistai* occupy certain definite geographical areas on the reservation and are not considered mediators or messengers to their Creator. Instead, they are principally pranksters whose tricks frequently get people in trouble. Little or no idea of religious significance seems to be attached to these invisible little spirits whose chief function is to annoy people.[22]

Another concept which the Montana Cree have that parallels the thinking in other regions is that of the Master Spirit. Each animal has one.[23] Hultkrantz writes:[24]

Conceptions of Nature's 'guardians' or 'masters' are well known, especially among the religions of the European and northern Asiatic peoples. One of the more prominent 'guardians' is the animal guardian. By animal guardian we mean here the genius *speciei*, which, as the supernatural representative for an animal species guards and directs the same. The animal guardian should be kept distinct from that spirit-animal which does, certainly, borrow the appearance of the animal, but is a supernatural power-being having no contact with the living animals.

Since each animal has its own Master Spirit which owns all of the animals of its kind, the Cree explain the idea by drawing a parallel with Christianity. "Jesus is God's Son, you white people believe," says Raining Bird.[25] "So are all the animals the children of the Master Spirit

---

[22] Verne Dusenberry, unpublished Northern Cheyenne field notes.

[23] Personal interview, Four Souls, August 30, 1960.

[24] Åke Hultkrantz, *Conceptions of the Soul among North American Indians* (Stockholm: Statens Etnografiska Museum, 1953), pp. 497–498.

[25] Personal interview, March 24, 1961.

that owns them. It is just like a large family." A hierarchy seems to have developed in their thinking, however, concerning the Master Spirits. The chief animal spirit is the Buffalo—prime giver of food in the old days. The Moose, however, is important also, for it is considered to have a kind heart, a strong mind, and is a representative of the Creator. Because it often protects people, an individual may offer the Moose a smoke or sing songs to it. Here the Woodland influence manifests itself. The Cree originally came from the Woodlands area, as has been pointed out in Chapter I. Moose are prevalent in those regions and furnish one of the main sources of the Indian's diet. To the typical Plains Indian, the moose are unknown. The Cree, then, despite the years they have been on the Plains, still retain an association with the animal and respect its efficacy, even though the Buffalo Spirit has superseded the Moose Spirit and is recognized as the Master of Life.

Each of the bears has a Master Spirit also. The Cree know that different kinds of bear exist—grizzly, black, brown, and white—and that each of them has a Master Spirit. The old people once knew where the bear spirits lived, supposedly near the cardinal directions. Consequently in the Smoke Lodge, the pipe is pointed to those directions in memory of the Master Spirits of the bears.[26]

When a person prepares to go hunting, he prays. Before he leaves his cabin, he prays first to *Ki-sei-men'-to*, for He is the Leader of all the Animals. Then prayers are said to the spirits, any of the indeterminate number of them, asking for their assistance in the hunt. The Eagle Spirit is one that frequently takes care of hunters and helps them, for its eyes are very keen and it can see a long way. Oftentimes a hunter gives some sweet-cooked berries to the Eagle Spirit, or perhaps a special kind of meat is put out for it. In the prayers said preparatory to hunting, a person may also promise to put up a sweat lodge for the benefit of the spirit if that spirit assists him.[27] Also the hunter prays to the spirits of his dead ancestors or close friends. These spirits have the power to bestow "luck" upon the living at the time of the hunt, so they are beseeched to give assistance now.

Fortified by his prayers, the hunter goes forth. Let us suppose that he sights a deer and is successful in the kill. He rushes over to the animal, cuts its throat to allow the bleeding, and then says a prayer to the Master Spirit of the Deer.

---

[26] Personal interview, Raining Bird, August 27, 1960.
[27] Personal interview, Raining Bird, March 24, 1961.

O *Kwas-kwi '-pai-hos*[28]
We know that it is wrong to kill.
You are our life.
We did not kill this child just to be killing.
We killed it because we are poor and hungry.
We need food.
Our children need food to grow large and have strong bodies.
Your child makes us strong.
That is why we have killed this child.
Forgive us for taking the life of your child,
But send us more of your children so that we may eat.[29]

Sometimes the hunter will rip open the animal and dissect a piece of the liver or some other part of the animal and offer it to the Master Spirit of the dead animal. Or he may give an offering immediately to the Master Spirit of the Eagle or whatever bird has assisted him. According to Raining Bird, this entire practice is still frequently followed by the Montana Cree.[30]

Trees also have a Master Spirit. At the time of creation, the Master Tree came into being. Springing from its trunk are branches that represent all of the different kinds of trees. One branch will be fir, another pine, another cedar, and others for each of the deciduous trees with which the Cree are familiar. This tree, which no one can locate but which is believed to be somewhere on the North American continent, is a collecting place for many of the spirits and has everlasting life. In one sense, this Master Tree is synonymous with the Tree of Life, a concept world-wide in its distribution. When a chopper cuts a tree down, he says a prayer to the Master Tree in much the same fashion that a hunter prays to the Master Spirit of the animal. He tells the Spirit that he has not destroyed the life of the tree just for the sake of destruction, but that he has cut it down so that it will provide warmth and comfort for the family. He may say that the tree will be used in a good way, for it will be manufactured into lumber or made into chairs or tables for people to use. These man-made objects, however, do not possess spirits, for the spirit of the individual tree departs when the tree has fallen. Some place those spirits reside, but the Cree do not know where.[31]

---

[28] The same term is used for both the Master Spirit of the Deer and the animal itself.

[29] This translation of an actual prayer was given me by Tom Gardipee, September 2, 1960.

[30] Personal interview, March 24, 1961.

[31] Personal interview, Raining Bird, March 24, 1961.

Thus with the Montana Cree, the animation of nature is deeply tinged with elements from the supernatural. This thinking penetrates their lives, envelopes their actions, and surrounds their every move. With them, it is a part of their religion—another element that has endured and is enduring in the latter half of the twentieth century. Their reticence in discussing these matters is noticeable; not until one is completely accepted by them will they bring up the subject of spirits. To them, it is a very serious subject, something that has set them aside and apart from the white man and a belief that is theirs. They cherish the concept for it is part of what they term "the Indian way of thinking." It gives them distinction; it keeps them Cree.

CHAPTER VIII

PURIFICATION RITES

The Montana Cree are conscious of the necessity of purifying themselves. Not only do they consider this as a definite necessity to be done prior to their participation in any kind of ceremony, but they also feel that it is the one way in which they can commune with the spirits or their Creator. Again, this custom is one that they carefully conceal from their white neighbors for fear of ridicule and misunderstanding. At the same time, they carefully point out many of the parallels that exist between their practices and Christianity. Particularly do they mention the use of incense in the rites of the Roman Catholic Church and how similar it is to their own use of herbs that carry their messages to the Creator.

The Cree recall the directions of their Creator when He related to them the means of communing with Him. Through the medium of sweetgrass and tobacco (in the pipe), one could send his prayers directly to *Ki-sei-men'-to*. Here, then, is a practice they consider to be distinctly their own, a means they have of communicating with the supernatural that was not given to the other inhabitants of this earth. And because they have been rejected in a certain sense, because their lot in the white man's world has been difficult, because the struggle for identity has been trying, they hold in common these practices that their Creator gave them. Thus, with their persistence in following these purification rites, the rites themselves have become extremely significant to the Montana Cree.

Tobacco is the main thing, say the Cree.[1] When a person asks for something, he always gives tobacco. It was to the old Indian what money is now—a medium of exchange. No ceremony of any kind is ever done without using the pipe and tobacco. The very presence of a lighted pipe in a room changes the atmosphere of the place, for it indicates that those present are seriously requesting favors from their Creator. If one smokes and takes four puffs from the pipe and then draws a little

---

[1] Personal interview, Paul Big Child, August 29, 1959.

of the smoke into his lungs, the Cree know that the Creator will give him a good mind.[2] Regardless of how addicted present-day members may be to cigarette smoking, they never associate sacred tobacco with their habit. Tobacco in the pipe is a thing sacred; tobacco in a cigarette is for pleasure.

Sweetgrass is another significant plant. Raining Bird says[3] that grass is one of the most important items in the world. When the water falls as rain in the spring, the grass revives and becomes green. The animals eat that grass and grow fat. Man kills the animals and eats the meat. In the old days, the Indian was completely dependent upon grass. To a considerable degree, they feel that man is similarly dependent today. Grass, then, is essential to man's life. Sweetgrass is one very special kind of grass; thus over the years, it has become representative of all the grasses to the Indians. With it, man is able to carry his messages to the Creator. The Cree gather the sweetgrass in mid-summer, braid it into a rope, and allow it to dry. Ends of the rope are then burned as one wishes to send the messages as he prays.

Another plant used extensively in prayers and ceremonies is sage. Sage means "buffalo sweet grass."[4] The buffalo itself is not a particularly clean animal. At the time of the first creation, the Creator took all the bad things and put them into woman where it would be discharged each month. The spirits are afraid of blood, but the buffalo is not. In the old days, a woman wore a napkin made from buffalo skin to protect her when she was menstruating. Thus, while other animals feared women when her period came, the buffalo did not. And that is why the Indians believe that the buffalo was not a really clean animal. Wherever the buffalo lived, however, there was plenty of sagebrush growing, Hence, sage became associated in the Indian's mind as "buffalo sweet grass."

In time, one particular species of sage (*Artemisia ludoviciana*) was selected as the one for purification. It may be distinguished from the other types in that it grows individually and has soft leaves on a single stock that rise eight or ten inches from the ground. Never are the coarse leaves of the big clumps used. By censing himself with sage, one can purify his body and protect himself from bad spirits that might come close to him. Also, in cases where it is absolutely necessary for a menstruating woman to enter a room or a tipi where sacred bundles or objects are kept, she can purify herself by wearing a buffalo dress and

[2] Personal interview, Raining Bird, August 26, 1960.

[3] Personal interview, December 30, 1959.

[4] Personal interview, Raining Bird, December 30, 1959.

covering her vagina with sage. Tom Gardipee states[5] that sage and sweet-grass each has about the same power, but sweetgrass is the cleaner. He points out that sweetgrass cannot be kept in a house when a woman is menstruating whereas sage can be.

Another purifier that the Cree use is one that they term "cedar." Botanically, it is not cedar but Alpine fir, (*Abies lasiocarpa*). Since "cedar" is the Cree term for the tree, that term will be used in referring to it. The Cree say that the cedar they use comes from a "Crow tree."[6] In the Pryor Mountains on the Crow Reservation in Montana can be found a certain bird with brightly-colored tail feathers. This particular bird stays all the year around and likes this one particular kind of tree. Symbolically, the bird represents the cold wind. And because of its propensity for this tree, the tree is known as the "Crow tree."

One can pick the needles from the tree anytime of the year that is convenient. Once gathered, the needles are dried and kept in a special bag. Perhaps because of its convenience in handling, the Cree seem to use these needles in their homes more than they do sweetgrass or sage. In many homes on the Rocky Boy reservation, one may see a shallowly hollowed rock or brick sitting on the top of the heating stove. At first glance, it looks like a crude over-sized ashtray. On closer examination, its appearance more closely resembles a primitive metate. Many families burn cedar needles in this container every morning when they first arise. It is particularly used to avoid or alleviate sickness. Not only does the aromatic odor cause one to feel better, but the smoke that goes upward "talks for us as we pray."[7]

Cedar is also used in many ceremonials. It is burned during the Sun Dance and is used extensively in the rites of the Native American Church. There, nationally, one always finds a "cedar chief" whose duty is to spread the needles over the fire. From my own observation, I feel that the Cree burn it with greater frequency than do either the Crow or the Cheyenne.[8] Tom Gardipee says[9] that cedar is put on the fire to cleanse the room each time a person goes out or comes into a room or tipi at every peyote meeting.

The commonest means of purification on the Rocky Boy reservation,

---

[5] Personal interview, September 2, 1960.

[6] Personal interview, Raining Bird, December 30, 1959.

[7] Personal interview, Raining Bird, December 29, 1959.

[8] Personal observation. I have attended meetings of the Native American Church on all three reservations in Montana where the cult exists.

[9] Personal interview, November 4, 1959.

however, is by all odds the sweat lodge. While historically this has been common among many North American Indians, the frequency with which the Cree use the sweat lodge in contemporary times makes it significant. Members of the Crow and Flathead tribes use the sweat lodge for pleasure as well as for personal hygiene. The Blackfeet and Cheyenne restrict its use primarily for ceremonial purposes. The Assiniboine and Gros Ventre have forgotten how to make a lodge and know nothing of its purpose or significance. But to the Montana Cree, the sweat lodge is a vital element in their lives.

The type of sweat lodge used is often classified as the "water vapor bath." Writing about it, Lopatin says:[10]

This from the very beginning has been an artificial type of bath evidently invented in a northern country. It has been common only in the countries with long cold winters and only much later was diffused to warm countries. Today it is very common among the Great Russians, Swedes, Norwegians, people of Finland, the Esthonians and the Latvians, and among certain agricultural Finns. In the New World it has been very common among all of the American tribes in North America and has been also known among some South American tribes.

The commonest kind of sweat lodge now used by the Montana Cree consists of a dome-shaped structure made from sixteen willows. Ordinarily, it is covered with canvas—the commercial kind purchased in stores. Sometimes old blankets are used or a heavy blue material which looks like faded blue denim covers the structure. Occasionally, a yellow plastic rain-repellent material is thrown over the other cover so that the moisture cannot escape.

Sixteen rocks are also used. These are heated outside the structure, but are carried to the spot in the exact center of the lodge where an excavation has previously been dug. Before the ceremony starts, one of the men carries several large live coals into the lodge and puts them around the already hot and burning rocks. The Crows follow almost the same pattern, as their sweat lodge has its excavation for the rocks in the exact center of the structure. They do not, however, carry any burning coals into the lodge. The Flatheads always have their rock pit dug near the edge of the structure, just to the left of the doorway. Consequently, they merely roll up the side of their sweat lodge covering and push the heated rocks into place.[11]

---

[10] Ivan A. Lopatin, "Origin of the Native American Steam Bath," *American Anthropologist,* Vol. LXII (1960), p. 978.

[11] Personal observation from having sweat with all three tribes. Parenthetically, I might add that Indian men on all three reservations are extremely modest and never

When all of the preparations have been made and all of the men have divested themselves of their clothing except their shorts or an improvised breechcloth, they enter the structure. Once the entrance covering has been pulled down and fitted closely to the ground so that no air can escape, the men remain silent while the sweat begins from the direct heat from the hot rocks. During this time, they usually sit cross-legged and seem to be in a meditative attitude. Once the sweating actually begins, the leader picks up the bucket of water which he has previously brought into the lodge and begins to sprinkle the water on the rocks according to the number of willows and rocks that have been used in the construction of the lodge. (It is well to bear in mind that the willow and the rock as well as the water are spirits.) If sixteen is the number of willows and rocks utilized, and as has been pointed out before that is the number most frequently used now, the leader sprinkles the water over the rocks sixteen times on the first round. He uses a brush made from slough grass to sprinkle the water in the pail (which now is an ordinary galvanized or enamel bucket) over the hot rocks. This brush can be used to hit oneself with while he is in the sweat lodge. It is particularly effective in removing pain from an individual if he goes into the lodge with an ache in his arm or leg or any place in his body.

The leader prays or sings while he is sprinkling the water on the rocks. At the conclusion of the first round, which consists of sprinkling water on the rocks four times, the men who are sweating may go outside. They remain outside approximately five minutes after which they again enter the sweat lodge and the same procedure is followed, although it is not necessary to sprinkle the water just sixteen times. Any number can be used now except that four prayers and songs are always given. Once more the men go out, visit for awhile and return to the enclosure. This same procedure is followed until four rounds of sweating have been accomplished.

At the conclusion of the sweat, the men may jump into a stream of cold water, or some of them may simply take an empty bucket or gallon can that is usually lying near the stream and throw cold water on themselves or on the backs of others. There is not the great drive among the Cree to jump into the flowing water that one finds among the

sweat completely nude. That they take this attitude because of my presence is negated by their leaving their breechcloths hanging on shrubs near the sweat lodge so that they may be there for them to use whenever they come to sweat.

Flathead who consider the ablution in the cold water an essential part of the sweat lodge ceremony.

In the old days, a new lodge was constructed each time a sweat occurred. Now, one can be used over and over again. The sedentary life of the people may account in part for the repeated use; so too may be the more or less indolent attitude that the pattern of their contemporary life has caused them to adopt. The Cree believe that repeated use of the lodge increases its efficacy. Each time prayers are repeated in the structure, more power or *muntua* is added. *Muntua* means something sacred—a great power. The Creator has this power as do the spirits although theirs is not as great as is *Ki-sei-men'-to's*. If one depends sufficiently upon the Creator, he can secure much of this power for himself.[12] Thus, whether through rationalization or firm belief, the Cree feel that constant use of the same structure enhances the *muntua* or power of that particular lodge.

The leader of the sweat lodge ceremony in contemporary times is selected by the men who are going to sweat. When they are all assembled within the lodge, the leader tells what the purpose of the sweat is going to be. He then prays to *Ki-sei-men'-to*. He may also pray to Jesus Christ. Or he can pray to the spirits, for in the sweat lodge, one can talk to the spirits easily. Among the things that I have heard the present-day Cree pray for while they are in the sweat lodge are their health, the education of their children, better ways of living, peace for the country, good luck for each other, and happiness for all the Indians in America. Once when I sweated with the Cree, the leader prayed at the beginning in English. He explained to *Ki-sei-men'-to* that he was using an alien tongue just so that I could understand his prayers more easily. He prayed for my health, for the success of my work,[13] for personal happiness for me, and for a happy Christmas for all of the children.[14] After these prayers were said for me, the leader changed into his own language and continued praying in the Cree tongue.

Occasionally, one may vow to put up a sweat lodge if he is ill or if someone in his family is sick. When the person has recovered, he takes

---

[12] Personal interview, Raining Bird, August 27, 1960.

[13] I spent the Christmas holidays, 1959, doing field work with the Cree and had arrived just the day before I sweat with them.

[14] Christmas and other Christian festivals are recognized by the Cree, not in a particular religious sense but rather as holidays. Many of them have trees lighted by electric candles at Christmas time and exchange gifts just as do their white neighbors. Again at Easter, the bunny and candied or colored eggs are noticeable, but all of it is done in a strictly secular sense.

sweetgrass and the pipe and goes into the sweat lodge and sings some special spirit song—any one that he knows. If he has felt that some particular spirit has assisted in his recovery or that of his relative, then he sings particularly to that one spirit.[15]

Or, in a more common vein, a person may secure help from the sweat lodge if he is just tired or lonesome. The sweat lodge provides an excellent opportunity to pray to the Creator and to the spirits. Oftentimes, people will make a promise or a vow within the sweat lodge and because of the spiritual strength that comes through their communication within the lodge, they are able to accomplish their desires. Sweating is also important to the Cree because the sweating helps the body and the mind. The spirits help the individual to drive the bad thoughts out of his mind and give him a peace that he cannot attain by himself.[16] Also as one cleans the pores and purifies himself, he is emotionally as well as physically more alert.[17]

Although not practiced as extensively as in the past, curing is another aspect of the sweat lodge ceremony. For this purpose, the lodges are always constructed by using twenty willows and twenty rocks. The pipe and sweetgrass are in the lodge, also. Here the order of smoking differs from the usual Cree practice, for in the sweat lodge, the pipe is offered first to the East, then the South, then the West, and finally to the North. Lastly, the leader points the pipe down to the fire. The men open the door four times during the ceremony. Between each round, the men eat berries.

In the old days, the shaman always accompanied the sick person into the lodge and stayed and prayed with him while he was sweating. Inside the lodge, the medicine man could talk better to the spirits than he could outside; consequently, he depended to a greater degree on what the spirits told him while he was inside.[18]

Today, very few of the Cree follow this practice completely. Raining Bird occasionally takes the pipe in the sweat lodge with him and prays with it. Curing practices still occur but are frequently augmented by the use of patent medicines commercially manufactured and sold in drug stores. For example, I had a slight cold when I entered a sweat lodge one December day during a visit with the Cree. The men were solicitous and advised me to use Vicks Vapo-Rub prior to entering the

---

[15] Personal interview, Raining Bird, March 24, 1961.

[16] Personal interview, Tom Gardipee, September 2, 1960.

[17] Personal interview, Pete Gardipee, July 3, 1960.

[18] Personal interviews, Tom Gardipee, November 4, 1959 and December 20, 1959.

lodge. They maintain that the effects of this medication are greatly enhanced by using it in the sweat lodge.

Ceremonially, the sweat lodge is still used in connection with the rites of the Sun Dance. Only a few people have either been given or have inherited the powers to construct this particular type of lodge. Earl Big Bow is one of the few men on the Rocky Boy reservation today who is capable of making the Sun Dance Sweat Lodge. Prior to the construction of the lodge, he gives a feast, one in which he has to serve service berries. All of the people whom he invites, and these must include all of the Sun Dance leaders, pray. The pipe is present. The actual lodge is made from willows. Any number of willows between twenty and forty is used. The same is true of the rocks. The important thing here in the construction of the lodge is that there must be the same number of rocks as there are willows and both must be in even numbers. Inside the lodge, there is sweetgrass as well as the pipe. The people pray to any of the spirits, but especially to the Thunderbird, because it is the special symbol of the Sun Dance Sweat Lodge.[19]

Since the Cree consider the sweat lodge to be their oldest ceremony preceding in time the Smoke Lodge, the Ghost Dance, or the Sun Dance, they feel that it can be a substitute for the Sun Dance. If a person cannot vow a Sun Dance because of lack of time or money or any other reason, he can erect a sweat lodge and finish his promises there. He fasts for two days prior to the erection of the sweat lodge and goes through some of the other preparations necessary for the Sun Dance.[20]

In addition to the ordinary and ceremonial use of the sweat lodge by the men, some of the women sweat. Other Algonquian women, such as the Blackfeet and the Cheyenne, abhor the idea of sweating and feel that it is a prerogative reserved for the men. Other tribes have various practices. The Crow women sweat with their husbands while the Flathead women not only sweat but frequently keep the fires burning and change the rocks while the men are sweating. Those Cree women who sweat have received the power from Mother Earth shortly after the time of creation. These women have handed the power down from one generation to the other and hope that they may, in turn, pass the power to their own daughters. My informant's mother learned it from an old woman now long dead. The following account illustrates the practice followed today on the Rocky Boy reservation.

[19] Personal interviews, Tom Gardipee, December 22, 1959 and Raining Bird, August 27, 1960.

[20] Personal interview, Raining Bird, September 3, 1960.

When Mrs. Yellow Plume is ill, her mother prepares the sweat lodge for her. When all is ready, they go into it together and the mother sings a song. Then the old lady pours the water on the rocks and blows the spot on her daughter's body that is sore. Next she prays to the unknown spirit that gave the power to the old woman who had given it to her and asks forgiveness if she does anything wrong. She tells the spirit that she herself has not been given the power by the spirit; hence, she may not know just exactly how everything should be done. In her prayers, she also dwells upon her daughter's afflictions and asks repeatedly that they be removed.

The general procedure followed is the same as in the men's sweat lodge. Four rounds of water are sprinkled on the rocks. The mother does the pouring of the water. When she lifts the covering of the lodge, she says, "Let the sickness out." When the steam rushes out of the door, it is important that no one be standing in the doorway because the sickness goes out with the steam.

Occasionally, mishaps occur. Once when I was on the reservation, Mrs. Yellow Plume burned her hip rather badly while she was in the sweat lodge being treated by her mother for another ailment. The burn posed quite a problem because it did not respond to native remedies. Mrs. Yellow Plume considered going to the infirmary and asking the nurse there to dress the burn or to give her some medicine for it. She hesitated in going, however, for she did not wish to explain to the nurse how she had received the burn. In the end, the burn healed and Mrs. Yellow Plume was subjected to no embarrassment.

The Cree men have developed a propensity for sweating. Every Friday night all of the male members of the peyote group sweat. They do this to purify themselves and their bodies before the prayer meeting the following night. Also, they do it so that they can be clean and relaxed and thus able to pray better the following evening.[21] But Friday night is not the only night in the week that men sweat, nor is it only those who belong to the Native American Church who sweat on Friday night. Some of the men sweat two or three times a week.

One middle-aged Cree informant becomes quite annoyed when he discusses the number of times a week these men must sweat. "It's all right to sweat once in awhile," he said, "but it isn't necessary to be sweating all of the time. It's just like taking a drink of whiskey. You and I could go into a saloon, have a drink of Scotch and walk out and that's

---

[21] Personal interview, Tom Gardipee, December 22, 1959.

all right. Some other fellows go into a bar and stay there drinking all night. And that's no good. It's the same way with these fellows who're always sweating. Why, I've known men who had good jobs in town (Havre) and they couldn't hold them because they had to be back here sweating."

The self-image that one of the informants gave includes a statement about sweating. He said, when speaking of himself, "Look at him. He's no good. He don't work much, sweats all the time, lives on relief." The wife of another informant said, "I can't get my husband to fix this cabin up or do anything. He's too busy sweating." Another time when I was on the reservation, a fire got out of control and swept up the mountain side. The women accused some of the men, whose sweat lodge was near the base of the mountain where the fire started, of allowing the smoldering embers of their fire to go untended and thus cause the fire. The men denied it completely.

But despite these irritations, the sweat lodge continues as an integral part of Cree life. "Isn't it better for our younger men to go into the sweat lodge frequently and pray and cleanse themselves than it is for them to run around and get drunk like some of them do?" asks Raining Bird.[22] Perhaps in some degree, the frequency of sweating among the Cree can be explained by Lopatin,[23] who says:

> Similar to the Sauna type of northwestern Europe, the native American sweat bath has always favored social intercourse and has been a focus for communal life. In this respect the Sauna type of bath has been the antithesis of the plunge or the ablution bath, which in the course of the whole history of mankind has always suggested the idea that ablution is a strictly private affair.

True it is that a deep bond exists among the men who sweat together. One of the men who has sweat with me told me that after men sweat together, their relationship changes and that they are always much closer friends. But it appears that the continual sweating that the Montana Cree practice has a much deeper meaning.

Here is their oldest ceremony—one given them by *Ki-sei-men'-to*. Here is a practice completely unknown and overlooked by the whites. Here is an Indian way of praying that is rapidly disappearing among other Indian tribes. Here is a method which they—the Montana Cree—persist in following because only Indians can thus commune with the supernatural. And they are Indians. So here, also, is another illustration of

---

[22] Personal interview, August 27, 1960.
[23] Lopatin, *op. cit.*, p. 986.

the sense of tribalism that comes from the persistence of a religious practice. In another way, it may be that the sweat lodge to the contemporary Cree represents symbolically Mother Earth's spirit. The shape of the lodge represents the womb, the position the men assume in it is almost foetal. There in the security of the lodge can the men retreat from the rebuffs and the inconsistencies of the Caucasoid world that surrounds them and pray for a better tomorrow for themselves and their children.

CHAPTER IX

DANCING

Dancing provides a good example of the misinterpretation the white explorer and the missionary gave to Indian culture when the contact with it began. Always associating dancing with secular practices, or more particularly with Satanic influence, the white man looked upon the Indian dance with contempt. To these early whites, dancing was a sin— here again, the Indian under the influence of Satan was merely reveling in debauchery. To Christianize the Indian meant that dancing had to stop and the missionaries were not slow in putting pressure upon the United States Government to adopt such steps. Consequently, throughout the settlement of the West, and at the time when the Federal government was imposing more and more restrictions upon the Indian, dancing fell into bad repute. Finally, in 1882 an all-out ban on dancing occurred.

To the Indian, the prohibition of his dancing was a regulation completely mystifying. Dancing and religion to him were one. Why, he asked, should there be a prohibition of one of his means of following his Creator's instructions? *Ki-sei-men'-to* had said that dancing would help people to be happy. In the "good place" where people would go after death, there was always a promise of feasting and dancing. Furthermore, the Creator gave the Indians many different kinds of dances so that there would be one to fit any occasion.[1]

So despite the regulations and the resentments that inevitably followed, the Indians have kept on dancing. Here is one thing that is common to all of the Plains Indians—the ability to execute the difficult and intricate steps while they are arrayed in their colorful garments. On every reservation in the West, these dances are held, usually coinciding with some holiday of the white man. The Christmas season, New Year's, George Washington's Birthday, Memorial Day, and Veteran's Day are particularly favorite times of the year for large dances to be held.

The dances are conducted in large community halls. Practically all of the members of the tribe will be there, while visitors from other reserva-

---

[1] Personal interview, Raining Bird, December 30, 1959.

tions attend, usually bringing with them a group of singers, drummers, and dancers. Some time during the evening a contest is conducted with judges posted at the four cardinal directions to watch the dancers. An elimination is made early so that only about six men will compete for the final round. Not only the intricacy of the steps is judged, but also the rhythm of the dancer is watched carefully. Generally, visitors win the contest and get a cash prize of ten or fifteen dollars.

In the smoke-filled rooms where the dances take place, the women sit patiently and complacently on the tiered seats surrounding the room. They hold their small children who eventually fall asleep and are then placed on the bleacher-type seat to sleep until early morning when the dance ends. A big supper served about midnight always characterizes the event. Frequently, some wealthy white cattle rancher who has leases on the reservation donates a beef for the occasion. Women boil the meat in large copper washboilers and from the broth make a delicious soup which is served earlier in the evening. The people bring their own containers, usually enamel cups, for the soup. Later, the washboilers filled with the meat are carried around by two men who hand a piece of meat to each person. Store-purchased bread, rolls, and cookies complete the menu.

Indians drive two or three hundred miles to attend these social affairs which are unnoticed and unattended by white people. The Cree hold a dance on Christmas night and another one on the following evening. The next night, the Assiniboine along the Milk River near Harlem, Montana, have their dance. Although the distance is about eighty miles, many of the Cree attend, coming in their old cars filled with children and old people. Perhaps the next night the Indians rest, but the following night they drive another forty miles to Hays, where the Gros Ventre entertain with another dance. The next two nights the Assiniboine at Lodgepole take their turn as hosts—another fifteen miles away. The Assiniboine dances always end on New Year's Eve. But there will be Sioux and Assiniboine from the Fort Peck reservation, two hundred miles away, who will be present. Perhaps some visiting Blackfeet will come. Occasionally, I have met Sioux from the Standing Rock reservation in North Dakota at these dances.

Usually, a collection of money is taken during the evening. Men go through the audience holding out their hats and asking for contributions. The host group uses the money thus obtained for prizes to be given the outstanding dancers. If enough money is obtained, the leaders will call a halt to the dancing and distribute the money to the visitors from other reservations, each receiving from one to five dollars depending upon the amount collected. The leaders announce that this is "gas money" and give the largest amount to those people who have travelled the greatest distance.

Many times the dancing begins with a tribute to the American flag which is prominently displayed. The national anthem is sung at the beginning of the dance. The people always sing the song in their own language accompanied by the drummers, and while neither the tune nor the words are recognizable to the white visitor, the Indians stand in rapt attention during the song. If one of their sons happens to be home on furlough from some branch of the military service, he stands near the drummers and is honored while the song is being sung.

The dances are always orderly. A uniformed Indian policeman stands at the door and allows no intoxicated person to enter. While children may run and play, they are not allowed into the center of the room where the men are dancing. If they go there, one of the older men walks slowly around them and quietly herds them back toward the bleachers where they may resume playing or climbing the rafters.

Participation in the dance is limited chiefly to the men and boys. Nearly one hundred men in full Indian dress danced at the Rocky Boy celebration on Christmas night, 1960. Most of these were young men in their twenties, although many middle-aged and older men were likewise present. Since most of the men now wear short hair, improvised or purchased wigs are prominently displayed on the heads of most of the men. A goodly number of little boys, dressed in costumes identical with those of the older men, is always on the floor. Very small boys, two or three years old, are sometimes fully outfitted in Indian style and always elicit attention and admiration, both from the dancers and the spectators. Several benches along one side of the room are reserved for the dancers. A "whip," some man in the host tribe selected by the dance committee in advance, carries a decorated stick and serves as leader for the dancers. If they do not respond to the drummers and are prone to remain on the benches smoking and visiting, the "whip" goes among them, touches them with his stick, and starts them back to the floor to dance.

Several times during the evening, the drummers who sit in the center of the room and pound a large drum (which now is usually a manufactured one) stand up. Four or five of them will take small hand drums and start singing a different type of song. This signal indicates that an owl dance where men and women dance in couples holding each other side by side is to start. The man stands on the left of the woman and places his right hand around her waist, as she places her left hand around him. He holds her right hand in his left one, and following the beat of the drum proceeds around the room. The other couples follow the leader so that a large number of dancers encircles the room. Variations of the old shuffle dance or round dance where men and women dance beside each other in a large circle also occur.

At these dances, women and girls often participate. Girls are outfitted in buckskin dresses which are elaborately embroidered in beads; women wear colorful dresses made from satin or some shiny material. A shawl that reaches well below the waist covers their shoulders. The women and girls dancing alone never execute the intricate steps of the men and boys, but their restrained grace gives beauty to the dance.

These social dances, engaged in by all Plains Indians in western America, fulfill a definite need for the Indian people. It is a social outlet for them. Here where they are visiting friends, where they are vying for attention as the best dancer, or where they are merely looking on from the crowded doorway, they are engaging in something that is distinctly their own. And while most of the dancing now is purely secular, it is the Cree who has retained the religious overtones.

The most popular dance to be performed at these social affairs is the "Grass Dance." According to Densmore,[2]

> The grass dance may be said to exist at the present time among all the tribes of the northern plains. ... The name Omaha identifies it with the Omaha tribe, from which it was received by many other tribes. ... According to Miss Flechter, the dance originally was connected with the Hetu'shka society of the Omaha, a society whose object 'was to stimulate an heroic spirit among the people and to keep alive the memory of historic and valorous acts.'

The Cree, however, have their own explanation as to the origin of the dance.

A long time ago, a sick woman was left alone while the other moved. She lay there sick and helpless for several days. Finally, the spirits reached the woman and talked to her. They showed her what to do. They instructed her to sing certain songs and to make a definite kind of drum. They also taught her how to make the clothing necessary for the dancers to wear and what steps the dancers were to use. The spirits warned her not to mention which ones of them had appeared to her and had given

---

[2] Frances Densmore, *Teton Sioux Music* (Bureau of American Ethnology Bulletin 61, 1918), p. 468.

her these teachings. As a result of these teachings, the woman recovered her health and returned to her home.

When she reached the others, she began fixing things just as she had been told to do. She made the first headdress from porcupine skin and fixed the feather belt and other items for the dancers in accordance with her teachings. Then when all of her preparations had been completed, she told the people that the spirits had appeared to her and had taught her these things and that the people must now dance. She also said that whenever anyone became ill he would recover if he made a promise to dance the new dance which she called the "grass dance." So people who had been sick heard the woman and made their promises and danced this new dance and recovered.

Because the people did not know what spirits had given the instruction to the woman, for according to her promise she refused to reveal the identity of the spirits, the dancers represent different kinds of spirits. In fact, they may choose their own. One of the principal ones whom they like to represent in the grass dance is Thunder. He has a lot of feathers, for, of course, he is a bird. He is also represented as carrying an eagle bone whistle, so very often the person who represents the Thunderbird makes a long and fancy whistle for his use.

The drum that the woman taught the people to use always had a wooden rim. Inside the rim, the woman showed them how to paint pictures; on one side were pictures of animals while on the other half would be pictures of birds. The outside of the drum, that which is pounded, was painted half in blue and half in either red or yellow. These paintings represented sky and earth. The drum used for the grass dance always hung outside the tipi. Sometimes people would hear it being pounded four times. When anyone heard those four beats on the unattended drum, he knew that the spirits wanted a feast and a dance. Someone in the camp always complied.

The grass dance then was associated with the spirits. The pipe was always present. Some old man took the pipe into the dance and sang a special song, lit the pipe and offered it to the four directions, and then gave it to the singers so that each of them could smoke to the spirits who had given them the dance. At these affairs, too, people confessed their sins and made public announcement of their bad deeds. What with the pipe present and the dance initiated by the spirits, the people knew that their confession and renunciation would bring them good luck.

In the old days, too, no women ever danced the grass dance. They had their own separate dances such as the round dance but they never entered the grass dance itself. Oftentimes, the leaders of the dance, in recognition of the fact that a woman had received the first vision about it, would invite two or four pure women to come forward and assist the singers. Sometimes, they would dance a few steps themselves but their dancing was very limited and very modestly done. Their selection by the men themselves was based on their chastity and purity. These women were known as *o-ki-tchi-ta s-kwe-wak,* respected women.[3]

Grass dances that have supernatural implications are still held. Sometimes if people have been ill or have someone sick in their family, they will vow to give a dance if the person recovers. For instance, the last one of such character to be held on the Rocky Boy reservation was given by a woman whose little girl had been quite ill with tuberculosis. The mother promised that if her child recovered she would give a dance. The youngster recovered so the mother gave a big dance out of gratitude. Another example occurred a few years ago. The mother of one of the boys who had served with the United States Army in Korea at the time of the outbreak there promised that if her son came home she would give a dance. When he returned, she surprised him by giving a large dance and having lots of food.[4]

Other instances, too, afford examples of the correlation between dancing and religion. For example, the Cree hold "sings" at various intervals before the dance is held so that people may contribute whatever cash they can afford to give to support the expenses of the dance. These affairs are held in people's homes. I attended a "sing" at the Fred Alexander home on Saturday night, one week before the Christmas dance in 1959. The affair, very informal in nature, was distinguished principally by the drumming and singing as the musicians rehearsed the songs that would be given at the dance. These men sat in one corner of the room. People came and went at will. The hostesses served coffee, sweet rolls, and sandwiches. One man had a tape recorder and taped the music. One woman, treasurer of the group, had a cigar box and a pad of paper. As each person walked over and made a deposit of money in the box, she wrote the individual's name down on her pad. Once or twice one of the song leaders, who between numbers enjoyed a cup of coffee along with the other singers, announced how much money had been contributed during the evening. But the religious element manifested itself

---

[3] All these details about the Cree grass dance and its origin were given me by Raining Bird, September 2, 1960.

[4] Personal interview, Raining Bird, December 30, 1959.

through the pipe. One of the older men had the pipe, lighted it and offered it to the four directions and then gave it to the singers, just as was once done regularly at every dance. At the conclusion of the round of smoking, the same man offered prayers for the success of the dance.

A religious aspect of the Christmas dance which would have been completely unnoticed by the average person in attendance was that of praying over the food before it was served.[5] In a small room adjacent to the dance floor, various women and girls dished out the food on individual paper plates. Before these plates were distributed to the guests, however, one of the holy men of the tribe smoked the pipe, offering it to the spirits as he asked for the good luck and good health of the people during the coming year. As a result of that blessing, the Cree do not like to see any of the food wasted or thrown away. What is not consumed at the dance must be wrapped up and taken home. With the invocation to the spirits made prior to the distribution of the food, it would be disrespectful to them and thoughtless of the people to leave food lying around uneaten. Then, too, the ghosts who come to dance with the participants, as has been pointed out in an earlier chapter, would be able to indulge themselves and have much fun with the food that is left. Consequently, all blessed food must be eaten or taken home by the visitors.

The Cree have another explanation why prayers are necessary at this time. Whenever they serve food, they remember what *Ki-sei-men'-to* told the First Man and the First Woman. He instructed them to pray over food at every ceremonial they ever gave. Hence, although it may seem incongruous to the outsider, prayers are never forgotten at what appears to be a social dance. There are others among the Cree, too, who recall the story of some people in the old days who went to the land of the dead and were allowed to return. These travellers told the others to pray over all the food they ate, regardless of where they were eating it and to remember the dead as they were praying. If they do that, they were told, the food that is thus offered to the soul of the dead will reach its destination.

Another dance that the Cree remember and occasionally give is the

----

[5] I would never have known this detail had I not been asked to take my car and go and get an elderly Indian who lived about three miles from the dance site. His wife and sister-in-law accompanied me. It so happened that none of the holy men were at the dance, or if they were there, they did not have their pipes. Consequently, it was necessary to send for one, and I was chosen to run the errand.

Ghost Dance, which they call *kwas-kuts si-mun* or "jumping dance."[6] Bearing no relationship to the one practiced by the Sioux that led to the Wounded Knee affair, this one is not reported by either Mandelbaum[7] or Skinner[8] in their studies of the Plains Cree. Peeso, who knew this particular group well in 1905, reports[9] it and calls it the *che-pa* or *se-mo-wen*. He wrote:

When a person died, a lock of the hair was cut off and placed with tobacco and sweetgrass and made into a bundle, a foot or fifteen inches long and wrapped in a skin or cloth. As others died, the bundle was added to. Each year a piece of skin or cloth was added to the wrapping. In the course of time these bundles became quite large. They were tied at the ends, and hung up in the lodge. Once a year a Ghost Dance was held either in the spring or fall. Each family would bring its bundle, which was called *Ne-ya-che-kwa,* which implied that it was always carried along. Each family bringing a bundle was supposed to bring a kettle of soup or some other contribution to the feast. On the first round, the dancers made the circle holding up the bundles, which are then hung up in the rear of the dance lodge. Then the dance is continued and concluded with a feast.

Raining Bird emphasizes the fact that the translation of the name of this dance is incorrect—that "Ghost Dance" is incorrect and stems only from a misinterpretation of the real meaning. He says[10] that the essence of the dance lies in the communication with the dead. At the big feast, which is an integral part of the ceremony, the spirits of the dead return and tell the participants about the way of life after death. These spirits also warn people to follow the teachings of the Creator else dire results will follow. According to him, several of these dances are held on the reservation.

Sometimes just the feast is held. But, whether it is a dance or a feast, the participants pray to the same spirit, *Ki-tcha-tchak,* for he is the one spirit who has the power to chase away Matchi Manitou, the Evil One.

Seemingly, the Cree have now added some of the features of the Ghost Dance to their Give Away Dance. In essence, the description of the Give Away Dance as done by the Cree on the Rocky Boy reservation

---

[6] Personal interview, Tom Gardipee, August 31, 1960.

[7] David Mandelbaum, *The Plains Cree,* Anthropological Papers of the American Museum of Natural History (New York, 1940), Vol. XXXVII, Part II.

[8] Alanson Skinner, "Notes on the Plains Cree," *American Anthropologist,* Vol. XVI (1914).

[9] F. E. Peeso, Unpublished manuscript, typewritten copy, p. 55.

[10] Personal interview, March 10, 1960.

follows closely the one witnessed and reported by Mandelbaum.[11] Now, a connection seems to exist in the minds of the Cree that in this dance a certain communication can be made with the dead, but instead of using the bundles Peeso mentioned in his description of the Ghost Dance, sacks of lard are used. Several substitutions of articles have also been made. For instance, where Mandelbaum saw a bladder filled with hardened bone grease, the Rocky Boy Cree use lard which is usually put into a sack rather than a bladder. They paint a face on the sack, again, one that is commemorative of one of their dead relatives. Also, at this dance all of the people dance with the sack of lard rather than just the four leaders whom Mandelbaum saw. The dance lasts for four nights, and during that time, numerous gifts are exchanged. The Cree welcome children at these affairs. For instance, Allan, the teen-age son of my informants, recently attended one and came home with a lariat and some moccasins that he had received. A few tabus characterize the dance—no woman can dance if she is pregnant or if she is menstruating.[12] Some of the guests or participants at these dances bring the bundle of hair from their deceased relatives and place it in certain areas where it commands a great amount of respect—another feature that undoubtedly has come from the Ghost Dance.

The Montana Cree also recognize that they received this dance from *pa-kak'-kas,* whom Bloomfield calls the "Bony Specter."[13] My informants[14] report that the Cree received the dance from "a tall skinny spirit who is a man but is nothing but bones. He runs the Give Away lodge." This spirit gets his perfume by putting his finger in the rectum of a hunter. Once, a hunter wrestled with the spirit and secured the knowledge of how to do the dance. However, he did not live long enough to practice it.

One more dance which the Cree know but which they no longer perform is what Mandelbaum calls the "wihtiko-like dance."[15] Peeso designates it as the "Wetekokan" or Cannibal Dance.[16] This masked dance, in which the dancers make masks out of old lodge skins, or old pieces of canvas or burlap bags, is interesting because Raining Bird does not

---

[11] Mandelbaum, *op. cit.,* pp. 275–276.

[12] Personal interview, Ruth Gardipee, March 10, 1960.

[13] L. Bloomfield, *Plains Cree Texts,* Publications of the American Ethnological Society (New York, 1934), Vol. XVI, p. 204.

[14] Personal interview, Ruth and Tom Gardipee, November 4, 1959.

[15] Mandelbaum, *op. cit.,* p. 274.

[16] Peeso, *op. cit.,* p. 55.

associate it with the cannibal, Witigo,[17] and also because the dance is performed regularly by the Assiniboine who consider that they received it from Inktomi at the time of their creation. Among them, it is known as the "Fool's Dance," and is one of the very few native performances that the Assiniboine still follow. The dance is not given regularly; the last one held in Montana was given in 1957 at the conclusion of a Sun Dance which the Assiniboine had asked the Cree to conduct for them. Aloysius One Sound is the leader of the Assiniboine dance. His powers to perform the dance were given him by a great leader, Medicine Bull, and yet One Sound is not always too careful in following the directions according to some of the local informants. Therefore, he does not give the dance annually as he is supposed to do.[18] The Assiniboine say, "The world was made in mischievousness. The world will fool everyone. That is the way it was created by Inktomi. That is why we have the Fool's Dance."[19]

Skinner[20] has an interesting interpretation of this dance which he says can be found only among the Assiniboine, the Cree, and the Bungi (Plains Ojibway) on the Northern Plains. He believes that it is the result of Iroquoian influence. According to him, a good many similarities exist between the rites of the masked clowns of these Indians and the False Face dancers of the Iroquois. "The prime function of the Iroquois society is to exorcise demons and cure the sick; this is one of the great duties of the windigokanuk. ... Both tribes wear dirty and tattered clothing and carry staves."[21]

All the Indians in Montana dance or enjoy dancing. It fulfills one of their greatest social needs. It is something that keeps them distinctly Indian. But the Montana Cree still retain the religious overtones to their dancing that characterized that of their forebears. Not only do they dance for social reasons, they also dance because in doing so they remain distinctive from other Indians; in their dancing their religious beliefs come to light and weld them together.

---

[17] For complete references to Witigo, see Chapter X.

[18] I attended the last Fool's Dance the Assiniboine gave and learned many of the details there.

[19] Personal interview, Rex Flying, September 5, 1958.

[20] Alanson Skinner, "Political Organization, Cults, and Ceremonies of the Plains Ojibway and Plains Cree Indians," Anthropological Papers of the American Museum (New York, 1914), p. 504.

[21] Ibid., p. 505.

VISIONS AND DREAMS

Although the Montana Cree have not practiced a formal means of seeking spiritual help for at least fifteen years,[1] belief in the spirit helpers still persists. On the reservation today, older men recall their own experiences and point to the success they have achieved through the utilization of such help. They instruct the young men, particularly boys of fifteen and sixteen, about the ways and means of achieving power in the older days and tell them that it is still possible to achieve visions even without the complete sacrifice in isolated places. By thus indoctrinating the young men in the belief, the Montana Cree carefully and skillfully show the superiority of Indian belief over the teachings of the white men.

Unknown to the Cree, though, is the fact that visions are common to all religions, even those of the white man. As Murray writes:[2]

... Christians have met their Lord in dreams of the night and have been accounted saints for that very reason; Mahomed, though not released from the body, had interviews with Allah; Moses talked with God; the Egyptian Pharaohs record similar experiences. To the devotee of a certain temperament such visions occur, and it is only to be expected that in every case the vision should take the form required of the worshipper. Hence the Christian sees Christ and enters heaven; Mahomed was caught up to the Paradise of the true believers; the anthropomorphic Jehovah permitted only a back view to His votary; the Egyptian Pharaohs beheld their gods alive and moving on this earth.

As expected, then, the Montana Cree behold their visions in the context of their belief.

While in essence the older means of securing a vision compared in general with that of other cultures, it might be well to give the Cree version of the vision quest as practiced in an earlier time. In the first place, it was deliberately sought, much as it was throughout North

---

[1] Personal interview, Tom Gardipee, September 2, 1960.

[2] Margaret Murray, *Witchcult in Western Europe* (Oxford: University Press, 1921), p. 15.

America outside the pueblo area.[3] Rossignol gives a picture of the experience of the Canadian Cree when he writes:[4]

Every Cree had a guardian spirit or spirits whom he honored and invoked and to whom he made offerings. At the age of fifteen or sixteen, at the behest of his father or of the chief, the young man went off all alone into his retreat. Normally, he climbed a tree and settled himself among the branches where he might sleep for the purpose of dreaming. For three or four successive nights he received in his dreams the visit of spirits. He saw them coming to him in great numbers, offering to serve him. He had only to choose. According to the ancient custom, he attached several to himself by tacit, or occasionally express, contract, under which contract in return for their help and protection he agreed to respect them, invoke them, and make offerings to them. These protectors were called *pawaganak*.

Mustus, a Cree of brilliant intellect said, 'All the young men on reaching the age of puberty went to dream all alone and to vow themselves to the protection of the spirits who came to visit them in their sleep.'

An historical reconstruction of the vision quest is valuable here only because of the differences in thinking that are manifested on the reservation as the older men discuss the formal method of the past. Four informants of varying ages related the manner in which the spirit was invoked. Two of them told similar tales; the two other ones are more nearly like the report by Rossignol. Pete Favel, the oldest of the informants—somewhere in his seventies—and thus presumably closer to the time when the practice was extensively done by the Cree, gives this description of the quest:[5]

When I was a young man boys went out into the hills and cried and cried until the spirit came. It was part of their education. It is Indian education. Some boys cannot learn anything in school; others can. So it is with this business of finding the spirit. A good honest boy will be sure to see the spirit while others will never be able to do so.

When the spirit first comes it scares the boys. The spirit looks like a man and can talk like a person. Then if the boy does not recognize him, the spirit tells what one he is. It could be the Sun, Moon, Wind, or any animal—bear, goat or porcupine.

The spirit does not leave a souvenir. Instead, it puts the spirit in the boy's body. The wind or a stone or an eagle or anyone might put the spirit in the body. The jackrabbit is a very fast runner. If it has put its spirit in the body of the boy, no one can outrun that boy. The spirit tells the boy what he is

[3] Robert Lowie, "Supernatural Experiences of American Indians," *Tomorrow* (Quarterly Review of Psychical Research), Vol. 4, No. 3 (1956), p. 10.

[4] M. Rossignol, "The Religion of the Saskatchewan and Western Manitoba Cree," *Primitive Man* (1939), Vol. XI, pp. 67–71.

[5] Personal interview, December 26, 1959.

going to do for him. Maybe it will be instructing him how to doctor or save lives or whatever it can do. Then the boy will know what spirit helps him and what his special talents are.

Tom Gardipee, who is in his late thirties and a World War II veteran, relates the experience as follows:[6]

When a boy was about sixteen years old, he would be ready to go out and find his spirit helper. He would sweat and fast and then head off for the hills or any clean place where he could be alone. On this reservation, Baldy or Haystack or Centennial Butte were good places.

The boy goes and fasts as long as he can stand it or until the spirit comes. It might be two days, but it could go right on up to ten days. It must be even days. If they are lucky, the spirit comes to the boys who seek them. The spirit when he comes is formed like a man. He appears first as a spirit which the individual cannot see, but then he turns into a human and says, 'What do you want? Go back where you came from.'

If the boy is brave, he stays and asks for help. He has his pipe with him and now he smokes and asks the spirit to smoke with him. He also asks the spirit to show him something good. The spirit then will give the boy a song or songs and put words in them. Then the spirit tells you what kind of spirit it is, for it may be the wind, the eagle, thunder, or the sun, or any of the other spirits. It shows the boy how to be good and how to do good things. Then one knows it is a good spirit. If it shows one how to kill and be mean, it has been sent by Matchi Manitou.

Once you know the spirit, it will come to you and will stay with you always. You can ask it to come by singing certain songs—the ones it has given you. The spirit loves the boy. The boy knows the spirit and any time that he sings the song the spirit had taught him, the spirit will come.

Windy Boy, whose age is somewhere in the sixties, tells this story of the spirit quest:[7]

Sometimes different ways were taken to get boys to get their gifts from the spirits. My grandfather had four boys. He put them under the ice. Before that, he had made a box for them and put them in that box. He kept them there eight nights under the ice. Three of the boys died; the other one lived and became my grandmother's father; his name was Two Standing.

I knew of another boy who was put into a nest in the top of a tree. Then his father took an axe and cut the limbs off the tree and the boy had to stay there. Some other boys were tied up to a tree. And some others were tied to pickets that were driven into the ground. The boy's arms and legs were tied to the pickets and he could not move.

---

[6] Personal interviews, December 22, 1959 and September 2, 1960.

[7] Personal interview, December 26, 1959. In Windy Boy's story one finds him using the old Cree kinship terminology. From our standpoint, the man who put his boys under the ice was Windy Boy's great-great grandfather. The boy who survived became Windy Boy's maternal great grandfather.

Raining Bird, a man in his fifties, gives still another account.[8]

Sometimes people went out in the hills and when they were there they never ate anything. They thought of *Ki-si-men'-to*. After a while they became thirsty and hungry. The spirits took pity on these people and went to them and told them something. The spirits said they would teach this person and be his friend. When a boy would be out there in the hills crying, he would feel very humble. The spirit would come and say, 'Don't cry. I am going to give you something that will help you.' So the spirits taught people healing powers, what kind of medicine to use, and what herbs would cure a sick man. They always gave the boy a song or songs to sing, too.

In some cases, an animal might come to a person and would give that person its power. That would be no more helpful, though, than if it were just an unseen spirit, for the spirits have everlasting life.

These spirits who come to a person like that are his friends for life. Like friends you have to call on them. Maybe later on that boy needs help. He has learned the spirit songs, so he sings one of them, points the pipe to the four directions—for he is offering the pipe to the spirits, wherever they are—puts live charcoal around different places and burns some sweetgrass. Then the spirits come.

The thing to remember is this: As a man goes out to pray he prays to his Creator to send him a vision or to direct his life. The Creator sends the spirit to the person. Sometimes we can see the spirits whom the Creator sends, but we cannot see the Creator.

Before any analysis of these beliefs can be made, perhaps it would be expedient to review briefly the methods by which Plains and Plateau Indians secured their visions. Long ceremonial purification and intentness upon supernatural communication, isolation in the mountains at puberty, acquisition of power and song of the guardian spirit are all part of Benedict's type picture of the North American Guardian Spirit complex.[9] Lowie writes,[10] "For the Crow and their neighbors, the tutelaries are likely to appear first in human guise but when vanishing they identify themselves by reverting to their true shape." Among the Pend d'Oreille, a Plateau tribe, the supplicant after a long ceremonial purification went to the mountain to pray. An animal appeared to him, disappeared, and returned in human guise. It was the person, however, who spoke to the supplicant and promised to assist him. After the promises were given, the human figure disappeared, the animal returned for a few minutes before it vanished. Among the first things the supp-

---

[8] Personal interviews, August 24, 1960, August 27, 1960, and August 31, 1960.

[9] Ruth Benedict, "Concept of the Guardian Spirit in North America," Memoirs of the American Anthropological Association (Menasha, 1923), Vol. XXIX, pp. 10–11.

[10] Lowie, *op. cit.*, p. 15.

licant noticed after the animal had left was that a token or keepsake remained.[11]

Consequently, from the conflicting stories told by the Montana Cree several elements can be distinguished. Likewise, by comparing these elements with the findings of anthropologists who have studied other Indian tribes, a pattern reveals itself. In the chart that follows certain elements may be seen as being similar in varying cultures. By the same token, Rossignol's study of the Canadian Cree reveals a strong similarity to the story of the vision quest as reported to me by the Montana Cree. A chart listing these characteristic elements follows:

	Lowie Plains	Dusenberry Plateau	Rossignol Cree	Favel (70's)	Gardipee (30's)	Windy Boy (60's)	Raining Bird (50's)
Isolation							
Mountains	×	×		×	×		×
Trees			×			×	
Others						×	
Fasting	×	×	×	×	×	×	×
Praying	×	×	×	×			×
Weeping					×		×
Appearance of Visionary							
Human first	×			×	×		
Animal first		×					× [a]
Spirit or spirits[12]			×				×
May turn into man					×		
Gifts of Visionary							
Reveals true self	×	×		×	×		× [a]
Promises assistance	×	×		×	×		×
Leaves tangible evidence		×					
Gives songs	×	×				×	×
Puts spirit in body				×			

[a] Not an absolute element; it may or may not occur.

While fasting and isolation occur in all of the reports, Raining Bird's account seems to concur more with the one Rossignal reported from the Canadian Cree than do any of the others, for both of them not only

---

[11] Verne Dusenberry, "Vision Experiences Among the Pend d'Oreille Indians," *Ethnos* 1959: 1–2, pp. 54–55.

agree on these points but upon the spirits as well. No doubt Plains' influence has had its effect upon Favel and Gardipee. Favel's further element, that of the animal putting the spirit into the body, may be his own interpretation.

With this historical background, we can see that it was firmly entrenched into the thinking of the Montana Cree. And even though it no longer functions in an active quest for assistance, the belief remains as well as the informal means of securing help. Even today, people fast in preparation for certain rites, and during that time, birds frequently come to them and teach them something that is good such as how to treat someone who is ill or how to live in accordance with the wishes of *Ki-sei-men'-to*.[13] Visions occur to people who participate in the Sun Dance; coverage of that phenomenon will be treated in another chapter.

Helpers also appear to persons in dreams. These are given the same name as those who come to the individual when he definitely sought them in the old days. *Po-wag-an* is the Cree word for them. This word is practically synonymous with that recorded by Rossignol except that he has added the suffix, *wak,* which infers or includes people. "*Po-wag-an* is a word for the spirit that you know in your dreams. It is the person that tells you how to doctor or how to do something towards the good way or the praying way," explained Ruth Gardipee.[14] People today seem to depend more upon the appearance of the *po-wag-an* in their dreams than they do in actively seeking for it.

But the appearance of spirits or helpers in dreams is not a new thing for the Montana Cree. Four Souls, son of Little Bear—the leader of the Cree in their attempt to find a home in Montana—said that his father frequently communed with spirits in his dreams. He cites one instance[15] where Little Bear had the power to look into the future and see his own destiny illustrated there.

Once when he was a young man, Little Bear started out to visit a neighboring camp which he thought was close by. He became lost and wandered for two or three days. One morning when he was very hungry, for he had eaten the supplies he had taken with him, he walked into a prairie-dog town. He had his bow and some small arrows, so he shot one of the dogs and hit it in the throat. The arrow went into the rodent in a

---

[12] Spirits here refers to those innumerable intermediaries between God and man who may or may not be morphic.

[13] Personal interview, Raining Bird, March 24, 1961.

[14] Personal interview, August 31, 1960.

[15] Personal interview, August 30, 1960.

lateral fashion which prevented the wounded prairie dog from retreating into its hole. He killed the animal and ate bits of it. Then he lay down and went to sleep. As he slept, someone whom he recognized as a spirit came for him and told him to follow. The spirit took him into a large painted lodge. Sitting in the tipi was an elderly man whose hair had started to turn gray, whose face was stern and commanding, and whose belly was quite large. Playing near him was a little boy. The spirit told Little Bear to go sit where the old man then sat.

When Little Bear did that, he realized that the old man was he and that his life would be a long one. He also knew that the little boy was his son, so he was assured that some time his wife would bear him one. That stood him in good stead in later years, for despite the fact that his earlier children were all girls, he knew that eventually a son would be born to him.

Another time, Little Bear fell asleep. The same *po-wag-an* came to him and took him to a place where he could see many horses. "When you grow older, you will have lots of horses," said the spirit. "See that pinto over there. You will have that horse for a long time. See that bob-tail. You won't have to cut the tail of that horse, for it will be natural. You'll raise seven bob-tailed horses. The seventh one will be alive at a time when there will be a great war and everyone, Indian and white, will be fighting." The pinto horse that he saw eventually became his and lived to be thirty-two years old. The seventh bob-tailed horse that he raised was born in 1914 while the group was still wandering in search of a home. That summer, World War I broke out.

In another instance, Little Bear was very sad because of the death of his grandchild, a little boy who had died at the age of five. Little Bear went out on a hill and sat there weeping. As he cried, a bird flew down and lighted on the ground not far from where he was sitting. Suddenly it began to sing:

> *Ki-sei-men'-to's* Thunder
> It is Holy.
> His Thunder is Holy.

Four Souls sings this song in the Sun Dance today.

Many other illustrations of the efficacy of dreams are referred to by the Montana Cree. Some of them have been re-told in other parts of this study. Sufficient is it to state that the Cree are conscious of the power of the dream and of the spiritual helper that so frequently appears and gives them assistance. Even the young men do not scoff at these appearances, for they know the significance of them. It has been told and re-told to them. And as it has been something distinctive to these people, so is it something that is helpful to them. In their own struggles with the outside world, here is another element found only among their own kind that is capable of assisting them in their never-ending struggle to adapt to the superior culture around them.

CHAPTER XI

LEGENDARY BEINGS

Before any discussion occurs about the supernatural or legendary beings in whom the Montana Cree believe, some distinction must be made between myth and legend. These terms are used so loosely, and in some cases so falsely, that a definition of terms is essential. In general, I agree with the statement expressed by Hultkrantz[1] who defines myth as follows:

> The myth is an epic narrative dealing with figures belonging to the supernatural sphere: cosmic beings, gods and spirits. The action of the narrative takes place in a remote prehistoric period, but in principle the once consummated course of events is still of topical interest, timeless and eternal as the course of the planets. ... The myth gives instruction concerning the world of the gods, and therewith concerning the cosmic order; it confirms the social order and the cultural values obtaining and it is in itself sacred.

In this setting of belief, all of the supernatural personages thus far described seem to fit. When the Cree mention their Creator, *Ki-sei-men'-to* or any of His host of helpers, or when they discuss the Evil One, Matchi Manitou, they speak of them as having once walked this earth and having issued instructions that must still be followed. While they belong to the past, their teachings and actions cause certain events to happen in the ordered relations that exist between themselves and their universe.

Legends exist among the Cree, but the Indians differentiate between them and their myths. Hultkrantz[2] categorizes the legend as 'an epic narrative ... whose main personages appear partly in the supernatural sphere, though without their necessarily remaining there. The action of the narrative takes place in the past, but is in general not so remote; the human figures who always appear in the legend are regarded as historical personages, and the action occurs at least in part in places with which the listeners are familiar.'

Again, this definition is acceptable as far as the ideas the Cree

---

[1] Ake Hultkrantz, *The North American Indian Orpheus Tradition,* (Stockholm: Statens Etnografiska Museum, 1957), pp. 12–13.

[2] *Ibid.,* p. 13.

entertain about certain peoples around them. The legend, in general, may be extended to cover those events which the creative mind attributes to certain personages and events that have occurred either connected with the supernatural or the natural world. In the main, the Montana Cree's legendary beings are those who have a tinge of the supernatural connected with their exploits.

Another class of tales falls into a category removed from myth or legend. Here are the stories that have been re-told primarily for entertainment. Hultkrantz calls them "fairy tales."[3] I prefer the term, "folk tale," to cover generically this large body of imaginative literature that characterizes all pre-literate people. In general, these stories are told to entertain although plenty of instances occur in which the stories are told to instruct. It seems that the folk tale is the result of man's creative ability to construct stories from his environmental situation. Thus, it is altogether possible to find folk tales that deal with the supernatural beings that may, in other instances, people the myths or the legends.

Among the Montana Cree, we find examples of stories that could fit into the three classifications just mentioned. Wi-sak-a-chak, for instance, figures in the myth of the second creation as a Transformer; he is legendary in the sense that he is considered a real person whose place of departure from this earth is well known and as one whose return is expected. Furthermore, as the Trickster, he occurs in thousands of folk tales. Many of these stories are told for pure enjoyment. In others, however, Wi-sak-a-chak becomes a symbol and his stories are told to children to instill in them certain moral values. Because in most of the stories, Wi-sak-a-chak does everything wrong, the children can laugh at his antics, but by negatively emulating him they can learn many valuable lessons.[4]

In fact, Wi-sak-a-chak seems by all odds to be the one figure who is most alive in the thinking and the story-telling of the Cree. Children on the reservation grow up listening to his exploits; older people, men especially, like to tell of his affairs—particularly those that are somewhat vulgar—in much the same fashion that the so-called "dirty stories" are told in white society.[5]

---

[3] *Ibid.*, pp. 13–14.

[4] Personal interview, Pete Gardipee, July 3, 1960.

[5] For example, I was visiting in one home on the reservation when one of the neighbor men came in and began regaling me with Wi-sak-a-chak stories. The woman of the home protested vigorously. "Get that old man out of here," she said to her husband. "Him and his old Wi-sak-a-chak stories." Her protestations, increased by my presence perhaps, met with roars of laughter from her husband and visitor.

In telling the stories of their Trickster and in emphasizing the obscene elements, the Cree differ from their Algonquian neighbors, the Cheyenne, who emphasize only the traits of their hero, Sweet Medicine, that have been beneficial to them as a tribe. In all the years that I have known the Cheyenne I have yet to hear an indecent tale about either of their culture heroes, Sweet Medicine or Erect Horns (the latter was the hero of the Sutai and thus has occupied a principal place in Cheyenne belief since the Cheyenne absorbed the Sutai). The reticence on the part of the Cheyenne to discuss vulgar aspects of their culture heroes could be explained in part, perhaps, by their natural shyness and avoidance of obscenity. These attributes may stem from the same roots that Hoebbel develops when he calls them "sexually repressed."[6]

In contrast, then, to the reticence of the Cheyenne, the Cree, emphasizing the obscene elements, seem to enjoy the ridiculousness of Wi-sak-a-chak. Certain anecdotes have wide circulation. For example, Peeso recorded a tale that he had heard in 1905,[7] Skinner relates practically the same story from his informants in his work published in 1916,[8] and one of the Montana Cree told me the same story on Christmas Day, 1959. While the details vary a little in each case, the basic story remains the same. The following narrative is the one given to me:

One day while Wi-sak-a-chak was walking through the woods and brush, he found some red berries. He ate a great many. Finally, he asked, 'What is your name, *Me-sem?*'[9]

'*O-ke-han,*' answered the berries.

'You must have two names; everything has two names.'

'Yes,' said the berries, 'you are right. We do have another name. But that is not important. Anyone who eats lots of us will scratch his behind and will break wind.'

'All right,' said Wi-sak-a-chak. 'I am not worried.' So he went right on eating berries.

After a while Wi-sak-a-chak saw an elk and he took an arrow and was about to shoot when he broke wind loudly and caused the elk to run away. Soon after that he saw a moose and the same thing happened. Just as he took aim, he broke wind again and frightened the moose.

Then Wi-sak-a-chak was mad. He said to his rump, 'I'm hungry. Now if you

---

[6] E. Adamson Hoebel, *The Cheyenne: Indians of the Great Plains* (New York: Henry Holt and Company, 1960).

[7] F. E. Peeso, Unpublished manuscript, typewritten copy.

[8] Alanson Skinner, "Plains Cree Tales," *Journal of American Folklore,* Vol. XXIX (1916), pp. 341–367.

[9] Wi-sak-a-chak always addresses the person or object to whom he is speaking as *me-sem,* my younger brother. Peeso Ms.; Cree informants.

make another noise, I will burn you.' A short time after that he saw another elk and just as he was taking aim, the same thing happened. Now he was mad.

'I am hungry and you will not let me have meat. You frighten away all the animals. Now I am going to burn you,' he said to his rump. So he built a fire and put stones in it. He left them there until they were so hot they became yellow. When he decided that they were as hot as they could get, he lifted up his robe and sat down on the hot stones. He sat there until his *ches-s-s* (anus) was burned. 'O-hoh, I am burning you,' he said. 'Now you will listen to me when I talk to you.' But when Wi-sak-a-chak stood up, he found that he was so sore that he could not walk well and that he had to keep his legs stretched far apart.

After a while he came to a hill. It was too steep for him to climb because of his sore spot so he started walking around to the left. He kept walking around the hill and pretty soon he came to the spot where he had started. Then he took the same trail again and started once more walking in a circle around the hill.

'Ah ha!' he said, 'Somebody has been here before. I will track him.' So he followed the trail the second time. As he was going along, the scab from the place where he had burned himself fell off. Wi-sak-a-chak did not notice that, however, for he kept walking around. The third time that he encircled the hill he saw the scab and stopped to pick it up.

'Oh good,' he said. 'I am hungry and my grandmother must have been here and lost some of her dried meat. Now I can feast.' So he started eating the scab that he had lost.

'Wi-sak-a-chak,' a little bird called to him. '*Wi-sak-a-chak,* you are eating yourself. You are eating yourself. You are eating yourself.'

'You are a liar,' he answered. 'My grandmother has left some of her dried meat here for me to eat. It is dried meat that I am eating,' and he went on, eating as he walked away.

While the preceding story is typical of the ones that the Cree enjoy telling and is one that is representative of their folk tales, the Montana Cree do associate him with good deeds somewhat in the same vein as the Cheyenne consider Sweet Medicine or Erect Horns. From the Peeso collection of unpublished Wi-sak-a-chak stories the following is taken.

When Wi-sak-a-chak was very small, there was a great animal which was half man and half elk. This elk killed people and ate them. At this time Wi-sak-a-chak lived alone with his mother. One day, he said to her, 'Why is it, my mother, that you always live here alone?'

'Yes,' said his mother. 'It is true that I am all alone. But there used to be many people around. There was a great camp here.'

'Which way have they gone, all those people?' asked the little boy. 'Where are they now?'

'Poor little boy,' said his mother. 'Those people were killed long ago by the Great Elk. He ate all of them.'

'Well, my mother, where does he live—that Great Elk? I will go and find him sometime.'

'Better stay here with me,' his mother said. 'Don't go away anywhere for the elk might get you.'

'Tell me, my mother,' asked Wi-sak-a-chak a few days later. 'Where is my father?'

'Your father has been dead a long time. The elk killed him. That was before you were born.'

'All right,' he said. 'I am glad you told me about the elk. I will go and find him sometime.'

For many moons he played around the deserted camp picking up many things that had been left. He found feathers, buffalo hooves and elk horns and bear claws. He made a walking stick out of the horns; he polished it nicely and decorated it with feathers. He also made an eagle-bone whistle. Then he put white clay all over his body and head.

When his mother saw him, she became worried and said, 'You cannot harm the Great Elk. He is too brave to be frightened.'

'Well, I am going to try to scare him. Maybe I shall kill him, too.' So he started out after the elk. He climbed the mountain where he lived, Elk Mountain. Then the boy shook his stick. He thought he heard something.

'He-e-e-ya! Elk!' he called as he looked through the bushes. Sure enough there was something coming. 'I think the Elk is coming,' he said to himself. So he began to dance and pound his walking stick on the ground. He blew his whistle and danced like they do in the Sun Dance. He went up the mountain dancing all the time. Finally he heard the Elk say, 'Better quit for a while, although you make a good dance.' But Wi-sak-a-chak would not answer. He kept on dancing and blowing his whistle. The Elk called to him three times before he paid any attention to him. Then he stopped and struck the ground with his stick.

'Ho, ho! Why do you bother me for nothing? What is the matter? I never quit dancing until noon. I dance from morning until noon, and from noon until sundown. I stop twice, at noon and at sundown,' said Wi-sak-a-chak, saucily.

'I wish you would come to my lodge,' Elk said.

'All right,' answered Wi-sak-a-chak. 'Lead on.'

'No, you go ahead. I will follow.'

'No, I don't want to do that. I will go behind and you will lead,' said Wi-sak-a-chak.

'No one has ever gotten the best of me before,' said Elk as he went ahead. 'But you have beaten me. It is the first time.'

When they reached the lodge, Elk lifted the flap and said, 'Go in.'

'No,' said Wi-sak-a-chak, 'I won't go in first for it is your tent.' So Elk went in and the boy followed.

'I guess you are hungry,' said Elk.

'Yes,' answered Wi-sak-a-chak. 'I am very hungry.'

'What would you like?' asked Elk. 'What do you want to eat?'

'Show me what you give me,' requested Wi-sak-a-chak. So Elk brought out grease, pemmican and dried meat. He put it in a wooden dish and set it before Wi-sak-a-chak who looked at it and said, 'Eat it yourself. I don't want to eat people meat.' So the elk took the meat away and got some from the other side of the lodge. Animal meat—moose, blacktail deer, buffalo and bear, all nicely dried. 'This is the kind I want,' said Wi-sak-a-chak. 'I don't like to eat people. I like animals.'

'You have beaten me twice,' said Elk, 'I will take you for my friend. You travel a great deal. Why?'

'I am looking for a brave man who killed my father,' replied Wi-sak-a-chak.

'I think I am brave enough. Nobody can frighten me,' said Elk. 'I will go with you.'

'All right,' said Wi-sak-a-chak. 'I will take you for my friend. We will live together, but you must burn the people meat. I want you to stop killing people. If you don't stop, I will surely have to kill you.'

'All right, I will stop,' said Elk. They then went out to find the one who had killed the boy's father. After four nights, Wi-sak-a-chak said to Elk, 'I want to ask you something. Maybe we will find that man, so I want to find out what I shall do about you. Maybe you will be afraid of the man; I want to keep you close to me. Tell me what you are afraid of. What will kill you?'

'Elk horn,' answered Elk. 'If anyone should hit me with an elk horn it would kill me right away.'

'Oh,' Wi-sak-a-chak said. 'Tomorrow early in the morning, maybe, you will see the man who killed my father.' The next morning he said to Elk, 'I am going up on that little sand hill. You wait here and then see how fast you can run up to where I am. I want to see how fast you can run, so try your best.'

'All right,' said Elk, so Wi-sak-a-chak went towards the hill. Pretty soon he found an elk horn. Then he hid himself. When the elk passed his hiding place, he jumped up and knocked the elk down with the horn.

'Hai,' yelled Wi-sak-a-chak. 'Fool, you killed my father. You killed all of the other people. You will never kill anyone else.' He cut up the elk and burned him and then hurried back to his mother.

'My mother, I killed that elk. I killed him—the one that killed my father.'

'Sh-h-h. My poor boy, you can't kill the Great Elk,' said his mother sorrowfully.

'But I surely did kill him,' answered Wi-sak-a-chak. And from that time on people lived without any more trouble from that creature which was half man and half elk.

In this story, Wi-sak-a-chak emerges very close to the conventional role of the culture hero. Saving the people from starvation by destroying the cause is a familiar motif among many tribes and one that is traditionally accomplished by the culture hero. In this role, Wi-sak-a-chak approaches a mythical status. Endowed by supernatural powers, he performs his duties. Legendary, also, is his role as helper. In any case, the part he plays here is elevated from the lowly Trickster that he usually portrays.

A more serious note in the functioning role of Wi-sak-a-chak as a religious figure is noted in a story Raining Bird told me,[10] for here he appears as a prophet.

Wi-sak-a-chak used to go around visiting and doing funny things, some of which were bad. He stayed with some people quite a while and finally he said, 'Brothers, I have to leave you.'

'No,' said one of the fellows. 'You'd better stay with us.'

'No,' Wi-sak-a-chak replied. 'I have to leave you. I want to go because some day in the future you'll blame me if something bad is done or happens. Now, I'm going to teach you two things: One teaching is good; it is the way *Ki-sei-men'-to* wants you to act. The other teaching is evil and it comes from *Matchi Manitou*. That is why you will blame me. But I will come back to you some day—when the world is going to be changed. I will have to be here at that time. That time I am going to stay with you for good. And everything will be better.'

The Montana Cree believe positively that Wi-sak-a-chak left this earth at a certain place in southern Alberta (Canada) where there is a marked defile in the land. At this spot, Wi-sak-a-chak slid down a long clay hill where the marks of his buttocks are still visible in the formation of the hill.[11] And that they believe he will come again is manifested by frequent references to his return. In the spring of 1961, the Cree reported that they had heard a report that he had been seen in the mountainous area of western Montana, not far from the city of Missoula, Montana. He seemed to be directed toward the Rocky Boy reservation, for his large footprints and his six-foot stride indicated that he was travelling eastward. The informants[12] could not give a clear picture or description of Wi-sak-a-chak nor would they reveal the name of the person who had seen him. But the idea he had been seen gives credence to their strong belief in him and his supernatural powers.

Of course, the Montana Cree are not alone in their concept of Wi-sak-a-chak, for he is a familiar figure in the literature of the Northeastern Indians. Known by many names, including such various spellings as Wesakaychak or Wisukejak or Wisakedjak, and sometimes in translation as "Whiskey Jack," he is reported by Skinner[13] as follows: "All along the West coast of James and Hudson's Bays, Wesakatcak plays a prominent part as the culture hero and trickster, but the cycle seems to be

---

[10] Personal interview, December 31, 1959.

[11] Personal interview, Tom Gardipee, November 3, 1959.

[12] Personal interviews, March 31, 1961. Names purposely withheld.

[13] Alanson Skinner, *Notes on the Eastern Cree and Northern Salteaux*, Anthropological Papers of the American Museum of Natural History (New York, 1911), Vol. IX, Part I, p. 82.

unknown to the Eastern and Labrador Cree. At least all inquiries made in 1908 proved barren. Some of the Cree who are cognizant of Ojibway folklore identify Wisakatcak with Nanabozo."

The fact that he persists is important. And that he functions as a semi-spiritual person is evidenced by the name itself. The Montana Cree point out[14] that the main root in his name, *atchak,* is the term they use for a spirit. And although they cannot agree just what the prefix, *wi-sak,* means, they associate it which something that may mean both wise and tricky. But their very thinking and interpretation of the main root in the name indicates the status they give to Wi-sak-a-chak.

Another personage who is known by the Montana Cree and because of his supernatural background must be included in this discussion of legendary beings is Witigo. While it is nothing new, for the witigo psychosis has been studied and reported upon in much of the literature about the Cree and other Northern Woodland Indians, his presence among the Montana Cree is significant.

Because of its role among the Northern Indians, many scholars have studied and reported upon the witigo complex. The first reference is the statement made by Father Dablon in the *Jesuit Relations* for 1661.[15] He writes:

They (the Cree) are afflicted with neither lunacy, hypocrandia, nor frenzy, but have a combination of all these species of disease which affects their imaginations and causes them a more than canine hunger. This makes them so ravenous for human flesh that they pounce upon women, children, and even upon men, like veritable werewolves and devour them voraciously, without being able to appease or glut their appetite and ever seeking fresh prey and the more greedily the more they eat. This ailment attacked our deputies and as death is the sole remedy among those simple people for checking such acts of murder, they were slain in order to stay the course of their madness.

The next report comes from Umfreville who resided eight years at York Factory, 1771 to 1782, and who knew the Cree well. He describes their attitude toward Witigo as follows:[16]

They say that there is an evil Being who is always plaguing them. They call him Whit-ti-co. Of him they are very much afraid and seldom eat anything or drink any brandy without throwing some in the fire for Whit-ti-co. If any misfortune befalls them, they sing to him imploring his mercy, and when in health and prosperity do the same to keep in good humor. Yet ... when in

[14] Personal interview, William Denny, March 21, 1961.

[15] Reuben Gold Thwaites, *The Jesuit Relations and Allied Documents* (Cleveland: Burrows Brothers Co., 1896–1901), Vol. XLVI, pp. 263–264.

[16] E. Umfreville, *The Present State of Hudson's Bay* (London, 1790), pp. 189–190.

liquor they then run out of their tents and fire their guns in order to kill him. They frequently persuade themselves that they see his track in the moss or snow and he is generally described in the most hideous forms.

Speck reports[17] the same kind of creature among the Naskapi. Here, the witigo is a being human in form whose main object seems "to be killing and eating his fellow human beings without being detected. . . . In summer he lives like other people and eats the same food. But he changes completely in winter . . . and eats people."

Father John M. Cooper, in his extensive studies of the Algonquian people, has done considerable writing about the witigo complex. It is his belief that a connection may exist between Witigo and the Iroquoian Stone Coats, the bloodthirsty cannibal giants whose homeland was in the northern regions.[18] His suggestion as to the cause of the belief is found in his statement:[19] "The Witiko's heart of ice symbolizes an environmental condition, namely the icy winter of the north, and this note has become associated with the giant cannibal conception because winter time is the period of famine and famine conditions." He adds that he believes that this particular craving in the psychosis is directly traceable to prevalent environmental and cultural conditions in the northeastern Canadian woodlands, where death by starvation was very common and where the Cree, along with other native tribes, had a rigid tabu against and a horror of cannibalism.

A recent and comprehensive report on the subject is that done by Morton I. Teicher.[20] He lists four ways in which an individual may become a witigo:[21]

1. The witigo was once a human being who was transformed into his superhuman state of sorcery.

2. He was created out of a dream by a sorcerer and sent forth into the world to perform malevolent acts "carrying out the nefarious aims of the sorcerer."

[17] Frank Speck, *Naskapi* (Norman: University of Oklahoma Press, 1935), pp. 73–74.

[18] John M. Cooper, "The Cree Witiko Psychosis," *Primitive Man* (1933), Vol. VI, p. 23. It seems to me, however, that the Algonquian belief in witigo has a far wider distribution and that their obsession with cannibalism far outreaches Iroquoian influence.

[19] *Ibid.*, p. 24.

[20] Morton I. Teicher, *Windigo Psychosis*, A Study of a Relationship between Belief and Behavior among the Indians of Northeastern Canada. Verne F. Ray, ed., Proceeding of the 1960 Annual Meeting of the American Ethnological Society (Seattle, University of Washington, 1960).

[21] *Ibid.*, p. 3.

3. He represents all those who have died of starvation.

4. "God made them, like any other beings."

While Teicher stresses the fact in his study that the witigo belief was "built up by inductions from actual experiences of starvation and cannibalism,"[22] he stresses the fact that "an important element ... is that of spirit possession." And he points out that the witigo concept "appears to be an unique example of this phenomenon (spirit possession) in the Americas."[23]

While the Montana Cree have inherited the idea of the witigo and attribute the horror to "Matchi Manitou who went up to the North once and made the people misunderstand themselves,"[24] they firmly believe in the efficacy of such a super-human person. Two stories concerning Witigo, collected by Fred Peeso while the forebears of the Montana Cree were camped in Butte, Montana, in 1905, are included because they represent the type of stories our present-day Cree heard in their childhood.[25]

I

There were three brothers. The two older ones were married but the youngest was not. When winter came they moved—the three brothers and the two women. Finally, they came to a certain place and the oldest of the brothers said, "I guess this is about the best place to winter. There are lots of moose around here. Lots of marten and mink and lots of lynx and fisher, too. So they made camp. Then the oldest said, 'We will fix the camp up good, for we will have to stay here all winter.' They stayed there and snow came, lots of snow. So they made snowshoes. Then they began to hunt and to trap. They had good luck; they killed lots of moose and fur.

Along about midwinter, the youngest of the three men dreamed something; he told his brothers about it. He said, 'Now, my brothers, I am going to tell you something.'

'All right,' said the oldest.

'Let's get out of here,' said the young man. 'There is something going to happen here before long.'

'How do you know?' asked the oldest brother.

'I could see in my dream what is going to happen to us. It is all right for me, but to you and my other brother and my sisters-in-law something is going to happen. I think you had better take my advice and get out of here.'

'Well, I don't know,' answered his brother. 'I think I ought to know it

[22] *Ibid.*, p. 110.

[23] *Ibid.*, p. 112.

[24] Personal interview, Raining Bird, December 30, 1959.

[25] F. E. Peeso, Unpublished manuscript. One of Peeso's informants was Young Boy, father of my chief informant, Raining Bird.

myself, if anything is going to happen. I used to be pretty strong in dreams. Well, I will see tonight.' And he took his rattle and began to sing. When he had finished, he said, 'I do not see anything.'

'That is queer,' the youngest man answered. 'I am surprised that you do not know anything about what is going to happen, and me, I am young and I know it.' Because the young man knew what was going to happen, he dug back of the lodge next to his bed in the snowbank every night after he had gone to bed. Finally he had a hole large enough to hide in. Then he fixed it up good.

At last the night came he knew that the Witigo was going to come, and after all the others had gone to sleep he went into that snowbank hole that he had made, and he closed up the mouth of it with cedar boughs, leaving a small opening to look through. Along about midnight when all the people were sound asleep but the youngest brother, that Witigo came. He came into the lodge and made a little fire so that he could see better. First, the Witigo went after the oldest brother and hit him on the head with a tomahawk. Next, he went to the other brother and hit him on the head with the tomahawk, and so with the women. The young man was watching all this time and when the Witigo had killed them all, he went out and threw lots of wood into the lodge and made a big fire. Then he went out and got his old big kettle and hung it over the fire. Then he cut up all the people he had killed. The young man watched all this time. The Witigo ate all night. About daybreak, he had eaten everything—all those four people. The young man was still watching from his secret place. He just sat still and did not move. Then all at once the Witigo went out and brought all the snow shoes into the lodge.

Now the young man was frightened. The Witigo counted the snow shoes. There were pairs for three men, but he had only eaten two. After he had counted the snow shoes, he went out of the lodge. There were three trails leading to their hunting grounds and traps. He took one of these trails. After a while, he came back and counted the snowshoes again. Then he started out on the second trail which was a pretty long one, but at last he came back. He counted the snowshoes this time, too, and started out on the last trail, for he knew that he had missed one man. This trail was a long one. As soon as he left, the young man went out, grabbed his snowshoes and ran. He did not know where the other members of his tribe were and only had to guess the direction.

He ran as fast as he could in the direction where he had last heard the relatives were camped. He ran all night and all day and finally found a trail. Here he pulled his snowshoes off so he could run better. The camp had just been moved a little while when he arrived there. He stopped to look back and when he did he heard the Witigo coming. So he started running again toward the camp. Before he reached it, he came upon a party of young boys who were building a fire near the trail.

'Get out of here, boys,' he cried. 'A witigo is coming. He is behind me pretty close. Listen!' They listened for a minute and heard Witigo coming so they ran, all of them, into camp. He told the old people. Three of them and an old medicine man went out to meet the Witigo. They fought and killed him. Then, they found that the Witigo was a woman.

The young man told those people about his brothers and they went back but they did not find anything, hardly any bones at all. He returned with them to their camp and stayed with them, for now he had no place to go. His brothers were all dead and so were his sisters-in-law.

Here, as can readily be seen, we have the familiar setting. A small family group, camped by themselves in the frozen regions of the north, encounter the witigo. One person escapes and makes his way to other encampments where with the assistance of a person endowed with great supernatural powers the medicine man is able to kill the witigo, who turns out to be a woman. Sex differentiation is not a factor in the witigo complex.

Another story from the Peeso collection gives a further indication of the fear that the witigo inspired in the lives of the Cree, and illustrates, as well, how certain persons in camp could have the power to overcome the monster—a factor mentioned by one of my informants.[26]

II

There was a small band of Indians in the far north. There were three lodges and five men. They had moved out to their hunting ground where there was plenty of game and fur. This was far back, a long ways. They got plenty fur and lots of moose. There were no elk there or deer, only moose and bear. About midwinter they ran out of some things which was necessary to have, and it was a long distance they would have to go to get them.

One night the oldest man of the party called together the other four men. 'We will talk about what we shall do,' he said. 'We are short of many things and it is a long time till spring. I think it is best that we go where we can buy something—ammunition, tobacco, and other things we need. All five of us will go. We will leave the women here; nothing will bother them anyway.' So they all said, 'All right, we will do that. When will we go?' The oldest man said, 'I am ready any time.' 'All right, if you are ready any time we will start tomorrow. How many days will it take us to get there?' It will take us about four days if we travel fast," said the oldest. 'We all have good snow shoes, so nothing should break on the way.'

In the morning they pulled out. Each one had a load of fur on his back and they started for the nearest Hudson Bay post. They camped when night overtook them. They travelled a long distance that day. The next morning they started out again and when they camped that night, one of them said, 'Now, we are about half way. We will camp twice more before we get there.' So they travelled all the next day and camped. That night they said, 'We will camp once more and the next day we will arrive at the post. We will get what we need and the next day we will start right back.' In the morning while they were sitting around the fire, one of the men said, 'Something is going to happen at our camp. What shall we do? Shall one or two go back from here?'

---

[26] Personal interview, Pete Favel, December 29, 1959.

'It is too far,' they said, 'to go back from here.'

'There is a witigo coming to our camp in about four nights from now,' said the young man. 'But I will tell you one thing, my friends, our women know about it. They know a witigo is coming.'

'Well,' said the others, 'if that is the case, we will go on. We will not camp tonight. We will travel all day and all night.' So they started.

Now at the camp, one of the women told the others. 'A witigo is coming and all the men are gone.' The woman who knew this said, 'He is coming in two nights.'

There was a young girl in the camp who had no mother and no father. She was fourteen or fifteen years old. She said, 'No, that is not so. In three nights the witigo will be here.'

'Well, I am glad you know,' said an old woman. 'We can depend on the two of you.' So the old woman took a big pipe and gave it to the girl, as she said, 'Try your best. The best medicine you have. Use that.'

The girl took the pipe and said, 'All right. If anyone will help me, I think I can kill that witigo.'

'Yes, I will help you,' said the other woman. 'I think I can fight him, but I am not sure that I can kill him. He is pretty strong, this witigo. He has strong power.'

So the night came. It was cold, cold. They could hear the trees crack with the frost, and the girl asked the woman, 'Is there a gun here, a new one?'

'Yes,' answered the woman. 'We have a new one that has never been used yet. We have just kept it here.'

'Give me that gun.' So they gave the girl the gun. 'Give me some sweetgrass.' So they gave her some sweetgrass and she burned it and held the gun over the smoke. When she got through she took the ashes and loaded the gun with them. 'Now,' she said. 'I am ready. What are you going to use?'

The other woman took a little hatchet and painted the blade red.

'Now,' said the girl. 'We won't stop here because the children will be frightened. Put all the children in one lodge and then stop up all their ears because we will make a big noise.' The girl took off her moccasins and went out barefooted and they started off and went quite a distance from camp in the direction they knew the Witigo was coming from. They saw a big tree in a little open place. 'This is a good place to fight him. We will sit down here.' Not long after that they heard the witigo coming and the girl told the woman, 'I will shoot him and as soon as I knock him down, you cut his head off with your hatchet. Do not be afraid. Do not get scared.'

And the woman said, 'I am willing to fight. I will not be frightened and I will help all I can.'

They saw him coming. His eyes were like fire. When he came close to the women, he stopped and pointed toward them and said, 'There is nothing that will hurt me,' and he started on again.

When he came very close to where the woman and the girl were, the girl said, 'In the first dream I had, the thunder gave me power to kill anything I shot at.' So the girl shot the witigo and as she fired it sounded like thunder and he fell down like a big moose. The other woman jumped up and chopped his head off. Then she said, 'What shall we do now?'

'Get all the women,' said the girl. 'Tell them to bring their axes and come here, and we will burn him. If we leave any little bone, he will get up again,' So all the other women came with their axes and began to chop wood. They started a fire and burned that witigo. 'Burn everything,' the girl said. 'If you leave anything, even a little bone, he will get up again.' So they burned him good. They burned everything. There was nothing left but ashes.

The men started home. The young man who knew the witigo was coming to the camp said, 'It is all right now. We do not have to travel nights any more. The women have killed him. They have killed that witigo.'

'Which one killed him?' they asked.

'That little girl, the one who has no mother and no father.'

'Oh-hoh,' they said in surprise. They did not think that little girl had strong dreams like that—to kill a witigo. Finally, the men arrived at the camp. The women told them what trouble they had had. They said they had a great time killing that witigo. The men were glad. 'Now, we are all right. Nothing will trouble us after this,' they said.

Aside from the traditional pattern—that of the isolated family and the horror of Witigo—another element enters into this story that is worthy of mentioning. The girl saviour is somewhat unique. Stories from pre-literate people are filled with the exploits of a young boy saving the people from destruction. The Wi-sak-a-chak story quoted in this chapter provides a good illustration. But the girl is indicative of a different pattern. That such an instance is not unknown among the Cree is shown, however, by Bloomfield in his findings.[27] Two of his stories deal with the fact that a girl is able to save the camp. In one story, "Burnt-Stick", Wi-sak-a-chak instructs the girl how she could evade Witigo; in another instance, "The Foolish Maiden," Witigo captured the girl and took her home to be eaten. Instead, she escaped and he ate his grandmother. In each case, then, the girl was definitely the saviour, and hence, must have possessed supernatural power.

This phenomenon is not unknown among the Montana Cree. At the time of a girl's first menstruation, she stayed away from home and ate little or nothing. This period might last from four to eight nights, and during that time she was taught not to cry, as well as how she should remain in the proper frame of mind so that she would be kind and be able to keep her temper in times of adversity. During this time, also, a spirit who usually dressed like a woman, came to the girl and told her what she should do as well as giving her certain supernatural powers.[28] In this way, she received a vision very similar to those that men secured

[27] L. Bloomfield, *Sacred Stories of the Sweetgrass Cree*, National Museum of Canada Anthropological Series No. 11 (Ottawa, 1930).

[28] Personal interview, Raining Bird, August 31, 1960.

in other cultures. The fact, then, that the girl who saved the camp and directed the kill of Witigo in the second story, had received her powers from the Thunder spirit is in keeping with Cree belief even unto the present time.

Now with these inherited beliefs and stories, the Montana Cree have a definite explanation that places the narratives in the framework of religion. "To understand Witigo," explained Pete Favel,[29] "you have to remember that there are two gods—*Ki-sei-men'-to* and Matchi Manitou. Matchi is the Evil One. He's the one that might come to a boy who would be crying up in the hills while he is waiting for his vision. Then, Matchi would give him the wrong one." As an example: perhaps the boy who would be seeking his vision might see a porcupine. Matchi would be responsible for sending that helper. Then later in life, if the boy accidentally tasted the meat of a porcupine, he would turn into a witigo. Within his body a cake of ice would form.[30] When that ice reached the size of a child, the witigo becomes a cannibal and has no sense at all. If he sees children, any child—even his own, that child will look like a young deer or antelope or some such young and tempting animal, and so he starts to eat the child. He begins with the mouth and starts eating across the flesh from there.

Although the Montana Cree associate Witigo with the northern areas, they are cognizant of his presence there even to this date. A report came from Canada early in the spring of 1960[31] that a woman had turned into a witigo during the preceding winter. Ice grew within her. Her husband and friends melted the ice with beaver grease applied to her while she was in a sweat lodge. A little later, however, the ice returned inside her body. This time, for fear of the consequences, she did not tell anyone about it. One night she ate her husband and child. Her friends, fearing for their own lives, told the police about her and so had her arrested and jailed on a charge of murder. The Montana Cree have never learned the outcome of the case.

Thus it is that the legendary creature, Witigo, the outgrowth of the particular culture that gave rise long ago to such a belief, still functions in a religious sense with the Montana Cree. That he is the result of supernatural forces still operative classifies him within the framework of religious beliefs.

---

[29] Personal interview, December 29, 1959.

[30] Personal interview, Ruth Gardipee, October 31, 1959.

[31] Information supplied by a resident of the Rocky Boy reservation whose name is purposely withheld.

In addition to the firm belief in the exploits of Wi-sak-a-chak and the horror of Witigo, the Montana Cree also believe in the presence of other supernatural beings who fall properly into the classification of mythology, legend, or folklore. These are the Little People whose presence on the reservation is known to all the inhabitants. Endowed by supernatural power, yet not completely understood by the present-day Cree, these Little People are part of the mythology of the tribe, for they come from the remote past. That they are legendary also is manifested by the fact that many of the residents of the Rocky Boy reservation have heard or have seen them, but as time goes on the appearances and sounds seem to have decreased. Thus they seem to be passing from the realm of reality into the sphere of legend. But the places that they have inhabited are still known.

Several high buttes abound on the reservation, one of which is called Haystack because of a fancied resemblance to a stack of hay. The Little People—*m-me-m-mege'-soo*—live around the Haystack area, and children playing nearby often hear them but not with the frequency that people did in the past. Evenings and early mornings are the best time to hear them, although occasionally one can notice them in the daytime. They sound just like a group of children who are playing and enjoying themselves. Their language is Cree. Their dress is reminiscent of that worn by the old-time Cree Indian, for everything is tailored from hides. No white-man's apparel is ever worn. They are shy little creatures who always hide their faces if anyone sees them, as if they are ashamed. In physical appearance, they are about two and one-half feet in height, but they are extremely strong for such little bodies. No instances are ever remembered where these little people have ever harmed anyone; rather, they try to be very helpful to man. Their knowledge of herbs and doctoring sick people is one of their main assets and something that they willingly share with man. They also make spear heads and small hammers and frequently leave these items where man can find them and use them. The flint chips one encounters in many spots on the reservation were left there by the Little People.[32]

The Cree tell a story about Poor Coyote, the man they consider to be their last great medicine man. He had many encounters with the Little People at his home in Parker Canyon on the reservation. He liked to camp alongside Parker Creek which runs through the canyon and frequently left his cabin which stood some distance away from the creek

---

[32] All these details and succeeding ones about the Little People were given me by Raining Bird, December 30, 1959 and in other interviews.

to pitch his tipi beside the clear and bubbling water. One spring some boys came to stay with him and brought with them their marbles with which they played games alongside the creek. The next time the old man went to his favorite camping spot, he saw the Little People playing with some broken marbles which the boys had tossed away. When next he went to Havre, Poor Coyote purchased some new marbles and took them to the spot where the Little People had been playing and left them. The next morning when he returned to the creek again, all of the marbles were gone. The Little People had appeared in the night and had collected the marbles and taken them with them.

As Poor Coyote was standing there, wondering just where the Little People had taken the marbles, he heard a noise that resembled the sound of hands clapping. He looked at the bank across the creek from which the sound seemed to come, and noticed that it was about four feet high.[33] As he watched the bank and listened more closely to the clapping sound, he saw a door open in the creek bank. He crossed the stream, and stooping to enter, he walked through the door into the bank of the creek. Inside the earth, it was light. There he could see extensive signs of the Little People—their implements, tools, and clothes all scaled in size to fit their needs. He stood there watching and looking around him but seeing none of the small folk. Presently the door opened again, and he walked out, crossed the creek, and returned to his tipi.

With him when he was inside the habitation of the Little People was a bag of powder that he used in curing people and in effecting other matters of supernatural nature. The next time he used the powder, he realized that its efficacy had improved and strengthened. Through using it after that visit, he could divine the future in many instances. He could find out whether people were good and if their intentions were correct, for when he was with an honest and true person, the powder would grow and enlarge. By contrast, if the man he was with were mean or suspicious or not to be trusted, the powder would shrink. Thus it was that the gift of power the Little People bestowed upon Poor Coyote proved to be extremely helpful to him as men and women came to him for assistance in his role as medicine man and miracle worker of the Montana Cree. His death in the 1920's has left a void, for while others have claimed supernatural power and have demonstrated it to a certain

---

[33] Raning Bird took me to this bank alongside Parker Creek. Erosion has crumbled much of the bank away now, but the height of its previous position can be well noted. I also saw the spot where Poor Coyote pitched his tipi as well as the place where his cabin once stood.

degree, none has been as successful or as respected as was Poor Coyote.

The Cree belief in Little People is practically at one with the well-nigh universal belief among North American Indians concerning such beings. The existence of little people or dwarfs plays an active part in the imagination of people everywhere, for that matter; but here on the North American continent their existence is taken for granted. Among such tribes as the Coeur d'Alene of the Plateau and the Paiute of the Great Basin, dwarfs are described as small supernatural mischief makers who frighten people but who seldom if ever do any real harm. Some live in the springs or rivers while others are found on land.[34]

The Cherokee are strong believers in dwarfs, some of whom are good and some evil. These little people live in rock caves on the mountain sides. While some of them are capable of throwing spells over people and causing them to lose their way, they can also be very helpful, especially to children who have become lost. By the same token, however, certain malicious little people who live in caves along the river bluffs cause children's diseases. Two especial favorites of the Cherokee are named Tsawasi and Tsagasi, both of whom are mischievous little fairies. Tsawasi is a handsome little spirit with long hair falling down to his feet. His great power is over game, especially the deer. The hunter who prays to him is able to slip up to a deer unnoticed. Tsagasi is also a helpful little fellow, but he is often a little too mischievous. For instance, if someone trips and falls while hunting, it is probably because Tsagasi has caused it.[35]

The Chickasaw called their little people "iyaganaske." They were about three feet tall and had certain powers which they could give to the people whom they selected. They "did not live in all places, but sometimes under high banks or along a branch which had high banks."[36] Not everyone could see them. The idea of fairy invisibility is found in Irish, Indian, Icelandic, English, Scotch, Welsh, and Lithuanian literature.[37] So the well-nigh universal belief in the existence of Little People

[34] Ermine W. Voegelin, "Dwarfs," *The Standard Dictionary of Folklore, Mythology and Legend,* ed. Maria Leach. 2 vols. (New York, 1949), Vol. I, p. 331.

[35] All material about the Cherokee is taken from "The Cherokee Indians," by James Mooney, *Annual Reports of the Bureau of American Ethnology* (Washington: Government Printing Office, 1898), Vol. XIX, pp. 252–254.

[36] John R. Swanton, "Social and Religious Beliefs and Usages of the Chickasaw Indians," *Annual Reports of the Bureau of American Ethnology* (Washington: Government Printing Office, 1928), Vol. XLIV, pp. 250–251.

[37] Stith Thompson, *Motif Index of Folk Literature* (Bloomington: University of Indiana Press, 1956), Vol. III, pp. 37–81.

is shared by the Montana Cree. By identifying the powers of the Little People, they have brought them into their world of mythology.

In one sense, these stories of Wi-sak-a-chak, of Witigo, and of the Little People could be interpreted as being the literary expression of a group cut off from the main spring of their own culture and divorced, too, from the dominant culture that surrounds them. But in a larger sense, the stories are more than literary. They help the Montana Cree understand their environment and bring him closer to the supernatural. And in re-telling these stories, the Montana Cree are distinctly Indian and particularly Cree. Thus it is that another element—the stories about their mythological and legendary beings function in the persistence of their religious beliefs.

PLATE II

Little Bear

Indomitable chief of the Cree who led his wanderers to a home in Montana.

PLATE III

Four Souls
A view of the courageous son of Little Bear.
(Courtesy Museum of the Rockies
Photo-archive, Montana State University)

PLATE IV

Four Souls

Now a progressive cattleman, successful farmer, and conscientious employee of the Bureau of Indian Affairs, Four Souls is one of the most highly respected members of the Montana Cree.

PLATE V

Cree Dancers

View of the Grass Dance that follows the Sun Dance.

PLATE VI

Cree Dancers

Above: Another view of the Grass
Dance. Below: Rocky Stump at
a winter social dance.

PLATE VII

Principal informants in this study and friends of the author

Above: Tom Gardipee, grandson of Little Bear. Below: Ruth Gardipee, Tom's wife. Daughter of Mr. and Mrs. Pete Favel.

PLATE VIII

Contemporary Cree Tipi

Above: The temporary home
of Mr. and Mrs. Paul Eagle-
man at the Montana Cree Sun
Dance, 1960. Below: Details of
the construction showing the
three-prong or "swallow tail"
effect, distinctive symbol of
the Cree Lodge. (Courtesy
Museum of the Rockies
Photo-archive, Montana State
University)

PLATE IX

Scenes on the Rocky Boy Reservation.

Above: The skeletal frame of the Smoke Lodge. The leaves at the top of the poles remain green throughout the summer following the ceremony.

Below: A view of the Parker school colony, home of several of the informants.

CHAPTER XII

NATIVISTIC MOVEMENTS

At a cursory glance, the Montana Cree might be considered as a group who provide a good example of nativism. On a closer examination, however, it appears that many of them have never moved away from their native beliefs. Some of them, those with the Chippewa background, particularly, have generally accepted the Cree belief or have become submerged with Cree thinking. In general, then, the Cree on the Rocky Boy reservation have had no great need to return to the past, for in many cases they have never left the thinking of the past. Yet, in a few instances, we do find examples of their return. It is well then to define the terms by which we examine this apparent desire manifested by the Cree to secure some values from the past.

Linton's classical definition of nativism, "any conscious organized attempt on the part of a society's members to revive or perpetuate selected aspects of its culture,"[1] provides the basis for this examination. Linton further says, when he defines his terms, that "conscious attempt" arises only when other cultures threaten and that "selected aspects" are concerned with one particular element of the culture, never with cultures as a whole.[2] And in continuing Linton's treatise on nativism, we find that he classifies the various forms he has observed. He calls one "magical nativism." According to that classification, ". . . people are attempting to recreate those aspects of the ancestral situation which appear desirable in retrospect."[3]

Therefore, with Linton's definitions in mind, we shall examine a few practices found on the Rocky Boy reservation today.

Chief among these practices are the Spirit Lodge, the Smoke Lodge, and the Native American Church. All of these have been introduced or re-introduced on the Rocky Boy reservation during the last few years. The peyote group came to the Cree in 1936; since the end of World

---

[1] Ralph Linton, "Nativistic Movements," *American Anthropologist*, Vol. XLV (1943), p. 230.

[2] *Ibid.*, p. 231.

[3] *Ibid.*, p. 232.

War II, the primitive rites of the Spirit Lodge and of the Smoke Lodge have been re-instituted. At the same time, the culture has been threatened —more so than at any time since the establishment of the reservation. The Bureau of Indian Affairs has given the impression that it is desirous of withdrawing many of its former services. Already the Cree have seen the health program turned over to the Bureau of Public Health. The agricultural extension program has been shifted from the Bureau of Indian Affairs to the Extension Service of the State of Montana. Beginning in the autumn of 1960, the Havre Public Schools assumed operation of the school system of the reservation.

All of these changes worry the Cree. School officials report that many of the parents do not want their children to progress further in school than they themselves have. That idea, however, is a result of a misunderstanding that is prevalent in the area. In defense of the Montana Cree, I feel that they do want their children to be educated in the white man's way, but at the same time they want them to "remain Indian,"[4] to the extent that they know and appreciate the Cree values.

The young people themselves are caught in this trap. On the one hand, they hear the virtues of the white man's education extolled; on the other they listen to their parents reminding them that they are not and can never be white. And with the Cree, especially, they are reminded of their religious background and are instructed and trained in carrying on the primitive beliefs that have served their parents so well. As a result, tensions grow. Some of the young people leave and stay away but their numbers are few. Others go, but torn between the two cultures and beset with a sense of guilt for forsaking the teachings of their fathers, return to the reservations. Still others complete their required school attendance, which may be until they reach the age of sixteen or in some cases until they finish high school. Some of these young people become actively interested in the beliefs of the older people and become leaders in many of the ceremonies.

In this spirit of unrest that many of the Cree sense (for they feel that their culture could be destroyed), they are re-examining certain aspects of their religion which were effective in the past. Selected elements that were desirable to another generation are now being re-introduced by the present-day Cree as another means of combatting the possible disintegration of their group.

The Spirit Lodge is a good example. Its diffusion throughout the

---

[4] Many Indian parents have so expressed themselves to me, often weeping as they talk about how their children are going to be "forced into being white."

Algonquian world indicates its thoroughness in that culture.[5] The Northern Cheyenne[6] practiced it extensively; their descendants on the Northern Cheyenne reservation in Montana can take a person to the spot where the last great prophecy was made on June 21, 1876. There, near the present-day village of Busby, Montana, one of their great shamans foretold, while bound in the shaking tent, that four days later the American army would attack the Cheyenne.[7] On June 25, exactly four days later, Lt. Col. George A. Custer and the 7th Cavalry met defeat when they attacked the Dakota and the Cheyenne at the Battle of the Little Big Horn. The Gros Ventre of Montana were familiar with the efficacy of the shaking tent and used it extensively in primitive times. Power came to the Gros Ventre through the spirit of deceased relative.[8] The rite was known to the Blackfeet[9] and also to other western non-Algonquian peoples, the Kutenai[10] and the Assiniboine.[11]

The Cree have had a long association with the shaking tent.[12] In fact, Ray suggests[13] that it was they who brought the conjuring complex to the Northwestern Plains and the Plateau. All of the older members of the Montana Cree tribe remember the ritual well, and some state that it has not been done successfully since 1904. But the rite was re-

---

[5] See *Primitive Man* (1944), Vol. XVII. Practically the entire issue is devoted to the shaking tent ritual as found in various tribes.

[6] George Bird Grinnell, *The Cheyenne Indians* (New Haven: Yale University Press, 1922), Vol. II, pp. 112–117.

[7] For these details I am indebted to William Hollow Breast of the Northern Cheyenne tribe who took me to the spot and told me the story. Some years ago, the Northern Cheyenne built a concrete frame about six inches high and four inches wide around the area where the tent stood and then covered the framework with chicken wire. Time and youngsters have pretty well destroyed these efforts to preserve the site, however.

[8] Regina Flannery, "The Gros Ventre Shaking Tent," *Primitive Man* (1944), Vol. XVII, pp. 54–59.

[9] C. Denny, "Blackfeet Magic," *The Beaver*, September, 1944, p. 15.

[10] H. H. Turney-High, *The Ethnography of the Kutenai*, Memoirs of the American Anthropological Association (Menasha, 1941), No. 56, pp. 173–176.

[11] Robert Lowie, *The Assiniboine*, Anthropological Papers of the American Museum of Natural History (New York, 1909), Vol. IV, p. 49. Verne Dusenberry, Unpublished field notes on the Assiniboine, 1958.

[12] Regina Flannery, *op. cit.*, and David Mandelbaum, *The Plains Cree*, Anthropological Papers of the American Museum of Natural History (New York, 1940), Vol. XXXVII, Part II, pp. 261–263.

[13] Verne F. Ray, "Historic Backgrounds of the Conjuring Complex in the Plateau and Plains," *Language, Culture and Personality*. Essays in memory of Edward Sapir (Menasha, 1941), pp. 204–216.

introduced to the Rocky Boy reservation about 1945; its leader is a Canadian Cree.

Not all of the Cree are in agreement about the effectiveness of the present leader. Opinion seems to be divided about his ability. In fact, adherents to primitive belief are divided about their estimation of him. Some of the leaders of the Sun Dance maintain that he is a faker and that he cannot conjure properly; instead, he uses his powers of witchcraft. His supporters, among whom one can also find Sun Dance leaders, are just as vehement in the other direction and believe that he is endowed in such a way that he communes with the spirits. To bolster their arguments, they relate their own experiences.[14]

A Spirit Lodge is designed so that people can pray and find out various things, say the followers. If they wish to locate some lost article, or ask about their relatives, or divine certain events in the future, they can go to the leader and ask him to build the lodge. Sometimes people ask for the structure just so that they can go in and pray. Usually, however, it is built for certain specific reasons.

Illustrations abound. During the summer of 1959, a group of the Montana Cree were disturbed about the unemployment situation and the general unrest among the tribal members. One of them suggested that they put up a Spirit Lodge. The leader complied. During the course of the evening, the spirits told the leader that too many people were forgetting about their Creator and His teachings. As a result, *Ki-sei-men'-to* was going to send an earthquake to remind people about Him and His power. Within a month, a devastating earthquake shook Montana and surrounding country and caused the death of many people. Only the Cree who had been at the meeting of the Spirit Lodge were not surprised.

Another illustration of the power of the Spirit Lodge deals with a child who was lost on the reservation a few years ago. A thorough search failed to locate the three-year old youngster, so his parents asked that a Spirit Lodge be erected. The spirits told the leader that the child was dead, drowned in a certain stream at a definite localized place on the reservation. Immediately, searchers went to that spot and there found the body of the child. Still another instance happened during the Korean war. Parents of one of the soldiers received word from the War Department that their son was missing. When no further word came about

---

[14] Names of the informants both here and later are obviously withheld, just as is the name of the Spirit Lodge leader.

him, his parents had a Spirit Lodge erected. The spirits told the leader that the boy was alive and well. Within a short time after the prophecy had been made, the parents received a message that their son was unharmed and well.

In 1956, a brutal murder occurred in Great Falls, Montana. The bodies of an airman stationed at Malmstrom Air Base near the city and his girl friend were found on a lonely road within a mile of the city. Absolutely no clues could be found. The sheriff's office posted a liberal reward for information leading to the capture of the criminal. Some of the Cree who live in Great Falls wanted the Spirit Lodge leader to find out who had committed the crime. He refused to do it, however, on the grounds that the government might intrude and take steps to stop him from practicing on the reservation.

Much less dramatic incidents are also reported. For example one of my informants had a considerable amount of trouble with her throat. Finally, the soreness became so intense that she could not sing and could barely talk. She went to the government nurse who treated her and urged her to see a physician. When the doctor's prescriptions produced no result, she went to the leader and had him treat her in the Spirit Lodge. As a result, she has had no further trouble with her voice.

These adherents to the value of the Spirit Lodge state that after they make a decision to have one, the first step is to secure the permission of the leader to conduct one. The next step is the construction of the lodge. Before the work on the lodge starts, however, the person making the request buys eight pieces of new cloth, each piece being two yards long. Any color but black may be used. Black is dangerous, for it resembles and is associated with Matchi Manitou. Then the men must secure some poles. The men go to the hills and cut four green quaking aspen and trim them until they get the desired length and size. These should be about three inches in diameter and five feet long. The men sharpen these poles to a point on one end, and then, when they have them at the spot where the rite is to take place, they drive them into the ground to a depth of about one foot. The four poles are placed in the ground in a square about one and one-half feet apart. Once these poles are placed in the ground correctly, the men fashion a cord out of willows and fasten the cord around the top and the bottom of the upright poles. On the top of the structure, they place a piece of rawhide so that it will cover the top as well as approximately the top half of the square formed by the poles. The purchased cloth covers the bottom half. Near the top some bells—the kind used in dancing—are placed. The bells are later sounded by the spirits and are used by the Blackfeet and the Assiniboine as well as the Cree.[15]

This structure differs somewhat from that of the Canadian Cree as described by Mandelbaum.[16] According to his findings, the Canadians use stout logs, four or five inches in diameter and about six feet in length, which are implanted in the ground about two feet. There is a similarity between Mandelbaum's report and one of my informants, who now does not approve of the present use of the Spirit Lodge. According to him, the Cree used logs about the size of those of the Canadians, but instead of building the structure in a rectangular fashion it was cone-shaped. A hole, some two or three feet deep, provided the base for the cone which was covered completely with rawhide so that no possible way was left for the leader to get out of the structure.

Today, these booths are built inside a cabin if the meeting is to be held during the winter time. An opening is made in the floor by removing some of the floor boards so that the posts can be set in the earth. In the summer, however, the booth is put inside a tipi. Hay or grass covers the ground or floor, while sage is placed on top of that.

The meetings always take place at night. Before anything starts, however, the people eat and pray over the food with sweetgrass and pipe. Berries are always an integral part of the feast. Following the meal, a few preparations are made. Four singers, who help the leader, sit on the right-hand side of the lodge. Each one has a small hand drum. The leader sings a few songs first to instruct the singers. When these preparations have been made, and if the meeting is being held in a house, the lights are turned off when the leader is ready to start. If the people who are requesting the Spirit Lodge desire to do so, they may then tie the leader in any fashion they wish. Sometimes they tie his fingers together; that is, the fingers on his right hand are tied to those on his left. The Montana Cree do not believe that tying the leader is necessary; it is usually done now only if doubters are present. Before he goes into the lodge, whether he be tied or not, he always offers a long prayer asking the spirits to come to him.

Once the leader gets inside the booth, the singers start beating the drums and singing. Shortly after they begin their songs, the spirits start coming. Inside the booth, they shake the rattle (which the leader has

---

[15] Donald Collier, "Conjuring Among the Kiowa," *Primitive Man* (1944), Vol. XVII, pp. 44–49.

[16] Mandelbaum, *op. cit.*, p. 261.

taken with him), and then shortly thereafter they untie the leader if he has previously been bound. As they untie him, they throw the ropes or thongs that have been used to bind him out of the booth so that the people can see them and know that they have arrived.

The spirits speak in Cree so those present can understand what is being said. Their voices are reminiscent of very old men. Their name for the Indians is *aks-ju-aski-wes-skin-hagun*, "Earth Made People." Thus since the communication is well established between the spirit and the person, each person knows when he is being treated provided that more than one person has asked for the Spirit Lodge. The one whom the spirit announces is going to be treated goes to the little doorway of the lodge, which faces east, and sits there. Additional yard goods drape this entrance, so the person sits enfolded in part by the material. In speaking to the person, the spirit tells him where his sickness is located. The spirit is able to determine the location by hitting the patient's body with the rattle; once the exact spot of the sickness has been found, the spirit pounds that particular area quite hard. The patient can also tell that the spirits are there by feeling the spirits' noses.

If something is lost, the spirits sing. One spirit then goes to look for the lost person or article—usually that spirit is a bird. While it is gone, the other spirits sing and tell the individual good things that he should do. Sometimes they suggest that the person should light the pipe and smoke it. The time that the spirit is gone is commensurate with the distance he has to travel. Sometimes he is gone but for a few minutes; other times it may take an hour for him to locate the missing article or person. When the other spirits start singing louder and louder, one of them can be heard saying, "He's coming back. Sing harder." When the spirit returns, he tells the location of the lost person, describes him, and relates whether he is alive or dead.

Toward the end of the meeting the spirits shake the rattle one by one. As they shake it, those people who are present know that the spirits are leaving. The last one to leave throws the rattle out of the booth where it had been returned if it were used in determining a person's illness. The leader emerges after the rattle has been thrown out. Then, if it is in a cabin, someone turns the lights on. And if the leader has been tied, they all look at his hands and feet and seek the thongs that they had previously bound him with. At that point the meeting ends. Usually healing is almost instantaneous. The Montana Cree say that the old name for the ceremony was "Bow Pole Dance," but today it is known exclusively as the Spirit Lodge.

One of my informants told me that when properly administered, the Spirit Lodge can be a very effective means of instructing people. The spirits can teach people things that are good as well as proper ways of acting so that when one dies, he can be taken to the place of the dead and see things that others will not have the opportunity of seeing.

The Spirit Lodge provides a positive means whereby the Montana Cree can teach their children the effectiveness of their own religious values. Cures for illnesses that the white man's doctor is unable to effect; insight into the future that is denied the non-believer; ability to ascertain the location of lost items or persons—these are all practical solutions to problems that can be determined through the use of the Spirit Lodge. The Cree have returned to its use, not only because of its powers, but also because of the practical effect it has upon their children.

The interest in the Spirit Lodge is growing throughout the western tribes. The Arapaho have been developing it for the past several years.[17] During the autumn and winter of 1960 and 1961, numerous Indians from several Montana reservations have gone to Wyoming to see the leader of the Arapaho Shaking Tent. He is reported to be a young man who has great powers in healing. Patients with cancer whose medical doctors have given up hope for their recovery have been cured. Lesser ailments have been treated as successfully. Consequently, a constant stream of cars heads south for assistance from this gifted leader. The Montana Cree are no exception, for they are going in goodly numbers. The young Arapaho leader who is capable of performing miracles to the satisfaction of the Indian people through the medium of the Spirit Lodge provides an excellent example of what can be obtained through Indian belief. He is one more bulwark against the threatening breakdown of their culture. His performances are excellent arguments for remaining "Indian" in their actions.

While not as dramatic in its effect as the Spirit Lodge, the Smoke Lodge is another ceremony from the past that is now gaining in respect on the reservation.[18] Peeso gives accounts of the Smoke Lodge and its use among the forebears of the Montana Cree in both his published

---

[17] Dr. Ake Hultkrantz has observed the renewed interest in the Shaking Tent ritual on the Arapaho reservation in Wyoming and has given the information to me.

[18] Alanson Skinner, *Political Cults and Ceremonies of the Plains Cree,* Anthropological Papers of the American Museum of Natural History (New York, 1944), Vol. XI, Part VI, pp. 538–540. See also Donald Cadzow, "Smoking Tipi of Buffalo-Bull the Cree," Indian Notes, Museum of the American Indian, Heye Foundation, Vol. IV (1927), pp. 271–282.

and unpublished material.[19] Mandelbaum,[20] who has written a comprehensive first-hand account of the ceremony, ranks the Smoking Tipi next in importance to the Sun Dance. Because of its recent importation on the Rocky Boy reservation, the Montana Cree probably do not rate it quite as highly as did the Canadian Cree with whom Mandelbaum worked twenty-five years before. But their respect for it is growing.

The Smoke Lodge was re-introduced on the Rocky Boy reservation as a result of a vow made by a young man when he went into the Air Corps near the end of World War II.[21] The ceremony then had practically died out. He publicly vowed that were he saved from death during the war he would institute the Smoke Lodge upon his return. Since nothing serious happened to him during the war, despite many adverse adventures in which his companions were killed, he returned home safely and has performed the rites of the Smoke Lodge every succeeding summer.

The Master Spirit of the Bear is the one who presides over the Smoke Lodge and the one to whom prayers are given. The Montana Cree refer to this supreme spirit as *o-ki-mau-o-ko-sun,* which can be translated as "chief's son." Sometimes they call him *no-neo-gateo-ai-sin-yu,* "four-legged human."[22] The Bear figures in the Smoke Lodge ceremony because *Ki-sei-men'-to* keeps a great white bear as a pet. "Just as man has a dog for a companion, so *Ki-sei-men'-to* has this bear," says Raining Bird,[23] who explains further that the ceremony stems from the story of Bear Child. Tom Gardipee agrees and related the incident that started the ceremony:[24]

Once some people were out picking berries in the spring and while they were there, they lost their baby boy who was two years old. The Bear came along and took the boy in the cave with him where the child ate with the bear and stayed with him. Bear prayed over the boy constantly, and as a result, he grew to be a man in a very short time. By the next spring, Bear knew that the people would come and find him and kill him even though the boy was fine and had grown to be a big man. Bear called the boy, 'my grandson,' and the boy followed Bear wherever he went.

'My grandson,' said Bear one day. 'When they kill me and you return to your people, I will come to you in your sleep. Tell your father to build a tipi

[19] Fred E. Peeso, "The Cree Indians," *The Museum Journal* (Philadelphia; University of Pennsylvania, 1912), pp. 50–57. Also his unpublished manuscript.

[20] Mandelbaum, *op. cit.,* pp. 271–274.

[21] Personal interview, Raining Bird, August 25, 1960.

[22] Personal interview, Four Souls, August 30, 1960.

[23] Personal interview, December 30, 1959.

[24] Personal interview, November 4, 1959.

in a clean place. Do not let a woman see you. Then I can talk to you. Someone who is different, a big liar, I think, is coming here to kill me.'

That is just what happened. A man came and killed the bear. The boy, now grown to a man, wept. Then he said to the man, 'He knew you were going to come and kill him. Go now to my father and tell him that I said to put up a tipi away from the camp. Put it in a clean place and I will come home.'

The man followed the boy's instructions. When they were completed, he returned home. No one in camp could believe that this grown man was the boy whom they had lost just the year before. Yet, he knew them all. He did not stop to visit any of them, however, but went directly to the tipi that he had told his father to erect. It was now standing at a nice clean place some distance away from the main camp. Without saying anything or greeting anyone, he entered the tipi and sat there and sang for three nights. His father looked in at him and brought him food, but he refused to speak or to eat. He just sat there singing.

The chief's daughter became quite interested in this young man who had come to the camp and who spent his time just singing. She heard that he was a very good looking boy. She tried every way that she could to steal a glimpse of him; each time, however, the men guarding the tipi insisted that she leave. On the fourth night, the guards fell asleep and the girl slipped by them, lifted the tipi flap, and looked at this young man who had been singing so beautifully.

Immediately, the boy stopped drumming and singing and cried out, 'That girl has seen me; I cannot stay here. I must go to my grandfather, the Bear.'

The boy's mother and other relatives came. They talked to him a long time, but despite their pleas and their tears, they could not get him to change his mind. He told them that he would give them instructions about a new ceremony that would help them in much the same way that the Sun Dance helped them, but that after he told them how to do the ceremony he would depart and that they would never see him again.

He proceeded then to tell them how to erect the tipi and how to conduct the ceremonies. He insisted that they must always have plenty of food there, for instead of fasting as they did in the Sun Dance, now everyone must eat heartily as they prayed through his grandfather, the Bear, to *Ki-sei-men'-to*. Next, he taught them the songs they were to sing and showed them how to use a rattle instead of a drum. When he was convinced that they knew the songs, for he had them sing the songs to him until he was sure they knew them, he began to sink into the ground. He was singing as he started his descent. Finally, no one could hear him or see him. The people knew that he had gone to stay with his grandfather, the Bear. That is why the people called him Bear Child, and why today people put up smoke lodges.

The lodge that houses the ceremony is made today just as Bear Child instructed. It is, in reality, a double tipi made from forty-four poles. The leaves at the top of the poles, which are not trimmed off as they are from the poles used in a regular tipi, remain green and fresh throughout the entire summer and do not wither and blow away as leaves from a cut tree usually do. I saw the skeletal poles of a smoke lodge in December, 1959, and although it had been used in July for the ceremony, the leaves were still intact at the top of the poles. Although they were dry, and this was accounted for by the freezing weather, they did appear green.

The Montana Cree remember a story told them about one of their ancestors who, before they left Canada, had a pet bear. He secured a cub bear and reared it and kept it with him all the time. He always took the bear into the Smoke Lodge with him. When the leader of the ceremony started singing, the bear went to the singer or singers and stood before them. If the leader sang the songs correctly, the bear rubbed his shoulder approvingly. If, however, the songs were wrong, the bear slapped the leader. Even though the people knew that the bear was cognizant of the songs through his association with the Master Spirit of the Bear, many of them would not sing because of their fear of the bear. Yet, he was never known to harm anyone.[25]

Despite the fact that the Smoke Lodge represents the special Bear Spirit, not every song has to be directed to him. One can sing songs to the Wind or the Thunderbird or to any spirit he wishes while he is in the Smoke Lodge.[26] In accordance with Bear Child's teachings, though, everything else is done as originally shown them by the boy. Participants use rattles. They remain within the lodge throughout the entire night, singing and eating. Berries must be included in the meal.

In time sequence, the Smoke Lodge follows the Sun Dance. Its simplicity in form and in preparation adds to its attractiveness. In effectiveness it accomplishes much the same purpose as the Sun Dance. One makes a vow. If one is then granted the condition of the vow, such as recovery from an illness or return from a difficult journey, he gives the Smoke Lodge ceremony. By renewing it on the reservation, the Montana Cree have more evidence of the strength of their religion. As will be pointed out in succeeding chapters, the Sun Dance is particularly attractive to the younger people. The Smoke Lodge is an addendum, in a way, to the Sun Dance. Its renewal is another illustration that by remaining Indian, young people have advantages over their white neighbors.

Another superiority that the Montana Cree possess, and one that they jealously guard, is their affiliation with the Native American Church. Here again is an element that is nativistically orientated. Not until 1936 did the peyote movement appear on the Rocky Boy reservation. Before that time, some of the Montana Cree had been attending services on the

---

[25] Personal interview, Raining Bird, August 25, 1960.
[26] Personal interview, Raining Bird, December 30, 1959.

Crow reservation. The Crows, in turn, had received the idea from the Northern Cheyenne about 1914. On the Rocky Boy reservation, the Native American Church has been under attack since its inception. Catholics and Lutherans unite in their denunciation and criticism of the movement. Wild rumors have been afloat about the sex orgies that take place at the meetings, and other fantastic lies have been spread.[27] A more distinct cleavage exists between members of the peyote group and other residents of the reservation than I find on either the Crow or the Northern Cheyenne reservations. Perhaps that may account for the fact that members of the Native American Church on the Rocky Boy reservation seem much more secretive about their services and much more reticent about talking about them than do members on the other two reservations in Montana where the Church is flourishing.[28]

Perhaps that attitude, too, may account for the fact that the Montana Cree do not want white people to attend their meetings. Although I have been attending meetings on the Northern Cheyenne and the Crow reservations for years and have always been impressed by the generous hospitality of these people as well as the evident delight manifested by them that a white man would come and worship with them,[29] the Montana Cree displayed an entirely different reaction. Despite the fact that the leader for the evening when I did attend had invited me and did everything possible to make it pleasant for me, most of the other members resented my presence. One of them was downright insulting. When the meeting ended in the morning, the warm feeling of comradeship and friendship that has characterized this period at other meetings was not evident. In fact, I was not invited to stay for the noon-day feast.

The meeting itself seems much more rigid than either the Crow or

---

[27] I have heard these rumors from Indian members of both churches as well as from white neighbors.

[28] These are my personal reactions.

[29] The Northern Cheyenne are particularly gracious about extending invitations to me to attend their meetings. Once I had occasion to be on the reservation on business shortly before I was due to leave for Europe. That night, which was Saturday, some of the men mentioned at a meeting that I had been on the reservation that day. One of the leaders, the fire chief, took his car and drove nearly fifty miles before he located me at a motel just off the reservation. He insisted that I return with him to the meeting so that the members could "pray for my good trip across the water." My arrival there caused the tent to be so crowded that one member left, I later learned, and sat all night in his car near the tent. "I can always go to a meeting and you can't," he explained to me the next morning when I apologized to him for taking his place.

the Northern Cheyenne meetings are. In fact, among the Northern Cheyenne, more informality and individuality appear. Participants may walk in and out as they please. Due reverence is always given to the seriousness of the meeting, yet there is a feeling of individual independence associated with it. The Crows have a service that might be compared more to the Anglican High Church ceremony in that a good deal more emphasis is placed upon form. In both of these services, where the participants are as serious minded as they can be, they still manifest a close feeling of fellowship. The Montana Cree, on the other hand, hold a service that seems more comparable to the Fundamentalists in Christian sects. No sense of enjoyment is present. The participants look serious and weep frequently. Weeping, one of the members explained to me, is a Cree trait.[30] By shedding tears during a religious experience one becomes closer to his Creator. Weeping is a means whereby man can humble himself before *Ki-sei-men'-to* and communicate with him. One of the busiest men at the meeting is the cedar chief, for he is censing people continually. To an observer, the Montana Cree participate in the peyote meetings without the sense of comradeship or happiness that is displayed elsewhere. It is a serious business—a church founded by Indians for Indians, and one from which white men are to be excluded.[31]

"The peyote meetings are just as powerful as the Sun Dance," explains Tom Gardipee,[32] a member of the group and a occasional leader. "There must be a reason for these meetings," he adds. It may be held to ask for the recovery of a sick person, or it may be held as a result of a vow made if a person recovers from an illness. The person who gives the meeting always tells the others the reason for the meetings. Sometimes they have meetings to doctor a sick person who attends and the participants pray all night for him. Anyone can smoke for him or pray to the peyote to let the person get well. They can also pray for better homes, for the education of their children, for the health of the old people, and for peace. Sometimes they have birthday meetings where they pray for the

---

[30] William Denny explained this fact to us at the meeting, October 31, 1959.

[31] Again, these are my own reactions to the meetings of the Native American Church on the three reservations in Montana where the church operates. With me at the one meeting on the Rocky Boy reservation which I attended were two graduate students in anthropology from Montana State University and one young instructor from the same school. One of the students had been with me at a meeting on the Crow reservation. His reaction to our reception was identical with mine. One Cree did say that he was glad to see us there. Since four was their sacred number, it was good to see four of us present.

[32] Personal interview, December 27, 1959.

luck of the child's future. When the conductor of the meeting asks the sponsor to tell what the meeting is for, he always explains why he is giving it. When he finishes telling about it, all of the people are asked by the conductor if they want to request a special prayer. These special prayers are made during the smoking of the tobacco. This is the time when they ask things for themselves.

A man can be a Sun Dance Leader or a medicine man or any other kind of leader who possesses power and still be a peyote leader. The Montana Cree tell about one of their relatives who came down from Canada and attended a meeting of the Native American Church. He claimed to be a very active healer who not only knew over three hundred spirits but who had the power to conduct the Spirit Lodge ceremony. It is claimed that one night while he was face to face with the Peyote Spirit at a meeting, he realized that his spirits were not as powerful as was Peyote's. In the morning he publicly admitted his realization. While it is difficult to ascertain if the statement, relayed in a second-hand fashion to me, is propaganda for the Native American Church, it is significant since the teller is a strong leader of the Church.[33]

"There are no conflicts in religion," says one of my informants. "Since we are all the children of one God, whether it is *Ki-sei-men'-to* or the God of the white man, it's all the same thing. So a man can be a Catholic and a leader of the Spirit Lodge or the Smoke Lodge or the Sun Dance. He is just following the instructions of the Creator in different ways. He can also be a leader of the peyote church, for here again, one is just following the Creator who has put all this power in Peyote. You see, he can take part in all three of these ways of doing things, for all the prayers lead to the same place in the end."[34]

That there is no conflict in this configuration is evidenced among the Montana Cree. Sun Dance leaders as well as the Spirit Lodge followers and some Catholics and Lutherans belong. A number of young men are not only members but active participants as well. At the meeting I attended in October, 1959, the leader was a man in his mid-thirties. His assistant was a fellow of about the same age—both World War II veterans. The cedar chief was a boy just turned twenty-one and the fire chief a man not over forty. All of these men I had seen participating in

---

[33] This information and the quotation cited come from an informant whose name is purposely withheld.

[34] Raining Bird explained this interpretation to me, December 31, 1959. See also O. C. Stewart, "Three Gods for Joe," *Tomorrow* (1956), Vol. IV, iii, pp. 71–76.

other ceremonies on the reservation. I also recognized some of the members as people whom I had seen at other religious meetings.

Peyotism, at least with the Montana Cree, seems to be a symptom of unrest. Their acceptance of something new and something different from the old way indicates the adjustment that has forced them to compromise in a different religious pattern—one alien to them. Yet they militantly defend it. The approximate fifty percent of the reservation who are affiliated in one way or another with the movement praise its virtues. Although the Native American Church is perhaps nearer to Christianity than any other type of observance found on the reservation, the Montana Cree believe that again they are practicing a religious belief that is superior to the white man's. Born then out of the need to cling to some values of the past, the members present an united front against their critics.

Other nativistic movements aside from the peyotists and the followers of the Spirit Lodge or the Smoke Lodge may be found. The Montana Cree have turned toward Canada to institute the painted tipi cult, although in general the attempt has been abortive. Still, a few followers may be found. My informants say that an old man in Moose Mountain, Canada, attempted to establish a church some years ago. He was a good and powerful man, who had the ability to forgive the sins of the people. While insisting that he received his vision directly from *Ki-sei-men'-to*, he also added that his was the last religion the Supreme Being made for the Indians.

To worship in this manner, one had to construct a tipi and have symbolic emblems painted on the outside of it. For example, the one belonging to the late Mrs. Mary Favel[35] has a design on the top of it that shows teeth marks. Thus, if a person talks too much about the owner, there will be chewing on the tipi instead of on the individual. Or if the owner talks too much about someone else, the message will stick at the top of the tipi, for the teeth will hold back the message. At the rear of the tipi is a little door or lodge-like painting which represents the spirit lodge in the afterworld. The Moon and the Sun are painted on the tipi, too. A little person with a spear, who is painted on one side of the tipi, symbolizes the soul of an individual. On the front of the tipi is the wind bird. (The wind is something we breathe and hence something that takes care of the whole universe.) The wind bird re-

---

[35] Mrs. Favel's daughter, Ruth Gardipee, gave me this information. Since then the owner of the tipi has died. I am positive that the tipi will be left in the hills for the spirits.

presentation has hair fastened to its forehead. When the wind blows the hair completely down to cover the face of the figure, people know that a cyclone will occur.

To put up this lodge requires the use of special rattles and pipes as well as songs and prayers. Springtime is the occasion for the erection of the tipi. New ribbons may be added to the designs, especially to the sun painting. These new ribbons must be smudged first in sweetgrass smoke. Certain tabus affect the tipi also. No woman can sew on it or repair it while she is menstruating. No woman can walk behind the fire within it either—just men are allowed there. People often hold feasts in the tipi and then they sing songs, some of which have holy words. Revelations sometimes occur to people who go into the tipi, while others feel that by going in and singing and praying they become cleansed. One woman on the reservation went in to be cleansed once and became so affected by the powers that she fainted and had to be carried out.

Four tipis of the same design can be made by copying the original one whose owner received her instructions from the founder of the religion. Each time, a ritual must be carried out when the designs are transferred to the new tipi. When a person dies, the tipi cannot be sold or given away, but must be taken into the hills and left there for the spirits. Neither can it be sold during the lifetime of the individual. It is a sacred entity given to that one person who may pass along the secret to three other people and that is all.

My informant states that despite the fact that the religion has many fine and helpful elements, it has never flourished as other kinds have. Those who have practiced it, though, have found it to be very helpful. Apparently, the development of this religious celebration has never had any great impact upon the Cree, either in Canada or in Montana. Its presence, however, gives another indication that the people are continually attempting to find some interpretation of the supernatural and have deliberately turned to the past to see if they can discover some of the elements that sustained their forebears.

Another example of what I interpret to be nativism has just recently started on the reservation and seems to be thriving. During my stay with the Montana Cree in the winter of 1959, I witnessed a hand game played by the Assiniboine. On a return visit to the Rocky Boy reservation in the spring of 1961, I found the game well entrenched, for by that time the Cree themselves had learned the ritual and the songs.

Some years before, in 1956, Rex Flying gave me an account of the Assiniboine hand game when I was doing some field work with him.

The following description of the game comes from notes supplied me at that time. In 1882, the United States Government forbade the performance of the Sun Dance, so the Assiniboine made a nice adaptation of the well-known gambling game and gave it a religious connotation. While tribal members were worried over the loss of their most sacred ceremony and were confused and resentful toward a government that had stopped it, a voice came to one of their members, White Boy, as he dreamed.

"I am the Bright Morning Star,"[36] said the Voice. "They are stopping you from worshipping. Do it this way. Then it will only look like a game and it will seem that you are just enjoying yourself. Use the symbols this way, and I will know. Before you start playing, pray."

The bones that are used are similar to those that players have in the regular gambling game except that designs have been added. Two of the bones have a star on one side, symbolic of the Morning Star, while the other two have a bird carved on them, representative of the Crow. The one chosen to lead each side has a stick which he manipulates as he guesses the hand in which the proper bone is hidden. On each end of the stick are feathers—eagle feathers on one end and crow feathers on the other. The end with the eagle feathers guides the stick. Each player has one bone; thus the number playing the game is limited to four people on each side. When the group starts singing, each one of the players puts a bone in his hands. Through faith, the leaders, who walk up and down between the two groups of players while the singers and drummers sing special songs, can tell which hand holds the proper bone.

Four men usually play against four women. Perhaps a woman in the community is ill so her relatives play the hand game and ask that her health be restored. If the woman is to recover, the women will win. If she is destined to die, the women lose.

Originally, the players painted themselves with red to signify that they were children of nature, much as they had always done in the Sun Dance. Prior to the game, they bathed in the creek. After leaving the fresh-running water, they anointed themselves with sage and peppermint (*Mentha arvensis*). They could wear no metal upon their persons once they were dressed and ready to enter the game. During the progress of the game, a smudge of sweetgrass burned so that their thoughts would be on serious matters and nothing else. All of these details are reminiscent of the Sun Dance.

---

[36] Rex Flying says that the Assiniboine learned about the Morning Star from their friends, the Arikara, a Caddoan group, with whom they once were associated near the Mandan villages. Personal interview, October 17, 1960.

During the game, food is served. In the beginning years of the ceremony, only food prepared away from the scent of human beings was used. The menu included such items as chokecherries, service berries, Indian turnips and dried meat. Rodnick reports that part of the necessary food served during a hand game is puppy meat and relates how it was given to him.[37] Minnie Moccasin substantiated this statement as she reminisced about how the group had tried to keep Dr. Rodnick from seeing the preparation of the food. Laughingly, she told of Rodnick's appearance just as the women were singeing the hair from the strangled puppies.[38] Rex Flying emphatically denies any relationship between eating puppy meat and serving food at the hand game. According to him, those people who eat puppy meat will serve it at a hand game; those who do not eat it will not serve it. He maintains that puppy meat is not confined to nor related to the hand game. Mrs. Tavie Kipp[39] states that she has attended hand games among the Assiniboine in the Lodgepole area, and that puppy meat was never served to her or her family. At the meeting I attended with the Montana Cree, platters heaped with fried chicken were distributed to the guests as well as generous servings of bakery products.

The Montana Cree are interested in and are enjoying the hand game, or "feather game," as they refer to it. The meeting I attended was held in the home of Charles Writing Bird, a member of the Native American Church. The house, which is larger than most of the Indian homes on the Rocky Boy reservation, was crowded with visitors. The room in which the game was being played was jammed; others crowded the doorway of the adjoining room. They were quiet, respectful, and dignified. Numerous young men and women were present. They looked with interest upon the game as they followed each movement carefully. They watched with particular care when one of the Assiniboine young men led the group. He was about twenty-one, had just recently been discharged from the Army, and had married one of the Cree girls. The young Cree people seemed to respect him for his role as leader. Here, perhaps, was something worth knowing, they seemed to think; here was another instance of controlling the supernatural which could become theirs. It was Indian; it must be good.

In an attempt to convince their young people that the Indian way

---

[37] David Rodnick, *The Fort Belknap Assiniboine of Montana* (New Haven: Yale University Press, 1938), p. 123.

[38] Personal interview, July 5, 1956.

[39] Personal interview, July 6, 1956.

of communing with supernatural forces confronting them is superior to the white man's way, the Montana Cree have looked to the past and have taken certain aspects of their former religious values and have developed them. The Spirit Lodge, the Smoke Lodge, the Painted Tipi, the Hand Game are all illustrations. And by taking a new type of worship—that of the exclusively Indian-developed service and belief of the Native American Church—they can continue fortifying themselves against the encroachments of the whites.

CHAPTER XIII

THE SUN DANCE: ETHNOGRAPHY

By far the largest Indian ceremony in Montana is the Cree Sun Dance. Each year, Indians from all over the state, as well as from neighboring Alberta, Saskatchewan, and Wyoming come to the broad gently-sloping plain three miles from the agency center of the Rocky Boy reservation. And to this spot the Cree themselves return. Some of them come from as far away as California where they are employed in aircraft factories; they arrange their vacation time to coincide with the Sun Dance and return to Montana for that period. They often bring their trailers with them; those modern symbols of mobility take their places in the camp circle beside the tents and tipis of the other Indians. Cree living in Great Falls, Havre, Browning, or other places in Montana, likewise take their vacations and return to the reservation. Those who have left the reservation in early spring to follow the transient labor market around the Northwest are back. Those who have been left behind, even though they may be quite well acculturated, are there too. They may not have a tent or a tipi pitched, but they are there. And in numbers, there are usually at least one thousand people camped on that plain during the Sun Dance.[1]

"It is evident," said Rex Flying, an Assiniboine friend whom I visited at the Sun Dance, "that these Indians do not come to this Sun Dance out of curiosity. Look at them. Regardless of their education, they are Indians at heart and they will come a long ways to be here for one of these affairs. As long as there is an Indian alive, he will feel that way about the Sun Dance." And not only will they come, but their conduct will be excellent. While there, they are quiet, restrained and respectful. If the young men consume any liquor, it is in their cars away from the Sun Dance grounds and moderately done at that. None

---

[1] The impressions recorded in this chapter are those I received from attending the Montana Cree Sun Dance in 1953, 1954, 1956, and 1960.

of them appear intoxicated near the Sun Dance Lodge.[2] Fun and a carnival spirit come on the days following the conclusion of the sacred ceremonies when hand games and grass dances prevail.

During the four days of the ceremony, the camp is quiet and orderly. And the young people attend it in such numbers and behave themselves so well that they give an indication that the ceremony still has meaning for them and for another generation.

For the Sun Dance is the cultic symbol of all their religious values. *Ki-sei-men'-to* gave the Sun Dance to the Cree at the time of creation.[3] He showed them how to do each and every thing. Some of the songs that are used go back to the beginning also. One song *Ki-sei-men'-to* sang as He created the world. As the centuries have gone by, other songs have been added—songs that have been taught by the Buffalo, the Eagle, or the Thunderbird, as well as by other different spirits. The songs alone might serve as a unifying core to bring these people together—but the belief is much more significant. The Sun Dance represents the whole sky and the whole world. No matter now how varying may be the belief of the contemporary Cree—he may be a Roman Catholic, a Lutheran, a Peyotist, or one who practices only his Indian religion—at Sun Dance time he is unified with the feeling that here is something of which he is a definite part. Thus, he seems compelled to come. And come they do from every social stratum on the reservation as well as from the entire region.

But more than a sense of compulsion brings them back. They are doing what their ancestors before them did. The Cree were divided into eight loosely-organized bands.[4] Each band had its own general range, for they would have starved had they all tried to remain together. (The pre-white population is estimated at about 6,000 people.) During the summer months, runners went to members of these bands and notified them of the impending Sun Dance. Some summers only two or three

---

[2] A young Canadian Cree Indian who obviously had been drinking but who was not drunk stood near me at the entrance to the lodge one evening. An Indian police came to him and told him to go to his camp and stay there. The boy was quite surprised and started to remonstrate as he questioned the order. The policeman told him quietly but firmly to leave the area or else he would take him to jail. The boy left of his own accord.

[3] For this nice bit of ethnocentrism, I am indebted to the Sun Dance leader, Raining Bird. Practically all information in this chapter has been given me over a period of several years by Raining Bird.

[4] David Mandelbaum, *The Plains Cree,* Anthropological Papers of the American Museum of Natural History (New York, 1949), Vol. XXXVI, Part II, pp. 166–168.

ceremonies would be given; other times, each band would have its Sun Dance. With the dates set for early in the summer, the bands planned their migrations so that they could be with one of their groups when the Sun Dance was being held. The pattern is similar to that which exists today. The Cree scatter in the spring; some remain away from the reservation during the entire year. But like their buffalo-hunting ancestors, they return for the great religious ceremony of the year.

Each Cree knows that the sponsor of the Sun Dance has definite objectives in mind and that the ceremonial is conducted for some specific reasons. Perhaps someone in the tribe has been ill so his relative has sponsored the Sun Dance to petition aid for the sick person; or if the person has recovered from some sickness, the Sun Dance may be pledged from a sense of gratitude. It may be that the tribe faces difficulties which the sponsor seeks to overcome through the medium of the Sun Dance; or it may be for a wider brotherhood, all humanity, for whom the sponsor makes his appeal.[5] Recently, the Cree Sun Dance was dedicated to four things: good health for all the people; good luck for them in finding work; rain for the area; and peace for the United States and the world. And beyond these general aims, each Cree who comes to the dance makes a special vow of his own. He may show it by participating in the ceremony; he may also show it by fasting in the camp. But in any event, here on the Sun Dance grounds he is definitely a personage in his own right, displaying his own inheritance. Ethnocentric, no doubt; nativistic to a degree, perhaps. But whatever it does, in varying degrees to the thousand or more people there, it unifies the Cree. Being at the Sun Dance gives him a sense of continuation of former values—values that were good and workable in buffalo days; values that seem good to him now. And values that are significant to him as an Indian.

Just as it is with other tribes, the name Sun Dance is a misnomer. The ceremonial should be called "Thirsting Dance," or "Rain Dance." The latter term is used in Canada.[6] The Cree word for it is *ni-pa-kwesi-mo-win-ba*. The root carries with it the connotation of begging or beseeching so that literally it becomes a "beseeching-for-water-to-allay-the-thirst-dance." But it has been termed Sun Dance for so long in all the ethnographic literature, as well as in the minds of the Indian people themselves, that it shall be so designated here.

---

[5] Abel Watetch (as told to Blodwen Davies), *Payepot and His People*, Saskatchewan History and Folklore Society, (n. d.), p. 36.

[6] *Ibid.*, p. 36.

A Sun Dance is a completely planned and thought out performance. Much of its success depends upon the leader who works for months planning and preparing for the annual event. Sun Dance leaders, who receive their power from the spirits, must be men who are pure in thoughts and deeds. Preparations for a Sun Dance usually start on the Rocky Boy reservation after the New Year begins. If a person has a good reason for giving or vowing to give the dance, he can come to the leader and tell him that he wishes to sponsor the Sun Dance the following summer. If the reason given seems satisfactory to the leader, he gives his approval and before four nights have passed he must call a song ceremony. Here we find a little difference between the Montana Cree and those in Canada, for there a council of elders meets with the sponsor and after listening to his objectives and plans, makes the decision.[7]

An individual's dreams may be the reason for the person to request sponsorship of a Sun Dance. If he dreams of thunder or buffalo or the sun or of a cold wind for four times during the year, he has to sponsor a Sun Dance. If he dreams of any of these elements during the year, he must dance the Sun Dance although he is not required to sponsor it.

According to ancient custom, the sponsor appears before the leader very early in the winter, as has been pointed out. If permission is granted and a song fest has been held, the sponsor waits until he finds the first leaf in the spring. He takes that leaf to the leader who then sets up a tipi for the second song meeting where the leader, his three assistants, the two men who care for the pipe and the sweetgrass during the actual ceremony as well as the two men who are inside firemen within the Sacred Lodge, come to the second tipi for another sing. Other volunteers may also attend this meeting. Considerable time elapses between the first and the second meeting—in Montana, it may be from January until late in April. Because of weather conditions, these meetings do not have to be held in a tipi, but may be in the leader's home where it is warmer and more comfortable for the participants. Nonetheless, they are still referred to as being in the "first tipi" and the "second tipi."

Although it was necessary in the past for the sponsor to announce his intention to give the Sun Dance several months from the actual date, an adaptation has been made in recent years, which allows for emergencies. Let us asume that an unusual situation arises. For example, should an epidemic of influenza break out on the reservation in late March or April causing numerous people to become ill, the Sun Dance

---

[7] *Ibid.*, p. 37.

leader, because of the concern over the situation, can then announce that he will vow to give a Sun Dance to combat the epidemic. The preliminary rites can now be adapted to the time element. Nevertheless, the Montana Cree believe that the old method is the superior way. Whenever it is possible for them to do so, they still follow the custom of their fathers in having the first tipi in January, the second one in April, and the third one just prior to the date selected.

Four days before the scheduled opening of the Sun Dance, the leader and his assistants move to a secluded area and pitch their tents in preparation for the "third tipi." The Montana Cree have a traditional spot in the mountains where the last pre-Sun Dance ritual takes place. Here in varying numbers, they move each year.[8] According to Raining Bird, over one hundred tents and tipis were in the camp circle for the third sing in 1921; nearly forty years later, in 1960 when I was invited to spend these days with them, only four tents were pitched. These belonged to Raining Bird and his wife; their son, Louis and his wife; Big Bow and his family; and an elderly woman, Mrs. Samatte.

The group camps for three nights. The first night, after all preliminaries have been made, the baby Thunderbird is hatched. It is created from twists of tobacco that are fastened together to resemble the figure of the bird. The figure is wrapped first in sweetgrass, then in layers of clean blue cloth, and finally tied in four places with buckskin thongs. Like the youngest member of a family, the baby Thunderbird is loved and protected. It can never be left alone. Consequently, the bird is constructed at the third meeting now rather than at the first one as was done in earlier times and is reported as being done in Canada. Nowadays people have to go out and work or travel; consequently, they postpone the construction of the bird until the time of the "third tipi."

The first two nights the people are encamped for the third sing, they sing various Sun Dance songs. Other assistants aside from those who are camping there, come to the group and participate. On the third night, no singing is done. Before dawn, however, the leader arises and takes the baby Thunderbird around the camp. He pauses at each cardinal direction and offers prayers over it.

At about 5:30 a.m. on the morning of the fourth day, the people in

---

[8] Pete Favel says that these preliminary rites are held at a different spot so that the main Sun Dance grounds will not be dirty or cluttered before the ceremony actually starts. Personal interview, June 30, 1960.

the camp dismantle their tents and prepare to leave. The leader and his wife take all their possessions, including the sacred objects, and follow an old seldom-used wagon road in their automobile to the Sun Dance grounds. En route, they stop four times and pray, using the sweetgrass and pipe. These prayers are addressed to the spirits who are beseeched to grant safe journeys and good roads to all the people who will come to the Sun Dance. I left the preliminary site accompanied by the leader's son who directed me to the Dance grounds over a longer but better improved road. Consequently, we reached the grounds before the leader. His son asked me to wait at the entrance until his father arrived, for at this particular time, the leader must be the first person to enter the grounds. Raining Bird and his wife arrived some time later.

When the leader arrives at the grounds, he and his wife unpack the two tipi covers that provide the covering for the preliminary tipi to be used in the Sun Dance ceremony.[9] Poles for the structure are already on the grounds. While the previous meetings may be held in people's homes or tents, this fourth and last meeting before the regular ceremonies begin must be held in a tipi. Consequently, it is erected first, near the center of what will be the camp circle. Since it is made from two tipi covers, it is quite large. The tipi has no opening and can be entered only by crawling under the tipi covers. After the tipi is erected, the leader places a small cluster of green branches several feet away to mark the site of the Sacred Lodge.

The Sacred Lodge used in the Sun Dance the previous year stands close to the designated spot for the dance now in preparation. Streamers of cloth, somewhat faded by exposure to the elements, are still tied to the sacred pole. The colors, however, are clear—blue, red, white, and orange. Other sacred poles stand in the vicinity; the nest in each of them is still evident. The supporting poles and rafters have disintegrated or dropped away in most instances.

During this day before the actual beginning of ceremonies, cars arrive from various other Indian reservations as well as those bearing the Montana Cree who have been employed away from the area. Each family has its tent which is pitched by the members of the family working together. The local families frequently bring their tipis, since they either have the poles already prepared and stored for this occasion or else get new ones from the near-by mountains. They likewise put up

---

[9] The present tense is purposely used to describe the activity during the preparation for the Sun Dance as well as the actual ceremony. The step-by-step procedure seems easier to describe in this manner.

their tipis as family group. Usually the women supervise the construction although a goodly number of the Cree men are able to erect the structure, an accomplishment Indian men on other reservations seldom have. In the afternoon a truck arrives bringing a supply of fire wood which is deposited at intervals among the tents and tipis. By this time the appearance of a circle has begun to manifest itself. For despite the fact that the immobility of tipi poles has caused most Indians to utilize tents when they are thus camped, the primitive shape of the general camp remains—that of a circle.

Even though the appearance and convenience of a tent is unequal to that of the conical tipi used in primitive times, the Cree woman is an efficient housekeeper. While her permanent home is often barren and dreary containing just the necessities for living and nothing more, here in a tent, she has everything in order. And not only does she accomplish that, but the appearance is inviting. Just inside the tent door and squarely facing the visitor who enters is the stove—a large washtub that has been inverted and placed about two inches in the ground. Two holes have been cut in the bottom of the tub (which is now the top of the stove) and these provide an opening for firewood and for the connection for the stovepipe.[10] To the right of the stove are the food supplies and the dishes, usually china or a good grade of plastic; to the left, a washpan, soap and other cleansing materials are kept. A bucket of water is usually on the ground or on an oilcloth-covered wooden apple box. At the rear of the tent are mattresses, doubled and covered with blankets which during the day provide a pleasant place to sit. Suitcases are neatly placed along either side of the tent between the supplies and the bed. A woolen rug is on the ground in the space between the stove and the beds. In the evening, the family lights a kerosene lamp and places it on the rug. The orange-yellow light softens and cheers the interior.

Early in the evening of this first day, the leader goes to the preliminary tipi. He removes the tripod from behind it and carries it inside. From that time until it becomes dark, women go to the tipi carrying bundles of cloth that are to be blessed by the leaders and later placed on the sacred pole as offerings to all the spirits. At about ten o'clock, several

---

[10] These stoves which the Cree use are often called "Half Breed Stoves," since it was the Metis from the Red River settlements in present-day Manitoba who first adapted the washtub to such a different purpose from that for which it was intended. Information supplied by Joe Dussome, Zortman, Montana.

men gather in the preliminary tipi and sit, as Indians always do, in a semi-circle. At the north end of the tipi is the altar—a pole fastened horizontally against the tipi poles and covered with bright new cloth. This is the cloth that the people had brought in earlier and donated in memory of all the spirits that the individuals can recall. All of the sacred paraphernalia rests before the altar—a buffalo skull painted red, wands, peeled sticks, and four pipes. A fire burns in the center of the enclosure. Behind it, and facing the assembled men, the leader or sponsors sit as they pray and purify the material.

The purification ceremonies take about an hour. During this time the pipes, four of them, have been passed among the men who are in attendance. Each time the leader starts the smoking by accepting a pipe, which has been carefully lighted by an assistant who has used sweetgrass smudge to supply the fire. Each pipe is smoked four times. After it has been passed clockwise and everyone has finished smoking, the leader receives the pipe, purifies it again, and places it directly before the altar on a small rack made from peeled willow branches. By the time that the four pipes have gone round four times, the leader has finished the purification ceremonies and directs his assistants to distribute the sacramental food to the men. Cree bread, made from dough that has a leavening agent in it but that has been baked in the oven rather than fried in fat as most Indian women prepare it, and service berries constitute the food. Spirits, especially the bear spirit, like berries. That is one reason they are used; likewise they are the first fruits of the land, thus using them ceremonially, the Indian remembers with gratitude the sustenance that Mother Earth has given him.[11]

When all the men have eaten, the leader and one or two of his assistants face the altar and pray. They pray for peace, for the President of the United States, for representatives in Congress and for the leaders of other nations. All of the men remove their hats, stop their conversations and kneel, facing the altar. By this time it is eleven or eleven-thirty at night.

Finally one hears in the distance the sound of singing and drumming. As the sound intensifies, the leader's two assistants lift the sides of the tipi and place live charcoal at the entrance they have now created. When one can discern the figures of the men who are drumming and singing, he sees that they are not carrying the proverbial drum. Instead, they

---

[11] In 1960, canned blue berries purchased in a Havre store were substituted for service berries.

have a large flat object which is the dried, untanned hide of a buffalo.[12] Four times the men attempt to throw the raw hide into the tent; on each try they sing a song to the spirit whom they are beseeching. Roughly translated, the songs are something like this:[13]

Almighty Spirit, Our Creator, *Ki-sei-men'-to,*
I ask you to bless us at this time.
I am going to throw this buffalo hide in this place.
I am doing it for the good luck of these people.
I want them to have good luck in raising their children.
I want them to have good health.
I want rain to come so that grass will grow, crops will ripen and berries mature.
I want long life for all of these people.

To all the spirits that Our Creator made.
I offer my prayer to you—all of you.
I ask you to bless us at this time.
I am going to throw this buffalo hide in this place.
I am doing it for the good luck of these people.
I want them to have good luck in raising their children.
I want them to have good health.
I want rain to come so that grass will grow, crops will ripen and berries mature.
I want long life for all of these people.

Buffalo Spirit, who brought us food and who will return one day.
I ask you to bless us at this time.
Etc., etc., etc.

Mother Earth, I pray to you.
You have the power to make everything grow.
I ask you to bless us at this time.
Etc., etc., etc.

At the conclusion of the fourth stanza, the drummers throw the hide into the tipi, enter, warm their drums over the fire, and sit in the eastern quadrant of the tipi. Presently they begin drumming which continues throughout the remainder of the evening. Occasionally, it stops while the leader talks to the group. At this time, the leader selects the men who are to leave in the morning to scout for the tree that will become the sacred pole.

During the 1950's and later, it has been comparatively easy to follow

---

[12] Pete Favel explained that since the buffalo is the leader in the Sun Dance, the participants must have the buffalo head and hide in the preliminary tipi. "The whole ceremony is like an old buffalo trail," he added. "The trail leads to the Sun Dance, and all the people follow the trail." Personal interview, July 1, 1960.

[13] Personal interview, Raining Bird, August 2, 1960.

the primitive requirement necessary for the scout: Those selected to find the sacred tree must have had actual battle experience. Therefore, veterans of World War II or of the Korean conflict are chosen. The leaders feel that a touch of authenticity has been added to the Sun Dance now that they are able to use war veterans again, just as it was in buffalo hunting days when they used men who had fought the enemy. When the men have been selected, the singing and drumming suddenly stop. Without any further ceremony or sense of completion, all of the men present get up and leave the tipi. The leader and his assistants remain with the sacred objects. A goodly number of women and some men are outside the tipi—individuals who have been standing there throughout the ceremony.[14]

At approximately 4:00 a.m. the men who have been designated to scout for the tree come to the preliminary tipi. With them is an elderly man to whom the leader has given the sacred pipe and the sweetgrass. In the old days, a war party always carried a pipe with them; the pipe today is carried in much the same spirit, for the men's task is to emulate the old-time scouts who looked for the enemy. This time—as is done as a prelude to all the Cree Sun Dance ceremonies—it is to find the tree that will become the center pole, the one that will represent *Ki-sei-men'-to*. The older man who carries the pipe and sweetgrass is the leader of the expedition. In 1960, ten Cree war veterans comprised the scouting party; the group left the encampment in two automobiles, a scout driving one car and I the other, for one of the leader's assistants had come to the tipi where I was sleeping, awakened me, and asked me to come to the preliminary tent.

We travelled about six miles until we reached a timbered canyon. Leaving the dirt road, we followed a trail across a meadow and reached a clearing near the entrance to another canyon. Parking our cars, we

[14] In 1956 at the invitation of my friend, Four Souls, I sat with the men in the preliminary tipi for about an hour. While the men were friendly, they were aloof. Once, one of them offered one of the pipes to me. As I left the tipi that night, I overheard two men talking outside. "Maybe I shouldn't go in there," said one of the men. "I don't belong to this tribe you know." "Oh, that's all right,' replied the other one. "There's even a white man in there tonight."

At the 1960 Sun Dance, the attitudes were entirely different. I went into the preliminary tipi at the beginning of the ceremony with Tom Gardipee. Raining Bird, who was conducting the rituals, had previously invited me. Each time any of the pipes went round, I was offered it and I smoked it. When the bread and berries were passed, I ate of them, for it was indicated that I should. I stayed with the group until the ceremony ended. Some months later, I read my description of the preliminary rites to Raining Bird and received his corrections and approval of what I had written.

walked a few hundred yards into the timber and then suddenly turned into a cleared space to the right. Several large quaking aspen trees were growing there and one in particular had a large V-shaped fork in it about thirty feet from the base. Quaking aspen is the best tree to use for the center pole, since it does not necessarily have to grow near water as does the cottonwood. Were they to choose a cottonwood tree, the participants of the Sun Dance would suffer from thirst and would be unable to continue dancing without water. Even the smell of the cottonwood leaves or branches makes it difficult for the participants.[15] Therefore, quaking aspen, the only other large deciduous tree native to the region, is used.

When the scouts find the tree (and it is quite evident that it has been located and decided upon before) they clear the underbrush away from it. Then the men disperse in different directions to look for willow, dogwood, or chokecherry saplings that usually grow in the same region. They cut these small trees, strip the bark from the branches and make a crown and a belt for themselves. On the crown, they intertwine leaves. With their crowns on their heads they look like figures from ancient Greece. Since the Montana Cree are a handsome people anyway, as has been mentioned before, their appearance is particularly striking now that they have bedecked themselves with the crown and belt of leaves. In addition, they make for themselves a staff—a sapling about one inch in diameter and four feet in length with all of its leaves and branches cut off except for the branches at the top.

When they have completed these arrangements, the scouts return to the designated tree where the leader of the expedition now has a fire burning. When the fire is reduced to hot red coals, the leader places the coals in the four cardinal directions around the base of the trunk of the tree. He then takes the rope of sweetgrass that has been wrapped around the pipe and burns the ends of the rope. Saving the ashes from the burned sweetgrass carefully, he places them around the tree, also in cardinal directions. First the ashes are deposited to the South, then to the West, then to the North, and finally to the East. The pieces of yard goods that have covered the pipe and sweetgrass next are purified in the smoke of the sweetgrass before the leader ties them around the tree. When these details have been accomplished, the older man lights the pipe and prays for good things. He offers the pipe first to the Creator; second to the Master Spirit of the Tree; thirdly to the Thunder-

---

[15] Personal interview, Pete Favel, July 1, 1960. Crows and Shoshoni use cottonwood because the tree does grow in dry regions. Observation, July 4, 1961.

bird Spirit, and lastly to Mother Earth Spirit. He then takes four puffs from the pipe himself and presents it to the scout who stands to the south of the tree. (Just before he makes his prayer, four of the scouts place themselves in the cardinal positions around the tree.) The man at the south takes four puffs from the pipe and passes it to the man at the west who does likewise as do the men at the north and the east.

When the pipe has made its cycle, the older man finishes smoking it while the ten scouts arrange themselves in a circle around the tree. Beginning with the scout nearest to the south of the tree, each man takes a twig from the tree and tells of his experiences during the war. He emphasizes his hardest times during actual combat. When he finishes his narrative, he offers a prayer that all of those who take part in the Sun Dance will not have to experience the difficulty that he has had. He prays also for the good health and the good luck of all the Indian people as well as expressing the desire that the people may be allowed to stay a little while longer on this earth. Each prayer is directed to *Ki-sei-men'-to* who is beseeched to care for His people. At the conclusion of each scout's speech and of his prayer, he fastens the twig that he has been holding in his hand to the band of yard goods that is tied around the tree. When all of the men have finished praying, the scouts cover themselves with twigs and branches from the quaking aspen tree, take their staffs, return to their cars, and drive back to the camp. This practice is in contrast to the Northern Cheyenne whose scouts ride back to camp on horseback just as they did in buffalo days.[16]

It is between 6:30 and 7:00 o'clock when the scouts reach the camp. They try to come as quietly and as unobtrusively as they can so that the people will not be aware of their arrival. The older man brings the pipe to the Sun Dance leader and tells him that they have located the tree.[17] In the old days, the advance scout stole into the camp and brought

---

[16] Personal observation from having attended the Northern Cheyenne Sun Dances in 1954 and 1955.

[17] It was easier for the scouts to make their return to camp in 1960. Before we left the chosen tree, the leader, John Stump, asked me if I would take the sacred pipe and articles back to Raining Bird and notify him. He asked me to follow in my car the other car. When we reached a certain gully near the Sun Dance lodge, the other car pulled off on a side road and stopped. The men in my car joined the others, and I proceeded alone. A few people were up and stirring around the camp as I drove in and went straight to the preliminary tent. No one suspected that this white man was the carrier of the sacred bundle or was notifying Raining Bird. Few probably knew that I had stayed the night on the grounds. Thus, the coup was completed without arousing any suspicion at all.

presents to the chief who in turn announced the impending arrival of the scouts. Now, however, the Sun Dance leader comes out of his preliminary tipi, where the advance scout has reported to him, and makes an announcement. Between fifty and seventy-five men appear and form themselves into a double line whose base is the preliminary tipi and which extends toward the south. The men face each other with a distance of about three feet separating them. With the lines thus formed, and women and children coming from the tents and tipis and grouping themselves around each line, the Sun Dance leader sings four songs—each song representative of the four cardinal directions. When he finishes the fourth song, the scouts, now entirely covered with aspen leaves, suddenly appear. Acting as if they are sneaking upon an enemy camp, they run, crawl, and proceed carefully toward the lines of men. The men act as if they do not notice the approach of the scouts until they are about midway through the line. Then pandemonium seems to break loose. With loud cries, everyone—men, women, and children—swoop down on the scouts, strip them of their leaves which they exultantly put in their hats and belts.[18] The leaves are prime trophies because they represent good luck, good days, and good health. The leaves are kept by the people in much the same spirit that the blessed palms are kept by Christians.

When the foray for leaves ends, one of the scouts kneels down and speaks about the difficulties encountered in finding the tree. He eulogizes the tree, expresses regret that it has to die, but states that from the tree the Indian people will receive sustenance from *Ki-sei-men'-to*. When he finishes speaking, the leader sings another song, this time almost a keen, for it is wail-like in its penetration. One woman joins him in the singing as the line re-forms itself and the men remove their hats.

In the meantime, one of the leader's assistants offers a lighted pipe to the leader who in turn gives it to the scout who made the speech. The scout, as well as the leader, smokes. The leader sings four songs at this time, offering burning sweetgrass as he prays between each song. One of his assistants keeps the fire burning and attends to the sweetgrass. At the conclusion of the fourth song, the crowd dissolves.

The scouts enter the preliminary tipi along with the leader and a few of the older men. Inside the lodge, the leader and sponsors thank the scouts for having performed their duty so well. They also present the

---

[18] The scouts bring good luck to the village, just as they brought food, horses, or trophies in the old days. The leaves from the sacred tree are like life; hence they are much desired. Personal interview, Pete Favel, July 1, 1960.

scouts with a can of berries. Then the leader, or someone from the camp, invites the scouts for breakfast.[19]

While the scouts are eating and relaxing at the breakfast, a man, who has been selected to be the camp crier during the Sun Dance, rides around the camp and talks to the people. He tells about the difficulties of the time and asks that everyone cooperate to make this encampment a period of richness and happiness for the group. This is the time, he tells them, to remember *Ki-sei-men'-to* and to feel good. At the conclusion of his speech, he asks for volunteers to go for the tree, and for others to be ready to share the work in preparing the spot, digging the holes, and making preparations for the erection of the tree once it arrives on the campsite. Several men talk to him as he makes the encirclement. Others eat breakfast. Usually several cars of newcomers, often those from the Canadian provinces, arrive about this time and begin to pitch their tents.

Shortly thereafter, the leader and several other men leave the encampment to cut the sacred tree.[20] This time several cars as well as a truck make the trip to the tree. Once there, the men may have to cut and remove other trees so that the sacred one will fall in the direction that will make it easiest for the men to carry it out. While they are making these preparations, the leader builds a fire. Once the fire is burning nicely, he opens a bundle that he has brought with him and unwraps a pipe and a braid of sweetgrass. The men kneel in a circle around the fire while the leader burns the sweetgrass and prays. When he has finished this ceremonial element, he passes the pipe clockwise and remarks that everyone should be in good spirits that day.

While the assembled group is in this pleasant mood, the leader goes to the tree, unties the cloth, raises it higher on the tree, and places in it some sage which he has brought with him. He then chants and shakes a rattle. The Sun Dance rattle is made from rawhide with cherry pits inside it and is used as a substitute for the drum (*Ki-sei-men'-to* can hear it just as well). While he is singing and shaking the rattle, the sponsor stands beside him blowing an eagle-bone whistle. At the conclusion of the song, the leader and the sponsor return to the fire.

---

[19] The breakfast in 1960 was given in the tipi of Pat Chief Stick who came to me and invited me to eat with them since I had driven the scouts to find the tree. Generous servings of bacon, eggs, toast, jam, as well as doughnuts and rolls were served with coffee and tea. The men were all in a jocular mood and a pleasant atmosphere pervaded the meal.

[20] Again in 1960, I had the privilege of accompanying the men to cut the tree and witnessing the ceremony.

Again the pipe goes around. When the young men finish smoking it, they sing four songs. Then they rise and encircle the tree. The man who stands at the south and the man at the north are each supplied with an axe which they had previously purified in the smoke of the burning cedar that the leader had thrown on the coals of the fire. Because eventually these axes will cut the clean tree, the axes must be purified. The leader stands to the east of the tree. Suddenly, he chants and the two young axemen swing their axes toward the tree, touching it but not chopping it. The other men emit a shrill high-pitched sound—a means the Cree have of communicating with the spirits. The leader sings three songs with the young men swinging their axes and feigning to cut the tree at the end of each song.

When the leader sings the fourth song, all the men yell a hope that everyone will enjoy the next year. As they are yelling, two men shoot rifles in the air. When that happens, the men with the axes swing into the tree. Within forty-five seconds, the tree falls to the south. As it crashes, all of the men run to it and secure twigs and sprigs for themselves. The leader takes charge of the trimming of the tree and instructs the men to pay especial attention to cutting the forks correctly at the top. The limbs that are removed are carefully saved, for from these the men will make the nest for the Thunderbird later. When all of these details have been accomplished, the men load the tree and the branches on the truck, which has been driven as closely as it can be to the site, and then start back to the encampment.

By the time the truck carrying the tree arrives at the camp, several men, who have been working during the absence of the leader and his group have completed digging the significant holes, including the one for the center pole. The hole for the central post is dug first. Before they start digging the holes, the men offer the pipe to Mother Earth's spirit. Then it is pointed to the four directions beginning with the South. After that, they offer the pipe to all of the different spirits. When the men complete digging the hole for the sacred pole, which is on the spot previously indicated by the small bundle of limbs and leaves, they dig the holes for the four main posts. They begin with the one at the main door which faces the South and then proceed to the West and then North and last to the East. Beginning at the South, the men dig the holes for the other posts. The total number may be twelve, sixteen, or twenty.[21]

---

[21] When I first witnessed the erection of the sacred lodge, probably in 1954, I noticed that the total number of supporting posts was twelve. I asked a Cree, who

When this work is finished, the men build a tripod from sturdy aspen poles, each about four feet long. This tripod is used to raise the base of the center pole prior to its erection.

A noon-time recess usually follows at this time. The men leave their work and go to their tents or tipis to have the lunch which the women have prepared for them. The whole camp scene is much alive, as many more cars arrive and people start visiting with their friends. The men tend to congregate before the concession stands, of which there are usually two or three that dispense pop, Coca-Cola, candy bars, as well as frankfurters, hamburgers, and coffee. There, they drink coffee and visit among themselves. Children of all ages run everywhere, laughing and talking but not screaming. Usually a very good spirit pervades the camp at this time—one of friendliness, cordiality, and goodness, yet one tinged with a certain amount of religious awe.

Early in the afternoon another truck arrives that carries the trees that have been cut to be used for the sides and the top of the Sacred Lodge. These poles which are used for the sides are approximately fifteen feet high. They are cut with a V-shaped notch at the small end. The supporting poles—the ones that form the rafters for the top—are longer and slenderer.

Several men begin work now to construct the Sacred Lodge. The first post to be implanted is the one to the South, followed by the ones at the West and the North and the East. When these four main poles have been securely fixed in the ground, the men begin at the South and continue clockwise placing the other upright poles in position. While this work is going on, other men decorate some of the longer poles that will be used as rafters with the yard goods that the people have donated. Others tie strips of cloth to the center pole, which is still lying with its base on the tripod. Near the fork at the top of the center pole, the men place a cross-shaped piece that they make from small poles which they cover with cloth. In the notch of the center pole and just above this banner, the men make a nest of aspen twigs and boughs which previously had been cut from the sacred tree. Much time and care is devoted to the construction of the nest—symbolic of the home of the Thunderbird. When they have finished decorating the top of the center pole, the workmen tie long streamers of cloth—six or eight yards in length—to the notch. The main streamer, and hence the longest one,

was sitting on the ground near me, why that number. He replied, "The twelve posts stand for the Apostles; the center pole is Christ." At that time I was a near stranger on the reservation; I have often wondered what the same man would tell me now.

must fall to the south and its color is blue, representing the Blue Thunder. The next one, red, must fall to the west, for it symbolizes the Eagle or Half Thunder. White must face the north—a cold white wind and a white bird with a dark head. To the east is orange, the Sun. Additional bands of cloth are tied around the pole lower down.

With these preliminaries completed, the time has come to raise the sacred pole. The men fasten four long ropes to it. Eight or ten men take hold of each rope. The leader steps forward and sings a song:

> Now they are going to come in,
> My Grandfather, the Chief Stick.

When he is finished, the men holding the rope shout a shrill and triumphant note as the leader gives a blast on his eagle-bone whistle. The men at the rope also feign to raise the pole. Again the leader sings:

> Now they are going to wake him up,
> My Grandfather, the Chief Stick.

The men at the ropes repeat the same procedure. When this second attempt has been made, the leader sings again:

> Now he is going to get up,
> My Grandfather, the Chief Stick.

The men repeat exactly the same shouts and actions. Once more, the leader blows his whistle and sings:

> Now he is going to stand up,
> My Grandfather, the Chief Stick.

While he is singing this last song,[22] the men remove their hats and bow their heads respectfully. When the song is finished, they put their hats on again. The leader blows his whistle and as he does, the men give a concerted pull on the ropes and the sacred pole starts up. Two men guide the base so that it falls into the hole prepared for it. Just as the pole almost reaches a vertical position, the lines of men holding the rope swing clockwise in unison and the pole stands in place. Two men standing behind it guide its progress by using two peeled poles (somewhat larger than those used for tipis) fastened together at the top.

The lines of men hold the pole in its proper position while others tramp dirt around its base. At each cardinal direction of the pole, a man drives a small aspen stick, about three inches in diameter and two

---

[22] The words to this song were supplied to me by the Sun Dance Leader, Raining Bird, August 26, 1960.

and one-half feet long, into the ground. Then more dirt is tramped in place to hold the sacred pole firmly in place. The long banners of cloth are draped and tied to the pole about two feet below the nest and about five feet from the base.

When the pole is firmly secured in position, the men place the cross pieces between each of the outside posts; they are then ready to add the rafters. Before doing so, however, they cut a V-shaped notch in the butt end of each rafter so that it will fit the cross piece at the intersection with the upright post. Two men stand on a truck bed and guide the rafter so that one end fits into the nest and the other end into the supporting cross piece. The rafters placed first are those in the cardinal positions. The first pole to be placed is the one facing the south, then those on the west and the north go on about simultaneously while that to the east is affixed last. When the east rafter is in position, the men return to the south and place the other rafters in clockwise position.

With the framework completed, the people turn their attention to building a concentric circle inside the Sacred Lodge. With the exception of an opening to the north, where the altar is to be placed and one to the south where the main entrance is located, there are no other openings in the circle which is bounded by a three and one-half foot high fence. First, the workers pound stakes into the ground at an interval of about five feet, while next they cover all of the intervening space with branches and leaves from the aspen, chokecherry or willow trees. Both men and women work at this fence, which stands about three feet inside the outer walls. Behind the fence, the dancers will stand during the ceremony.

Late in the afternoon, a dump truck manned by about twelve young men arrives on the grounds. The truck is filled with young aspen trees, fifteen to twenty feet high. All the boughs and leaves are on the trees. The workmen take these trees, trim them and fit them on the sides of the Sacred Lodge. They begin again at the south entrance and cover the western side, ending at the north. Beginning there, the men stretch a canvas so that it extends eastward and continues to the south entrance.

During the early evening the leader and his assistants work on the altar, located at the northwest side of the Sacred Lodge. It consists of an excavation about eighteen inches square and three inches deep. In the center and in each corner is a small, peeled peg. These four pegs and the one within represent the Creator and His four spirit guards (*Tse-mento-tos-knid-kma*). When *Ki-sei-men'-to* created man, He told him that the whole world would be his, but that His four guardsmen would help man to live. Man was instructed not to quit even if the times were difficult, for if man quits, the world will be changed. These four spirits or guardians once had names, but they are now forgotten and are merely called "Officers of God."[23]

When the altar is completed, the leader and his assistants leave the Sacred Lodge which is now ready for the ceremony. The Lodge itself represents Man and Woman. From the altar, the men will stand on the right side while the women will be on the left. Those positions represent the strength of men and the weakness of women. The lodge, however, represents all mankind. The entrance must face the south because that is the main direction of the Master Spirit of the Buffalo. The chief Thunderbird is the blue one whose home is also in the south. The sun, too, describes its main arc toward the south, especially in winter. Consequently, the opening of the lodge must be toward the south.

Once all the preparations are completed, some young men start a fire just north of the central pole, between it and the altar. When they have the fire nicely started and leave the Lodge, the structure takes on the air of expectancy that characterizes a Christian Church once the candles have been lighted and the services about to begin.

The leader and his assistants now take down the preliminary tipi and start a procession as they carry the holy objects to the Sacred Lodge. They begin at the rear of the lodge, proceed slowly around the east side, pass the opening to the south and then continue to the east where they stop. After a short pause there, they continue around again, stopping at the West and the North before they finally come back to the South and enter. Here again, as it had been at the preliminary tipi the night before, the entrance to the Sacred Lodge has burning coals in the doorway and again at three other places between the doorway and the altar. The leader and his procession carry all of the sacred items and place them very reverently and carefully between the lighted fire and the altar.

Then begins a long purifying process. Each item is carefully censed in sweetgrass smoke. The painted buffalo head, which the men carry foremost in their procession into the Lodge, is purified first in a long ceremony before the leader places it on the altar. The Montana Cree believe that the buffalo will come again to take care of the people; consequently, they continue using a buffalo head in the Sun Dance.[24] Four small hooked staves or crooks surround the buffalo head at the altar. These are placed there in memory of the Master Spirit of the Buffalo—"Stands

---

[23] Personal interview, Raining Bird, December 31, 1959.
[24] Personal interview, Raining Bird, August 26, 1960.

up Buffalo Walking," Since he stands on his legs and walks like a man, he carries a crook similar to the miniature ones that surround the buffalo head in the Sacred Lodge. All of this reverence to the buffalo stems from the fact that the Master Spirit of the Buffalo represents the spirit that supplies the food for the people of this world. When the white man destroyed the buffalo, they went under the ground in many places. Some time these animals will come back, the Cree say, and when they do, they will come from the four directions. The Master Spirit of the Buffalo watches these four entrances like a guard. One spot where the buffalo descended into the earth can be seen in a geological formation near Hays, Montana, on the Fort Belknap reservation, approximately one hundred miles from the home of the Montana Cree.

Once the buffalo head has been placed on the altar, the leader next opens the tobacco which is wrapped in blue cloth in a bundle about eighteen inches long and three inches in diameter. Four men each smoke this tobacco in representation of the four spirits of *Ki-sei-men'-to*. Each one puffs four times—to the South, West, North, East—before he offers it to Mother Earth. When they have finished, they put the tobacco again in the blue cloth, for they will repeat this particularly sacred smoking each day of the Sun Dance.

At about eleven o'clock in the evening, the censing will have been completed and the drummers arrive. They follow exactly the same procedure as on the previous night when they entered the preliminary tipi. Three times they pretend to throw the buffalo rawhide into the Lodge; each try is accompanied by the same song that they had sung the evening before. While these attempts are being made, other drummers and singers take their places in the northwest quadrant of the Lodge. One of the firemen places live charcoal in four places near the singers.

The leader arises and prays. His first prayer is directed to *Ki-sei-men'-to*. When he finishes that prayer, he moves four paces toward the opening, where the men with the dried hide are standing. He stops and says a prayer to the Master Spirit of the Buffalo, takes four more steps which take him to the entrance and says a prayer to Mother Earth. He receives the hide from the hands of the men who are holding it and throws it inside the lodge. As he stops to pray each time throughout his course to the doorway, the drummers have been drumming and singing. The sound is discordant. By the time he reaches the fourth prayer, the drumming becomes rhythmical and from that time forward, each singer follows the leader of the song.

The person handling the rattle is the leader for the song. Before singing, he shakes the rattle, says the words to the song, and gives the drummers the rhythm. In the meantime, the drummers go slow as they remember the tempo. When the leader has finished, the drummers chant the tune and pound the drums four times. Then the leader repeats the same performance but says different words. The drummers know the tune by this time, so they keep the same tempo of the song going. This same method is followed two more times, so that the total measures are sixteen. Only persons who own Sun Dance songs may be leaders.[25]

At the end of the first song, the dancers appear from behind the leafy fence. The men are on the west side, the women on the east. Each dancer fixes his eyes intently upon the center pole, which as has been indicated, represents *Ki-sei-men'-to*. Therefore, as they look at the pole, they concentrate on the prayers that they are saying. At the same time, they blow on their eagle-bone whistles. In the construction of these whistles, only the femur of the eagle is used. The eagle is the most powerful bird and his wings the most powerful part of him. Therefore, the whistle can carry the messages aloft, for, as has just been pointed out, the dancers are praying as they look at the Sacred Pole and as they blow the whistles. Never have the Montana Cree known of any one of them or their ancestors using a whistle made from goose bone or any other kind of bone but that of the eagle. Throughout the first evening, the whistles are extremely discordant and sound like a series of piercing shrieks. Seldom do two people blow at the same time, and seemingly, no one pays much attention to the drummers. The ceremony on this first night continues until about 1:30 a.m. Then the drummers leave the Sacred Lodge, the fire dies out, and the dancers lie down to rest.

A few hours later, about 4:30 a.m., the drums begin again. Soon the sound of whistles starts. The dancers look neat and clean, but none of them dress in anything except their ordinary clothing. Here is an interesting factor about Cree participants in the Sun Dance. Their clothes are those they would wear to Havre to shop, or for a special social occasion, or to attend a white man's church. Participants in many other Sun Dances in the Northwest (and this includes the Arapaho, the Piegans and the Bloods of the Blackfeet, the Cheyenne, the Crow, and the Shoshoni) all dress in outfits characteristic or reminiscent of primitive times. But the very fact that the Montana Cree use white man's clothes in the Sun Dance may very well indicate that they are not returning to the past, but rather that their religious experience (i.e., participation in

---

[25] Personal interview, Andrew Gray, a well-informed member of the Assiniboine tribe, June 30, 1956.

the Sun Dance) is entirely compatible with their present role in white civilization.

Not all of them dance at the same time—some may lie behind the fence and rest. Fatigue does not show in their faces as yet. They must abstain from eating; they can drink only water that falls in rain during the time of the ceremony. They are permitted, however, to smoke.

With but little change, the procedure is the same all of this third day. At about half-hour intervals the drummers change; new ones replace those who have been drumming. Otherwise, the steady monotonous beat of the drum and the shrill piercing cry of the whistle continues. During the late afternoon, one of the older men who acts as an inside fireman, lights a rope of sweetgrass, and as the grass burns, he allows the charred remains to drop into a bark trough. While these particles are still smoking, he deposits them at all four cardinal positions at the base of the center pole. When he has finished that, he takes the sweetgrass rope again and burns it in the trough. While it is still smoking, he walks around the circle of dancers, and with an eagle wing, he blows the smoke over each of the dancers.[26] Completing his circle, he lights one of the four pipes hanging near the altar and passes it to one of the four old men sitting near the fire. In turn he lights each of the other pipes and passes them likewise to the old men. The first pipe that he lit is the largest; when the old men have finished with it he walks to the center pole and holds the glowing pipe upwards so that *Ki-sei-men'-to* can also enjoy the tobacco. After he offers it to the pole, he moves to the dancers and allows each one of them to have one puff from the pipe. As the day comes to a close and night comes on, the rhythm becomes much more decided than it was at the beginning. The whistles are practically in unison.

On the morning of the last day, the dancers may be augmented by the addition of other individuals, for vowers have the privilege of pledging to dance either for a period of twenty-four or forty-eight hours. On this morning, a piece of bright cloth is unfolded before each dancer. The cloth, about a yard square, hangs on the outside of the fence and signifies that the vower has requested that prayers be given for his good luck. Each dancer's face is painted. Some of them have a considerable number of lines drawn vertically down their faces; others, just a

---

[26] People must be clean. It is natural for the human body to smell strong. That is why, despite the fact that the men have purified themselves in the sweat lodge and the women have bathed in clear cold water before entering the dance, they must be censed with sweetgrass. Personal interview, Raining Bird, December 26, 1959.

dab of red. When someone gets tired and needs help, he may get it by using special paint. In using the paint, though, the person has to pray for help. Younger people receive instructions in the use of such paint from their elders. The leader, a few of the men, and some of the women may wear eagle-down feathers in their hair at this time. The spirits once told the people about the use of these feathers.

The crowd watching the dancers usually increases on this last morning. A good many old women sit inside the Sacred Lodge in front of the fence separating the women dancers from the lodge interior. Old women may come into the Sun Dance Lodge and sit on the left side just as freely as the men come in and sit on the right side. These old women have passed the menopause; consequently, they are like children and have clean bodies as well as souls.[27] Many of the on-lookers, those who crowd the doorway, are fasting, even though they are not actively participating in the ceremony.

At regular intervals during the morning, the official camp crier makes extensive announcements. At the conclusion of each speech, a family comes forward, stands at the south of the center pole, and brings piles of clothing, especially new bedding—blankets and hand-made quilts. They pile the clothing and bedding beside the center pole as several dancers leave their positions behind the fence and join the family standing in the Sacred Lodge. The leader comes forward and prays over the gifts and the people while the drum leader sings a song. The family head gives rather a long speech in which he thanks the Creator for giving them the privilege of being re-united again beside the sacred pole. The speech is followed by a song, while the dancers who have come out from their accustomed places raise their arms toward the center pole, blow their whistles and dance up and down. The gifts that are being blessed for each family are later to be distributed, for by so doing it provides a means of showing thankfulness to the Creator as the people share their gifts with each other. It means that people are happy and in good health. This expression is an acknowledgement of their good feeling. It is done somewhat as is done at Christmas time when people want to do something to please others.

That this pattern of sharing material goods with others of the tribe is not new is evidenced by a statement from Goddard,[28] who quotes

---

[27] Personal interview, Raining Bird, August 25, 1960.

[28] Pliny Earle Goddard, *Notes on the Sun Dance of the Cree in Alberta*, Anthropological Papers of the American Museum of Natural History (New York, 1919), Vol. XVI, Part IV, p. 309.

from a report by Robert Jefferson, a man who had observed closely the traits of the Canadian Plains Cree. The statement follows:

On the second day (of the Sun Dance) most of the offerings are made. Wearing apparel, ornaments, household utensils, guns, horses, and equipments, any of the things that enter into Indian life, either as necessities or superfluities are offered as a sacrifice. The small things are piled in the open space in the tent, lifted up one by one by the master of ceremonies for someone to come forward to take. Horses are led into the tent. A few words will accompany most of the gifts—a reminder to listeners of the giver's virtues. The takers are mostly old people. ... The underlying idea of the offering is, that it may buy something the giver desires—health, long life, success of some kind, which will be contributed by the recipient. ...

Later in the afternoon the crier makes a lengthy announcement and the crowd in front of the Sacred Lodge, which now has usually grown to include hundreds of people, moves into a circle outside the Lodge. Both men and women sit on the ground, although a few may be sitting on folding chairs that they bring with them. Conspicuous are visitors from other reservations. Three or four men ordinarily assist the camp crier and drag all of the accumulated gifts—quilts, blankets, yard goods, and tanned hides—from the Sacred Lodge to the center of the circle formed by the people. When everything has been taken from the Lodge, the men begin distributing articles to the visitors. Frequently, several silver dollars are also distributed.

Thus from Jefferson's description, the Canadian Cree combined the two ceremonies into one. Everything was taken into the Sacred Lodge and there blessed but given immediately to the assemblage. The Montana Cree have no memory of this procedure, although they do recall that once people used to bring horses into the Lodge.[29] They like to pray together in family groups first; later the items may be distributed, and frequently are given to people who were not at the blessing ceremony.

Several of the old women—those who sit on the ground before the fence—cry, wail, and almost keen as the blessings upon the families is performed. Some of those who weep the loudest face the center pole, hold one arm out to it with the palm extended openly toward the pole. In fact, anyone who needs prayers, or who has sick relatives, or who has lost loved ones may come into the Lodge, touch the sacred pole and

---

[29] One of my informants became quite indignant when I asked if they brought automobiles into the Sacred Lodge now to give away, instead of the horse. A horse is a spirit, he explained, while a car is a man-made mechanism. I did not ask further about the man-made blankets and equipment that are brought to the tent for blessings.

weep.[30] Others who may have had sorrows, or want to rear their children so that they will become good people or else just desire to think about something good may also come. The Spirits hear them and take pity on them.

After the presents have been given out, the same censing program is carried out with the Sacred Lodge as had been done the previous evening. The sweetgrass smudge is burned and the coals are distributed to the cardinal points of the center pole. The dancers are censed. Each one receives the pipe. The pipe is passed to all of those who are sitting inside the lodge as well as the dancers, who by now may well reach one hundred or more persons; this ceremony takes at least an hour. When the last person has received his tobacco, two men come to the center pole and untie and unwrap the long lengths of cloth that have been fastened to it. The cloth then hangs in straight lines from the nest, and blows and waves in the breeze.

The largest piece of cloth is fastened just at the forks of the pole where the Thunderbird's nest has been built. That is the only piece of material that is older and has been used before. It is very long, very wide (at least two yards), and looks like a piece of stroud, an English product that proved popular in the early-day trade that the Hudson's Bay Company had with the Indians. Its color is red, symbolic of the Thunderbird's nest. The four long banners directly below the large piece are new material and will be left to distintegrate in the elements. The longest piece is blue, for it is given to the South, home of the blue thunderbird. The red one is given to West—to the Eagle who is half thunder; the long white one to the North, the home of the white thunderbird (the one we do not see or hear). The yellow one is given to the East, the Sun.

As the drummers start singing their last four songs, the first three of which are quite moderately pitched, the baby Thunderbird which has been lying at the right hand side of the buffalo head is purified with tobacco and sweetgrass. The men all stand back from it then, for the Spirits, who have been trying to get close to the baby Thunderbird, watch it start to fly. They circle around the Sacred Lodge and come close to the people, for they reach the minds of the people at this time.

---

[30] Father Schmidt, in his book *High Gods in North America,* writes: "The prayers of the Algonkins are not mere formulae to be recited only by the lips. The seriousness, the deep meditation and inner concentration of mind with which they are performed are attested by all writers. The strong inner commotion of the soul might, even with the bravest warriors, go so far as to break out into weeping and sighing, as is illustrated, for example, by the Western Cree," p. 81.

They are also capable of taking the message in the people's minds to *Ki-sei-men'-to*.

It is this time too that the participants see visions. While some of the dancers are able to experience visions at any time throughout the ceremony, it is at the close of it that most of the people experience them. Many of them see the Thunderbird, and that pleases them, for one of the Thunderbirds stays in the nest all of the time that the ceremony takes place and watches the participants. Only those who have the vision are able to see him, however. Others see colors. Or it could be that they see some of the spirits as they fly around the circle of dancers during these closing minutes of the ceremony. A spectator can see the rapt expression on the faces of some of the dancers, can observe the complete concentration, and can appreciate the deep insight that they are experiencing as these visions come to them.

All of this last part of the ceremony comes fast. The three songs are sung moderately, as mentioned. The last song is tremendously loud and shrill and high and ends almost with a wail. As it is being sung, one of the assistants clears the doorway of spectators and makes a path through the people who are standing on the outside of the lodge. This clearance is about three feet wide and its length depends upon the number of people who are crowding the entrance. This pathway is made so that the Spirits, who in these closing moments have been circling the dancers, may get out of the Sacred Lodge first.

By the time the drummers have reached their last high note and the pathway is clear, the dancers leave their positions and start out from behind the fence. There is no order in their going. They just leave, taking with them the squares of cloth that have been hanging on the fence in front of them. Those who have medicine bundles will put the cloth in them; those who do not will take the cloth to the hills, tie it on a tree, and leave it for the spirits. When the dancers get out of the Lodge and into the camp, they take a cup of water and cense it with sweetgrass and again ask that something good will happen to them during the next year before they drink the water. The same is true with eating—they purify food first and offer a prayer before they eat it.

Another Sun Dance ends. An ancient ritual has been performed again much as it has been done since its introduction to the Cree people in a now long-forgotten past. The lives of the participants have changed, the economy is different, the problems are unlike those of the past, but the basic values of the Cree's interpretation of the universe are unchanged.

CHAPTER XIV

THE SUN DANCE: INTERPRETATION

While no one is certain just where the Sun Dance originated, the Montana Cree are assured that *Ki-sei-men'-to* gave it to them at the time of creation. The Assiniboine have the same strong certainty as, no doubt, do most of the members of the other tribes who practice the ceremony. Be that as it may, certainly the Sun Dance has elements within it that are characteristic of mankind. In all times peoples have found a means through religion of strengthening life. And it is the enrichment of the content of life that forms much of the essence of religion, as Radin points out.[1] The form may be different; the core remains much the same.

One of the essential features of the Sun Dance is the center pole. Here is one of the oldest forms of ritualistic worship recognized by man, extending back through the misty past even to Paleolithic times.[2] The Tree of Life in India is another development of the same idea. On the northwest frontier of India, the Gilgats still recognize the efficacy of the *chili (Juniperus exelsa)*, a species of cedar that gives the power of fertility.[3] Hundreds of other examples abound. Among the Plains Indians on the North American continent, the center pole is the core of the Sun Dance, for it is common to all tribes who practice the ceremony. "... elaborating rites seem so much ceremonial embroidery on the web of essential features. In this I am assuming that the essential performance is simply erecting a pole within an encircling structure before which the votaries dance," Spier explains.[4]

But what particular tribe first developed the "embroidery" about the

---

[1] Paul Radin, "An Introductive Enquiry in the Study of Ojibwa Religion," *Papers and Records,* Ontario Historical Society (Ottawa, 1914), Vol. XII.

[2] Dr. Åke Hultkrantz, class lectures, Brandeis University, Waltham, Massachusetts, Summer, 1958.

[3] Sir James George Frazer, *The Magic Art and the Evolution of Kings.* 2 vols (New York: Macmillan Co., 1951), Vol. II, p. 50.

[4] Leslie Spier, "The Sun Dance of the Plains Indians: Its Development and Diffusion," Anthropological Papers of the American Museum of Natural History (New York, 1921), Vol. XVI, Part VII, p. 491.

pole and added the embellishments so that the ceremony took on the appearance it has today is unknown. Spier feels[5] that "the Arapaho and Cheyenne seem to be the center of diffusion with priority slightly in favor of the Arapaho. The Cheyenne received theirs from the Sutaio . . . who were presumably in close contact with the Arapaho. But whether the Cheyenne obtained their dance from the Sutaio or Arapaho cannot be proven." Clements adds[6] that "The originators may have been the Assiniboine, or perhaps the Arapaho and Cheyenne at the time the latter occupied the northeast section of the Plains." His correlations suggest further that there may have been two streams of diffusion, "one being carried by the Arapaho and Cheyenne toward the southwest while the other spread to the Dakota, Ponca, and Aricara and northwest by way of the Assiniboine."[7]

I do not feel that it is particularly pertinent to this study to engage in a lengthy discussion about the origin of the Cree Sun Dance. It is rather interesting, though, to note correlations that exist between the Cree ceremony and that of other tribes. Certain elements, then, will be discussed. Spier's work provides the basis for comparison, agumented by observations of my own.[8]

Name: "Thirsting Dance"

    Montana Cree   Utes
                                      Wind River Shoshoni
                                      Plains-Ojibway

Preliminary Tipi

    Montana Cree   Blackfeet
                                      Gros Ventre
                                      Assiniboine
                                      Sisseton Dakota

Altar within the preliminary tipi

    Montana Cree*   Blackfeet
                                      Arapaho
                                      Southern Cheyenne
                                        Oglala
                                      Ponca
                                      Assiniboine

---

[5] *Ibid.,* p. 492.

[6] Forrest Clements, "Plains Indian Tribal Correlations with Sun Dance Data," *American Anthropologist* (1931), Vol. XXXIII, No. 2, pp. 225–226.

[7] *Ibid.,* p. 226.

[8] My own observations about Cree traits are marked by an asterisk. Other references are those of Spier who calls them Plains-Cree.

Drumming on a hide
 Montana Cree*
         Blackfeet
         Gros Ventre
         Arapaho
         Assiniboine

Cutting of Sacred Tree — Accompanied by recital of martial deeds and shooting
 at it
 Montana Cree
         Crow
         Blackfeet
         Gros Ventre
         Arapaho
         Assiniboine

Men or women rushing in to strip off twigs or leaves as trophies or symbols
 of luck
 Montana Cree*
         Blackfeet
         Gros Ventre
         Arapaho
         Oglala
         Assiniboine

(In the old days men and women both went out after the tree. Now it is
 considered a man's job.)
Thunderbird's nest at the forks of the tree
 Montana Cree
         Arapaho
         Cheyenne (both Northern and Southern)
         Ponca
         Plains-Ojibway

Offerings of cloth in forks
 Montana Cree
         Kiowa
         Wind River Shoshoni
         Blackfeet
         Sarsi
         Arapaho
         Southern Cheyenne
         Oglala
         Ponca
         Assiniboine
         Gros Ventre

Center pole lifted into place with aid of coupled tipi poles accompanied by
 ritual
 Montana Cree
         Wind River Shoshoni
         Crow
         Blackfeet
         Sarsi
         Gros Ventre
         Assiniboine

                                        Hidatsa
                                        Arapaho
                                        Cheyenne (both Northern and Southern)

Three attempts to lift the the pole prior to successful fourth trial
        Montana Cree*   Ute
                                        Wind River
                                        Crow
                                        Gros Ventre
                                        Oglala
                                        Arapaho
                                        Southern Cheyenne

Recitation of prayers before lifting of tree
        Montana Cree*   Hidatsa
Sun Dance Lodge
    Roofed Type
        Montana Cree   Kiowa
                                        Wind River Shoshoni
                                        Blackfeet
                                        Sarsi
                                        Gros Ventre
                                        Arapaho
                                        Cheyenne (both Northern and Southern)
                                        Hidatsa

    Entrance at the south
        Montana Cree   Plains Ojibway
                                        Hidatsa

    Altar
        Montana Cree   Blackfeet
                                        Sarsi
                                        Arapaho
                                        Cheyenne (both Northern and Southern)
                                        Oglala
                                        Ponca
                                        Assiniboine

Hooked sticks before the skull
    Montana Cree
Pipes as a formal element in the altars
        Montana Cree*   Southern Cheyenne
                                        Oglala
                                        Ponca
                                        Plains Ojibway
                                        Canadian Sioux

Drumming on a hide preliminary to entrance of votaries and later during dance
        Montana Cree*   Kiowa
                                        Gros Ventre
                                        Arapaho

                    Southern Cheyenne
                    Oglala
                    Hidatsa

Leaning against the center pole and crying in supplication
    Montana Cree   Arapaho
                                    Sisseton

Fire in the Lodge—feeding sticks to it for each coup they can recount
    Montana Cree[9]   Wind River Shoshoni
                                    Blackfeet
                                    Gros Ventre
                                    Arapaho
                                    Southern Cheyenne

People and materials blessed during dance
    Montana Cree   Blackfeet
                                    Assiniboine

Leadership—individual without bundle
    Montana Cree   Assiniboine
                                    Plains Ojibway
                                    Wind River Shoshoni
                                    Ute

From Spier's ninety-two traits compiled from an analysis of the Sun Dance of nineteen tribes, the elements selected give some idea of the comparison of the traits followed in the Sun Dance by the Montana Cree and representative Western tribes. Three other elements, each important in its own right, should be mentioned—the bundle complex, torture, and woman.

The bundle is to the Blackfeet what the torture is to the Dakota and the woman is to the Cheyenne. A Sun Dance could not be conducted without it, for, as Spier mentions, the "fundamental concept is based on the medicine bundle. ... Yet it is emphatically a bundle ceremony. It ties in with their story of creation."[10] But the Montana Cree, as has been pointed out earlier, do not have the same idea about the bundle as the Blackfeet. Its place in the Sun Dance is mentioned by Raining Bird who says:[11]

---

[9] The Montana Cree realize that sticks of wood were once put on the fire to represent coups that had been counted. It is not done now, explained Raining Bird, for it is not the fault of the soldiers that they go to war. The government just takes them. Consequently, there is no need to show off publicly. Personal interview, August 26, 1960.

[10] Spier, *op. cit.*, p. 510.

[11] Personal interview, August 26, 1960.

214

There is no special ceremonial connected with the bundles in the Sun Dance ritual. A person can take his bundle in with him if he wishes. If he takes it along, he unties it in the Sun Dance Lodge at the beginning of the ceremony. Maybe he will have a special whistle or necklace or cap that he has wrapped up in the bundle. Then he will get that out. Or, maybe, he will have some sweetgrass or some other article that he wishes to put in the bundle. It is up to him. As I have told you, some of the dancers put the yard goods that hang on the fence before him during the dance in their bundle. It is up to him what he does. But just remember, the bundle doesn't have any place in the Sun Dance ceremony itself.

Bundles, then, so important to the Blackfeet in all their ceremonies and so significant and necessary to their Sun Dance have only secondary or personal meaning to the Montana Cree.

Likewise, torture is known but not practiced by the Montana Cree. Spier writes[12] that torture is of secondary importance in the Sun Dance everywhere except among the Dakota. "The Sun Dance is inconceivable without torture only from the Dakota standpoint,"[13] and continues by writing:

... torture centers among the Dakota and the Village tribes and is found in decreasing extent as we proceed from that center. Since this does not coincide with the ascertained center for other traits, torture must be considered of secondary origin in the Sun Dance of the majority.

Skinner reports[14] that among his Cree informants, torturing was done, but not to an appreciable degree in early times; later it was "an invariable feature." He gave as illustrations and reasons for torture the following information:

Some underwent the pain to cure sick friends or in fulfillment of a vow, others took part merely to show their bravery. ... Those who were to submit to torture came forward during the dance and presented themselves to the host who called on the medicine men, and they pinched up the flesh in two places on the breast, slit it with a knife, ran in wooden skewers, and made them fast to thongs attached to the central pole. Dancers flung themselves back, tugged, whistled and gazed skyward. This lasted from five to ten minutes. Some of the men fainted and were cut down disgraced. There was no effort to tear loose, but if this occurred the person was instantly freed. During the torture the sufferers wept and prayed continually.

Outside the lodge, men made the entire circuit of the camp trailing several buffalo skulls attached by thongs and skewers to their backs or arms, or with

---

[12] Spier, op. cit., p. 491.

[13] Ibid., p. 491.

[14] Alanson Skinner, "The Sun Dance of the Plains-Cree," Anthropological Papers of the American Museum of Natural History (New York, 1919), Vol. XVI, Part IV, pp. 291–292.

several guns carried in the same manner. Some, apparently those who dreamed of horses, would make their steeds fast also and would try to lead the horses, fastened by thongs made fast to skewers in their backs, into the lodge and around it.

Again, Raining Bird remembers hearing about the dancers torturing themselves. His interpretation[15] of it stems from what he thinks was a misunderstanding. He believes it was the work of Matchi Manitou, the Evil Spirit, who instructed people what to do. He also said that those who tortured themselves in the Sun Dance never had any children. If any were born to them, they always died. "People should fast and pray in the Sun Dance Lodge," he concluded, "and not try to show off."

The role of the sacred woman is missing among the Montana Cree. She is vital in both the Blackfeet and the Cheyenne ceremonies. In fact, it is her role that has aroused the ire of missionaries, especially among the Cheyenne.[16] Dorsey[17] has always seemed just a bit equivocal to me on this element. Some people read his reports and believe that he states that the sexual act between the Sun Dance leader and the sacred woman occurs just before the ceremony begins. Others, including myself, interpret his works to mean that the symbolism is there—that the man and the woman represent fertility—but that is the extent of it. Be that as it may, the Cree do not have any especial attention focused upon the women. They may participate. The old women, as has been pointed out, enter the enclosure and sit before the fence, but in no place does the woman feature in the Sun Dance.

Historically, the Sun Dance was a tribal ceremony for all Plains groups with the exception of the Crow (the River and Mountain divisions held separate ceremonies), and the Plains-Cree and Plains-Ojibway,[18] whose separate bands gave the ceremony. But as Spier adds, such instances only emphasize the fact that the political unit functioned at the time as a ceremonial unit. As has been mentioned before, the Plains Cree were divided into eight bands, each practically autonomous. Now that the Montana Cree have been separated from their parent stock, as well

---

[15] Personal interview, August 26, 1960.

[16] Mrs. Rodolphe Petter, whose late husband was a Mennonite missionary among the Southern Cheyenne from 1890 until 1905 and with the Northern Cheyenne from then until his death in 1947, stoutly condemns the Sun Dance on this very basis. She insists that an actual sexual union takes place and interprets it as a sign of moral degradation.

[17] George Dorsey, *The Cheyenne*, Vol. II, Field Columbian Museum Publication 103, Vol. IX, pp. 130–132.

[18] Spier, *op. cit.*, p. 459.

as having emerged from a motley group of Indians from many different tribes, the Sun Dance has become a distinctly tribal ceremony.

Its organization parallels to some degree the social organization of pre-white times. According to Mandelbaum[19] each band might have several chiefs, each with his own following. One of the chiefs was generally recognized as outranking the others, either because of age or of accepted superiority. An informal council, composed of leading men of the tribe including the chiefs, decided the matters of importance. In addition, the primitive Cree filled the offices of camp criers (usually two), callers (again two), and camp leader. The Montana Cree have at least two qualified leaders whom the people recognize as being capable of performing the Sun Dance—Raining Bird and Good Runner. When a man wishes to sponsor a Sun Dance he goes to one of these men, who then calls a meeting of the older men, much as the chief called his council. Three of these men are selected to be the leader's assistants. These four, in turn, select two men to take care of the pipe and sweetgrass during the ceremony, as well as two other men who act as inside firemen.[20] The leader asks for help from the other men of the tribe; many of them volunteer. So the system, while definite, has some of the characteristics of the old and informal social organization of the Plains Cree.

An interesting study that reveals the correlation of data concerning the Sun Dance is that of Clements.[21] Although some of the means may be questioned, his coefficient of association of the Plains-Cree with eighteen other tribes analyzed by Spier gives some interesting results. Clements did his study on the ninety-two specific traits that Spier had used in the nineteen tribes. Out of the ninety-two traits, sixty-six are absent in the Cree and Ojibway which are present in some of the other tribes.[22] The Cree possess twenty-six traits common to all, ten of which occur among the Ojibway who have no traits reported other than the ten they have in common with the Cree. Hence, all Ojibway traits are Cree, but not all Cree traits are Ojibway.

Clement's results, based on the coefficient of association, (Q), follow:[23]

---

[19] David Mandelbaum, *The Plains Cree*, Anthropological Papers of the American Museum of Natural History (New York, 1940), Vol. XXXVII, Part II, pp. 223–224.

[20] Details given me by Raining Bird, August 24, 1960.

[21] Clements, *op. cit.*, pp. 219–220.

[22] A later study would show that some of these traits are present now in the Sun Dance of the Montana Cree.

[23] Clements, *op. cit.*, p. 220.

Tribe	Q with the Plains-Cree
Ojibway	1.00
Assiniboine	.93
Wind River Shoshoni	.64
Gros Ventre	.62
Blackfeet	.59
Crow	.55
Ute	.52
Ponca	.51
Hidatsa	.49
Sarsi	.41
Arikara	.36
Canadian Dakota	.33
Sisseton	.25
Southern Cheyenne	.22
Northern Cheyenne	.22
Arapaho	−.01
Kiowa	−.03
Oglala	−.08

The correlations with the Ojibway are easily explained, for the two tribes have always been friendly. Their language is mutually understood; many of their beliefs are similar. For example, while the Grand Medicine Dance, the Midewiwin, is usually associated with the Ojibway, the Plains Cree practiced it. At the beginning of the settlement on the Rocky Boy Reservation, where both Ojibway and Cree were placed, the Midewiwin flourished at first. Over the years, those who knew how to conduct it died and finally no one was left who knew the ritual and songs. The last time it was performed there was in 1938.[24] Historically, the Plains-Cree came to the Great Plains before the Ojibway; hence, it is easy to conjecture that the Cree taught the Ojibway about the Sun Dance.

With the Assiniboine, it is a little different. We know of the long and friendly association those tribes have had since early in the seventeenth century. Spier says,[25] "The Plains Cree ... were intimately associated with the Assiniboine. Their sun dance is considered equivalent by the latter and was probably obtained from them. ..." Raining Bird states[26] that the Assiniboine Sun Dance is almost the same as that of the Cree. "Just little differences, but nothing of any great importance." If the Assiniboine had the ceremony prior to their separation from the Dakota,

---

[24] Personal interview, Raining Bird, August 26, 1960.

[25] Spier, *op. cit.*, p. 496.

[26] Personal interview, Raining Bird, August 26, 1960.

why is the torture element missing? Was it the Cree influence? Or was it only in late years that the Cree learned the ceremony from the Assiniboine? These questions seem to be largely academic. The essential point is that the Sun Dance functions strongly in the 1960's among the Montana Cree—a ceremony whose elements correlate with those reported in a ritual once performed by the Assiniboine.

But the Montana Cree have not been able to develop their Sun Dance to the tribal ceremony it is today—the high point in their religious life—without experiencing trouble. It is the result of long years of harassment, of subterfuge, of adjustment. Out of the years of trouble, out of the merging of the groups on the reservation into one unit, out of the caustic criticism of the white officials has come this symbol of Creehood that unifies the group and keeps them Indian. One example from the past illustrates the difficulties they have encountered.

Before Little Bear brought his group from Canada, the United States government had forbidden the Sun Dance. As early as 1882[27] the Secretary of the Interior, at the request of the Commissioner of Indian Affairs, had issued an order prohibiting the Sun Dance on government lands in the United States. Twelve years later when Little Bear's band was attempting to find a home in Montana and had started preparations for a Sun Dance near Great Falls, Montana, the second governor of Montana issued a proclamation not only prohibiting the ceremony but ordering the local officers to arrest the leaders.

The Governor's proclamation provides an excellent example of the failure to understand the aims of the Sun Dance, as well as showing the degree of intolerance a superior and dominating culture can display. He wrote:[28]

Investigation . . . convinces me that it is not only inhuman and brutalizing, unnatural and indecent, and therefore abhorrent to Christian civilization, but that its aims and purposes are a menace to the peace and welfare of communities. My information . . . leads me to regard the proposed exhibition as wholly inconsistent with Christian civilization. . . . The Cree Indians are refugees from Canada and therefore do not come within the restrictions imposed by the authorities on reservations. Whatever steps taken to prevent the Crees from repeating the Sun Dance must be by direction of the authorities of Montana. . . .

Therefore, I, John E. Rickards, by virtue of the authority vested in me as

---

[27] *Report of the Commissioner of Indian Affairs* (Washington: Government Printing Office, 1883), pp. xiv-xv. John Collier, Commissioner of Indian Affairs, revoked the order prohibiting the Sun Dance in 1934.

[28] *The Great Falls Tribune,* June 6, 1894.

governor of the state of Montana do hereby prohibit within the limits of this state the festival known as the Sun Dance and the local authorities of the several counties are directed to take such steps as may be necessary in their respective communities to enforce this inhibition.

Little Bear moved his straggling little band northward toward the sparsely-settled areas near the present town of Havre, Montana, and proceeded to continue his preparations for the ceremony. A newspaper reporter from the then small frontier community found the Cree and interviewed Little Bear. While the reporter made frequent references to the fact that the Cree were subsisting on "barb wire, dead gophers and rattlesnakes," his account of Little Bear's defense of the Sun Dance is significant. He quotes Little Bear as saying:[29]

We are here today to worship the Great Spirit. He brought us into the world and has taken care of us. My people take this method of expressing our gratitude. God put us here to love each other. Every day I and my people ask mercy of God and thank him for feeding us and keeping us healthy. For two days and two nights I do not eat. Ever since I was born I have worshipped my God at this season of the year. I do not think it right for the white people to stop me from holding the Sun Dance. It is my method of devotion and my people want it. We mean no harm to anyone, but want to save our souls. My people cut their skin in the shoulders. Christ was put on the Cross and had nails driven through his feet and hands the same as my people do. But if the white man objects we will not do this. We do not want trouble with the white race. They are good to us and when we get through with our devotion those Indians who came here to dance will scatter as the birds to pick up a crumb here and a crumb there on which to live. My people are good people and we will do no wrong. The light, the air, the water and the birds are free and we also want to be free and be good so that the Great Spirit will smile with gladness and call us his children.

While this rhetoric has some of the flavor of nineteenth century oratory, the essence of Cree belief is there. It reveals, too, that the Cree were using torture at that time, but by Little Bear's own admission, it could easily be omitted. But the most important thing of all is the fact that the Montana Cree know about this affair; Little Bear was the father of one of my informants and the grandfather of another one. Parents of many of my other informants were in the group. They have heard the tale of persecution, as they interpret it, told many times. They know, too, of many other instances, perhaps less dramatic than this one, in which the white man did all he could to stifle their belief. Neighbors of the Cree—Assiniboine, Gros Ventre, Blackfeet—were on reservations

---

[29] *The Havre Plaindealer*, June 7, 1894.

by treaty right. While their adjustment was difficult, these other Indians had annuities and rations. The Cree had none. The others were concerned, too, with the loss of their religious festivities and made certain adaptations,[30] but with their material needs satisfied to some degree they did not need to rely upon the supernatural as did the Cree. As they fought and starved for recognition, they turned more and more toward the spirits and the divine beings for help. And the Sun Dance brought all those values together. Seventy years later, the Sun Dance is forgotten or dying out on the surrounding reservations. Among the Montana Cree, the Sun Dance is a thriving institution. It satisfies their religious needs today, just as in the past. It is the focus of their belief.

A comparison of the elements of their belief with the Sun Dance practices illustrates how completely the Sun Dance brings together all of the varying religious details. For ease of reading, the comparison is presented in chart form.

Belief	Sun Dance
1. The High God Concept	1. Consistent recognition of *Ki-sei-men'-to* and the attempt to reach Him in prayers.
2. The Four Spirits who stay with *Ki-sei-men'-to*	2. The use of the four pipes in the ceremony in commemoration of these spirits.
3. Sweetgrass Man, always with the Creator	3. Sweetgrass is used constantly so that the prayers will reach him who will transmit them to the Creator.
4. The Thunderbirds, one at each cardinal direction	4. Creation and nourishment of the baby Thunderbird; nest for the black one at the forks of the sacred pole; colors for the other three expressed in cloth hangings on the pole.
5. Importance of Sun and Mother Earth	5. A yellow flag hangs to the east in commemoration of the Sun Spirit; Mother Earth is recognized with the pipe.
6. Master Spirit	6. Prayers to the Master Spirit of the tree prior to its felling; emphasis upon the buffalo whose Master Spirit still controls all food.

---

[30] For example, the Assiniboine Hand Game.

7. Spirits—messengers of *Ki-sei-men'to*

7. Spirits fill the Sacred Lodge during the ceremony and at the end carry the messages and prayers aloft.

8. The Sweat Lodge, the oldest ceremonial known to the Cree

8. All participants must sweat prior to taking part in the ceremony.

9. Visions

9. In contemporary times, more people experience visions at the Sun Dance than in the past according to informants among the Montana Cree.

10. Dancing as a means of expressing supernatural contact

10. The actual "dance" itself.

11. Seeking spiritual help by fasting and praying

11. Fasting and praying during the ceremony.

12. Smoking according to the Creator's instruction to First Man

12. Establishing contact with the Creator through constant smoking during the ceremony.

13. Use of cloth as offerings to the spirits

13. New cloth offerings hang on the rafters as well as the center pole of the Sacred Lodge; each participant has his own cloth.

14. Weeping as a sign of communication

14. Weeping at the center pole.

15. Bear Spirit feasts on berries

15. Berries served in the preliminary rites.

16. Bundles

16. Not necessary but may be used at the ceremony if the participant desires.

17. Sage as a purifier

17. The dancers stand on a bed of sage.

18. Tabus against women and menstruation

18. Menstruating women cannot dance; until the menopause, women are not allowed in front of the fence.

19. Drums talk and carry messages

19. Constant drumming during the ceremony.

20. Praying not the prerogative of the medicine man

20. Everyone prays during the ceremony.

But what does the Sun Dance do to the people themselves? First, let us allow the Montana Cree to answer that question in their own words. Raining Bird,[31] Sun Dance Leader, explains it this way: "The Sun Dance is kind of a new birth for the people. It is a thirsting dance when we ask *Ki-sei-men'-to* for rain so that the earth will have water and the grass will grow to feed the buffalo. Nowadays, of course, the prayers have changed because our life has changed. Now people are concerned with money and the education of their children so that they can learn something good. And we pray for other things that will help us. These prayers are not learned. They're just made up and said from the heart of the person. Doing things right at the Sun Dance and praying together makes us feel good, for this is the Indian way."

Pete Favel:[32] "The Sun Dance is the Road of God. If a man tries to do everything right, he can save himself trouble that often comes. Our voices go to God every morning and night. The people talk to God when the sun comes up and when it goes down. If the Indians quit the Sun Dance and follow the white man, it would be bad. *Ki-sei-men'-to* gave the Indian this way to worship. It is ours. We need to have it. The Sun Dance is for everything—water, good grass, good health. We pray for all the Indians at the Sun Dance, too—not just our own Cree. We pray for the white man and for the crops they have put in the ground. We ask the spirits to help make the white man's crops grow. The white man is smarter in lots of ways than we are. But they don't know how to ask the Creator for things and get them the way we do. That's why we ask for help for the white man at the Sun Dance. The Indians travel a long ways to come to the Sun Dance. They want to show God that they believe in it. That's why they come so far."

Pete Gardipee:[33] "The Sun Dance is a time for all the Indians to come together and give thanks for seeing that they've all come through the last year alive. It is also a time when people come to see if any miracles have happened. In a way, it is kind of like you folks crowding in to see Oral Roberts.[34] Not many of the Cree nowadays know the real reason for the dance. A long time ago it was done to harden a man's mind and spirit for the ordeals of life ahead of him while he was giving thanks for being alive. But today, that is most forgotten. The Sun Dance still brings people together and reminds them of the Indian way."

---

[31] Personal interviews, July 1, 1960; August 24, 1960.
[32] Personal interview, July 1, 1960.
[33] Personal interview, July 3, 1960.
[34] A prominent faith healer whose television programs are very popular with the Indian people, as well as whites.

Ruth Gardipee:[35] Everyone comes to the Sun Dance to join their prayers to the dancers and sponsors so that everyone will have good luck for the coming year. In that way, it is kind of a New Year's ceremony.

"I have five children. I pray to the lodge and the Indian beliefs that another year will see me there with my five children and that we will all be in good health and that I will be there with all the other Indian people."

Whatever the reasons, the Cree come. Participation or even attendance is a means of assuring "luck" for the following year. The Sun Dance is to the Indian what a combined celebration of Easter and Christmas would be to the Christian. For the Sun Dance is a renewal and a continuity of his faith—something that has come down to the Montana Cree from a now long-forgotten past. It matters not to him if anthropologists concern themselves with the when and where of its adoption. To the mid-twentieth century Cree Indian, living on a lonely reservation in an obscure corner of a sparsely-settled western state, the Sun Dance is a living memorial of the Indian's ability to triumph over his environment. Through their persistence in performing the dance each year, the Cree not only receive blessings for themselves and their families, but they can also demonstrate to their children the advantage of being Indian.

They point, too, to the Indians of the other reservations who come to the Sun Dance ceremony. Some of those people participate, but many of them just stand and look. They do not know the ritual; they have not been taught the knowledge the Cree young people have. There is no Sun Dance on their reservation; they are not active members of the Christian missions that dot their area. They are living in a religious wasteland, for they have forgotten the teachings of their fathers and have adopted little if anything from their contact with the white man. The grandparents of these people were eating meat and living in houses on reservations while the fathers and grandfathers of the Cree were wandering and being shunted from one place to another. But the Cree, so they claim, did not forget the teachings of their Creator. They stayed with their religion and their Sun Dance. Today, they have something of value to them that the others do not have. And this factor they never allow their children to forget.

For the children, the Sun Dance is a rare and wonderful experience. The family moves to the grounds, erects its tent or tipi, and camps in a

---

[35] Personal interviews, July 3, 1960; September 2, 1960.

large circle. Here is a chance for play, not only with their own friends, but with new ones who come from neighboring reservations. Here six or seven of them can ride a horse at one time and circle around the the camp and play at being Indian as Indians once were. Here fifteen or twenty little girls can flock together and play tag among themselves not worried by being teased by the little boys, for they are too busy climbing hills, charging the camp or raiding a tent or tipi for food. It is all part of the wonderful experience of growing up as an Indian child.

As the children grow a little older, they learn new things. By the time the girls are ten, it means dressing up in their store-bought clothes for the last day of the religious ceremony. It means looking with envy at one of their friends who is a year or two older and who is dancing the Sun Dance for the first time. She is an object of wonder and envy as she stands there, bobbing up and down, an eagle-bone whistle in her mouth, her cheeks painted, eagle-down feathers in her hair and dressed in new clothes. It is something to be looked forward to, something definitely to be desired. And at Sun Dance time, the children listen more carefully to the instructions of their parents about Indian religion. To believe the Indian values means that one can dance the Sun Dance; to participate in the Sun Dance is a proud manifestation that the child is a Cree.

Then come the days of celebration after the ceremony. Hand games, races, grass dancing—all the fun that any child could ask for is there. And for the adult, too, these days mark the social high light of an otherwise rather dreary life. Goddard wrote[36] a description of the social aspects of the Sun Dance years ago; it is just as true today:

Apart from its religious significance, the sun dance marks the yearly gathering of people whom the exigencies of life compel to spend the fall and winter in isolation, and it is looked forward to as such today. The young make, and the old renew acquaintances, and it is a general holiday.

The time comes for the affair to end. The people dismantle their tents and tipis, pack their cars, and head for their homes. The green leaves on the branches that cover the Sacred Lodge are already curling; soon they will die and blow away and the lodge will stand beside the remnants of those of previous years—symbols of an enduring and enriching belief.

---

[36] Pliny Earle Goddard, *Notes on the Sun Dance of the Cree in Alberta*, Anthropological Papers of the American Museum of Natural History (New York 1919), Vol. XVI, Part IV, p. 307.

CONCLUSION

In this present work I have attempted to investigate religion as it is practiced by the Indians on the Rocky Boy reservation in Northern Montana. Not only has an ethnographic account of the religion as practiced today been considered, but, as well, an inquiry has been made to determine why the primitive religion has persisted there while it is fading or being abandoned on other Indian reservations in Montana today.

In the first place, it is important to remember that the members of this reservation have come from many sources. The basic groups were Chippewa and Cree; mingling of blood lines from the Assiniboine, the Blackfeet, as well as from numerous other Indian tribes and from the French, brought peoples of diverging beliefs together. The two major groups, however, the Chippewa and the Cree, brought with them a religion that was Woodlands orientated, yet each had been under Plains influence for a goodly number of years.

Each one of the stragglers coming to the newly-established reservation in 1916 brought with him a history of struggle, of hardship, of deprivation. The Cree came out of Canada as a result of a rebellion against the Crown; hence they bore the stigma of being malcontents and murderers. And before the establishment of the reservation for them, they were never allowed to forget the fact that they had neither rights nor privileges on American soil—they were British subjects in the eyes of the Americans despite the fact that their forebears had roamed the country south of the International Boundary for centuries. The Chippewa had been separated from their parent stock in Minnesota or Canada for so long that they themselves had practically lost account of their origin. Living in city dumps in Montana, allying themselves with other recognized Indians on reservations, roaming at will throughout Montana seeking food, they were an isolated and fragmentary group without security, heritage, or recognition. Other Indians who joined the group on the new reservation and were duly enrolled came from various sources; many were women who had married a Cree or a Chippewa.

Others were men whose parents had been separated so long from their parent stock that they too had lost completely any identification. They were Indian—tribal lines were unidentified or forgotten. But they were homeless, insecure, and like the two major groups, anxious for the permanency of a home.

Securing a tiny reservation of their own did not solve their problems immediately. Certainly there was a sense of relief from the deprivations they had known before, but other factors faced them. No pattern of organization existed; Rocky Boy, the Chippewa leader, died the year after Congress provided for the reservation. Little Bear, the Cree leader, was aggressive, dominant, vigorous. During the last five years of his life, which coincided with the first five years of the existence of the reservation, he complained, cajoled, and threatened not only the Indians but the representatives of the government as well. Many of the Chippewa, unaccustomed to such leadership, resented him. Yet no other political leader seemed to evolve.

The economic situation on the reservation likewise seemed to put the Indian in jeopardy. While they now had whatever security may come from having land that was considered theirs to use, and the possibility was present of building cabins without fear of eviction, there was still little or no means of subsistence. The representatives of the government tried to help them get started. But with only meager funds available, for America was just entering World War I and was not too interested in providing means for a group of straggling Indians, not too much assistance could be given them. Then, too, to weld together a group as motley as these Indians required patience and tact beyond the potentiality of practically any agent assigned to them.

While these internal struggles were going on, it is well to remember that the other Indians of the West were well along the way to cultural disintegration. Since the 1860's, they had been under the dominance of the Federal government; by 1916, when the Rocky Boy reservation was established, their culture had been quite well destroyed. Much of their religion had been prohibited, their children had been gathered up and sent to boarding schools, their political structure eliminated. Yet they had their land and their rations—a security of a sort that was fast leading them to apathy and listlessness.

Thus while the process of disintegration was going on among the Indians of the established reservations, the internal dynamics of the members of the Rocky Boy reservation seemed directed toward another goal. They needed recognition; they were enrolled members of a reservation yet they had no tribal identity, no satisfactory political structure, no economic security beyond government rations, no one religion. At first, a mutually understandable language plus a sense of being outcasts finally thrown together, were the only common elements. To achieve any sense of cohesion as a group meant finding a common core. And in the end, the common core was religion.

Why these Indians followed the Cree tradition rather than the Chippewa is a matter for speculation. The domineering influence of the Cree leader, Little Bear, may account in part for the Cree ascendancy. His lieutenants after his death, especially Kennewash, Young Boy, and Poor Coyote, were forceful and respected men who insisted that their tribal rites be continued. During these times of stress in the early years of the reservation, these men along with many of the others, regardless of previous tribal affiliation, could contemplate the supernatural together. And the contemplation was the result of the Cree's interpretation. So it was, as the years passed, that the few religious leaders of the less aggressive Chippewa group saw their ceremonies decreasing. As death took many of their leaders, they realized that their rites were passing. The Great Medicine Dance of the Chippewa—the Midewiwin—finally was lost about 1938 with the death of their last leader. And for the younger Chippewa the transition to the Cree belief was not difficult. Too many of the elements were the same or so similar that no conflicts arose in their minds. Instead, this new bond of cohesion that religion afforded them began to give them a sense of belonging, of unity, of being "Cree."

The Indian Reorganization Act of 1934, although coming into being at a time when the group still thought of themselves as "Chippewa Cree," gave them some sort of political structure again. The government-operated schools on the reservation educated their children yet allowed them to remain at home. The families had the security of a home on the reservation; their other needs were met by welfare assistance and seasonal labor in neighboring areas. The practice of their religion, now that the other anxieties had decreased and more leisure was available, meant that they were no longer alienated. They were Indians, Indians who began to achieve recognition and a certain amount of respect from other tribal members because of their religious practices.

While this increased cohesion was developing, the values of the Indians remained more and more those of their ancestors. These values had always worked well for their people; why should such values not continue to work for them now that they had achieved a recognition of their own and had a religion of their own? Such was the thinking of these Indians as their cohesiveness developed. And such is their thinking today. Their main values are those drawn from the past.

The economic pattern is very similar to that of the past. Despite the fact that the Indians look and dress like their white neighbors, drive automobiles, shop in the supermarkets, have their cabins wired for electricity, own radios and in some instances television sets, the pattern of their lives parallels that of their buffalo-hunting ancestors. Just as in primitive times, the people have a home base, in this case the reservation, yet when spring comes, the men take their families and go to surrounding areas seeking work. Until late June they perform whatever work is available, but when the Sun Dance time arrives, they return to the reservation. Once that great ceremony has ended, they leave again to wander across the Northwest following the harvests. When the last potatoes have been dug in Idaho in late October, they pile their belongings in their cars and return to the reservation. Income from picking rocks, repairing fences, doing farm labor, harvesting crops has replaced the more dramatic and dashing search for the buffalo. But the pattern is the same.

And once they are back on the reservation, they have the time to contemplate and to perform their religious rites. White men may say that some of them are lazy, that they will not accept jobs away from home for an extended period of time, but as has been pointed out in an earlier chapter, months are required for the Sun Dance leader to prepare properly the minute details of the ceremony. No man can do that task properly and still be employed away from the reservation for the full year. And these men who have been away but who return during the winter give their assistance to the leader when he needs it as well as planning and participating in other religious practices. Hence, despite outward appearances, the Montana Cree follow very closely the economic and religious pattern of their ancestors.

That this phenomenon is not characteristic of them alone is noted by Caudill in his mention of the Mohawks.[1]

... there is a group of Mohawk Indians at Caughnawaga reservation just across the St. Lawrence, who, after three hundred years of being completely beaten down by Western society, very quickly became, by the chance building

---

[1] William Caudill, "Values," from *An Appraisal of Anthropology Today*, edited by Sol Tax and others (Chicago: University of Chicago Press, 1953). Based on an International Symposium of Anthropology, 1952, p. 357.

of a bridge next to the reservation, high steel bridgeworkers. There was an efflorescence of the old native religion; the men left to work on bridges and came back in the winter time to talk about their exploits. In general, there was a revival of a certain pattern of life, with different content but essentially the same structure as existed in the old society. Why this persistence?

It seems possible, then, that when aspects of a primitive culture are restored—even in a different context—anxieties are eliminated and time is available for the adoption of other elements or universals. The Cree, like the Mohawk, have adapted to the new material culture but at the same time have intensified their interest in other elements—especially religion.

With other values, we find much the same practice. The preoccupation with spirits recalls Radin's statement that has been quoted before, "... from among the heterogeneous mass of beliefs, the one which stands out most definitely is the belief in spirits who bestow on man success, happiness, and long life."[2] We have seen how the Montana Cree are constantly pre-occupied with the spirits in order that they may have success in finding jobs, health for their children, and "luck" for themselves. The concept of the Master Spirit and the subsequent offering to the spirit when the animal is killed reflects also something of the primitive idea of the supremacy of the male, whose role as hunter made him the dominant figure in the culture.

The buffalo as the Master of Life is another example of aboriginal thinking. While it undoubtedly came late to the Cree, as has been mentioned earlier, the concept of the buffalo as the giver of food is found in many ceremonies, particularly the Sun Dance. Yet, as has been pointed out, the Master Spirit of the Moose is not forgotten—the Woodland's influence is still being manifested.

Aside from these aspects, other values drawn from primitive thinking persist and flourish. The Sun Dance is an excellent example. Here is a splendid illustration of a ceremony that heightens the social cohesion of the group. While other dancing fulfils some of the same function, nothing equals the Sun Dance in bringing the group together and welding it into one unit. By the same token, the Cree have achieved a status through the continuance of the Sun Dance. They have witnessed the disappearance of the ceremony in other tribes; they have noted the nostalgia of the other Indians who no longer have the ceremony and

---

[2] Paul Radin, *Primitive Religion: Its Nature and Origin* (New York: Dover Publications, 1957), p. 6.

who come to the Cree dance sometimes to participate, more often just to watch. With the Sun Dance of the Cree becoming the last great expression of primitive religion left in the Northern Plains, Indian visitors are pouring into the Rocky Boy reservation to ascertain what the Cree are securing from this ceremony. The Montana Cree's Sun Dance is becoming another Mecca or another Jerusalem to the Indians of the West.

The Montana Cree recognize their superiority in this respect. Thus the primitive value of the Sun Dance has been enhanced. The effectiveness, drawn directly from past values, now takes on additional force through the attitudes of the other Indians. Parents can now point to their Sun Dance and teach their children the need for the perseverance of Indian religion.

The concept of the after life is purely primitive.[3] The "happy-hunting ground" is indeed just that. Buffalo are plentiful, skin tipis keep everyone warm and clean, campfires glow, dancing abounds. It is but another example of how people envisage the future life to be an idealized improvement over the present. The average Montana Cree sits and talks and dreams about how wonderful life was before the white man came and spoiled it. In his concept, then, the after life could be nothing but this "good place" where life is happy and comfortable, as they think it was during the days of their ancestors.

Those in the after life are close to their Creator and are presided over by the First Man. The dead, like the living, never address the great Kitchi Manitou by his real name. In this respect, the Montana Cree are like the Greeks and the Hebrews and many other peoples of antiquity—their god is too holy to be addressed casually. As Graves explains,[4] when speaking about the Greeks:

... a god so holy as Phoroneus the Fire-giver might well conceal his real name and expect his worshippers to address him by a periphrasis, or else retain only the consonants of his name while changing the vowels—as the Israelites did with the name 'JHVH,' which was not really pronounced 'Jehovah.'

---

[3] It is interesting to note that I arrived at these conclusions independently only to read almost verbatim the same results in Robert Murphy's account of the Mundurucu. In several instances, other than the ones I have mentioned, the Mundurucu study parallels the pattern of the Montana Cree. See Robert Murphy, *Mundurucu Religion*, University of California Publications in American Archaeology and Ethnology, Vol. XLIX, No. 1, (1958).

[4] Robert Graves, *Food for Centaurs: Stories, Talks, Critical Studies, Poems* (New York: Doubleday & Company, Inc., 1960), pp. 270–271.

So, the white man, to explain this phenomenon, has to depend upon a Polynesian term to describe it. The name becomes a *noa*[5] name.

And it seems irrelevant to worry whether the Kitchi Manitou is indigenous with the Algonquian Cree or whether it is the result of European influence. The significant thing is that these Cree believe, as did their immediate forebears, that *Ki-sei-men'-to* is their High God—no doubt the same one the white man talks about, but that He has a place reserved for them away from the contempt and the superiority of the white man. One realizes this tremendous respect for their High God as he sees the Cree worship Him and hears their prayers to Him. With complete certainty in His greatness, they throw themselves upon the mercy of their God. An observing Caucasian attending their Sun Dance, or a meeting of the Native American Church, or even listening to their prayers in the sweat lodge, cannot help but sense the sincerity and conviction by which they abjectly beseech their Maker for better days for themselves and their children. With this great sense of dependence and firm belief in their High God, what difference does it make if the concept was originally Algonquian or European? In the latter half of the twentieth century, the concept belongs to the Cree.

Their Trickster, Wi-sak-a-chak, is a vital figure among the Montana Cree as he was among their ancestors. His antics served as a mechanism for the expression of frustrations of the group, particularly the Cree group, during the days of their wandering.[6] He is, as my informants have pointed out and have demonstrated, an example of what Radin wrote about the Trickster of the Winnebago:[7]

> Trickster, of course, resolved nothing, except in so far as he demonstrated what happens when man's instinctual side is given free reign. He is the symbol for that instinctual side and, overtly, ... he can serve either as an object lesson or made to be ridiculous, and become a source of laughter and amusement. ...
> But the Trickster is not merely the symbol for the instinctual. He is likewise the symbol for the irrational and the non-socialized. For the Winnebago, for all primitive peoples, in fact, they all belonged together. ... Every man, they felt, possessed a Trickster unconscious which it was imperative for both the individual concerned, and even more so, for society, to bring consciousness lest

---

[5] From the class lectures of Dr. Åke Hultkrantz at Brandeis University, Summer, 1958. *Noa* is a term used to address animals or gods too great to permit one's saying their real names.

[6] For a fuller account of the Cree stories of their Trickster, see those collected by F. E. Peeso in 1905 included in Appendix A of this publication.

[7] Paul Radin, *The World of Primitive Man* (New York: Grove Press, Inc., 1960), pp. 338–339.

it destroy him and those around him. No man can do this for himself. He must call his fellowmen and society to his aid. In the career of Trickster all this is depicted. There he sees his own instinctual and irrational self, unanchored, undirected, helpless, purposeless, knowing neither love, loyalty nor pity. Isolated, he cannot grow nor mature. He can do nothing with the two fundamental appetites, hunger and sex.

Wi-sak-a-chak, as is evidenced by the frequency of the retelling of his exploits, is an inheritance from the past that is much alive today.

Witigo is another being that illustrates the closeness to the values of the past. Conceived in a culture that was constantly threatened by starvation, the cannibal-like monster devoured human flesh and threatened the existence of the people. In Montana, the Cree, too, have known starvation—not in comparatively recent times, although the spectre is still there. Thus witigo is not a dead figure from the past. He too may be considered as representative of another value they hold.

Other details could be cited, but sufficient evidence points to the fact that the Montana Cree are holding the values of their aboriginal culture. That these values have endured may be accounted for by their religious views. But that they are not completely freed from anxiety about their children is illustrated by the fear that many of them exhibit about the possible loss of tribal identity. Schools to them, particularly the public schools and the high schools in larger towns, are a threat. For in the school, the child is exposed to influences that may alienate him from his religious beliefs and cause him to lose his identity—an identity that these people have struggled to obtain. Hence, to combat the influence of the white man's thinking, the Montana Cree have in some instances turned to the past or have adopted forms of a modified Indian belief. We can see that factor working in some of the nativistic movements mentioned in this work and especially in the constant reminders that parents give children about the superiority of their own religion.

To indoctrinate one with religious values is a means, then, of keeping one's tribal identity—an identity and unity that has been achieved by the Montana Cree through a struggle and a persistence that has covered a period of seventy-five years of heartache, of contempt, and of roaming. Through their religion these people have achieved some degree of security, they have become welded into a new tribe, and they are jealously guarding their children lest the younger group be alienated from the factor that has unified the tribe. Thus their religion is functioning and persisting as it is on no other reservation in Montana where the tensions of life have not been so intense. Religion has bound them together out of disorganization;[8] it has made them the "Montana Cree."

---

[8] It seems to me that the entire story of the evolvement of the Montana Cree through the cohesive force of their religion is an example of one of the derivatives of the term. According to the *Oxford English Dictionary* (Oxford: Clarendon Press, 1933), Sir James A. Murray, ed., Vol. VIII, p. 410, the source of the word is as follows:

> *Religion* (AF *religioun* 11th c., F. *religion*, or ad. L. *religion-em*, of doubtful etymology, by Cicero connected with *relegere*, to read over again, but by later authors with *religare*, to bind.

Certainly, the Montana Cree illustrate the full meaning of the last source, *religare*, to bind.

APPENDIX A

Selected Examples of Cree Literature

F. E. Peeso collected the following stories from the Cree who had left Canada in 1885. In 1905, when Peeso worked with the Cree, they were camped near the present city of Butte, Montana. These stories, then, are the ones the parents and grandparent of the Montana Cree heard when they were children and hence are closely related to the original literature of the Cree Indians.

Ten of the stories concern Wi-sak-a-chak. I have selected them primarily because they are typical of the Trickster, for each one deals with the basic instinctive needs of man—hunger and sex—and, as well, because many of the same themes run through the literature of the contemporary Cree. Secondly, these stories have never, to my knowledge, been published before.

Five other narratives are included for much the same reason, although in these stories one sees instead of the antics of Wi-sak-a-chak, another common theme running through them—the boy saviour of the camp.

I

1. Wi-sak-a-chak and the Pe-che-ke-ke-tches
(Of Eyeballs and Headaches)

One day while Wi-sak-a-chak was travelling along, he saw some little birds with white stripes on the side of their heads—Pe-che-ke-ke-tches. They were throwing their eyes into the bushes and they would come back again into their heads.

"Ho, my brothers," called Wi-sak-a-chak. "What are you doing? Why do you do that?"

"Oh," they said. "We do not do that for nothing. We do it only when we have a headache."

Old Wi-sak-a-chak said, "Ho, that is just my trouble. That is just what I want. I have been travelling from place to place looking for that medicine. I feel very bad. My head is aching all the time. I wish you would give me some of that medicine."

Then one of the Pe-che-ke-ke-tches said, "I am not the oldest. Ask the oldest one."

He then asked the oldest, and he answered, "I do not know. Maybe you will not do it right. I will show you how."

Old Wi-sak-a-chak answered, "Sure, I will do right, the way you tell me. I will do right."

Pe-che-ke-ke-tches told him, "All right, I will give you three trials to do that."

"All right," answered Wi-sak-a-chak. "I am very glad, my brother, to get rid of my headaches."

Then Wi-sak-a-chak left his brothers. He continued his journey, and after awhile, he said, "My head aches very badly. I think it will kill me." And he rolled over and over on the ground. "Oh," he said at last, "My brother gave me some medicine. I will try it. Maybe it will cure me." Then he got up and took his eyes out and threw them into the bushes. He shook the bushes and they came back in. "Oh," he cried. "That does it. It is good. My head is all right now."

So he started again. He went only a short distance, when the same thing happened. He had another headache, and he said, "I know how to get cured now. It will not take me long." and he did it again. He took his eyes out and threw them into a bush, and when he shook it, his eyes came back in. "That is twice now, I have done it; I have one more chance." And he continued his journey, and soon his head was aching again. "Ah, that is the last one, but I have a very bad headache, and I must do it." And he threw his eyes again into a bush, and shook it and they came back in as they had before. "That is all, there are no more now." And he started on again. All at once his head began to ache. "Oh, I have another bad headache. I do not know what to do. My brother gave me three chances, but I will try it once more." And again he threw his eyes into the bushes, and shook them to make his eyes come back, but they would not come back. And he was blind. "That is my fault," he said. 'He gave me only three chances. I did it too much. Now what am I going to do?"

Then he started on again, without his eyes, blind. He kept on until he struck a tree. "What kind of a tree are you?"

"I am a poplar," it answered.

"That is not the kind." After a little while, he struck another tree. "What kind of a tree are you?" he asked.

"I am a willow."

"No, that is not the kind," he said. Then he went along again and struck another tree. "What kind of a tree are you?"

"I am a pine," it answered.

"Oh," he said, "dry land pine," and he went on and struck another pine, a swampy pine. 'That is the kind," he said and he felt the tree, running his hands over the bark. He picked off some white pitch, which he rolled up into two balls and made his eyes out of that. "Now I am all right," he said. "I can see again."

He made his eyes out of pitch. From there he started toward the north and did not come around that way again.

A-kwa-kwah. (That is all.)

2. Wi-sak-a-chak and the Bear

One day while Wi-sak-a-chak was walking along by a river, he saw a bear on the other side. 'Well, I will have some fun with her," he said to himself, so he called out, "Hoh, Hoh, ha-ya! If anyone crosses my path I will kill him."

And the bear then answered, "It is just the same with myself. I will kill anyone who crosses my path."

"A-e-yah, hai," yelled Wi-sak-a-chak. "If anyone talks loud to me, I will kill him." And the bear stood up on her hind legs.

"Look here," called Wi-sak-a-chak. "This fellow crossed my path and I killed him." And he pointed to a dead buffalo, but it had been dead for a long time. The bear looked over and saw something but she could not make out what it was.

"It is just the same with me," she said. "I kill anything that opposes me."

Then Wi-sak-a-chak said again, "If anyone talks loudly to me, I kill him." And he ran after the bear and chased her quite a distance. Finally the bear became tired and lay down. She was breathing hard. Wi-sak-a-chak said to his spear, "Ha, Cha-ke-cha-ka-nas (ha, my spear) if the bear moves kill her." And he stuck the spear into the ground close to the bear; it was a fine spear and many feathers dangled from the shaft. "If you move, the spear will kill you," he said and continued his journey. After the snows had set in Wi-sak-a-chak said, "I guess I will go and see how my bear is now."

When he found the bear, she was almost dead, there was nothing left of her but skin and bones. Whenever she looked up at the spear, it was shaking in the wind and the feathers were rustling, and she was afraid to move.

"Mas-kwa," asked Wi-sak-a-chak, "Ke-kwa-ye-ke-mo-chen?" (Bear, what do you eat?")

"I eat animals, birds, people, and any kind of meat," answered the bear.

"You must quit that," said Wi-sak-a-chak. "If you eat meat, I will fix you good. I don't want you to eat meat. You must eat berries, roots and such things. It is wrong for you to eat people and animals. Maybe sometime a great many people will eat bear meat. That is good, but you must not eat meat. If you do, I will kill you. You have been bad; you are still too mean. You get mad and kill people. Don't do that any more. In the winter you must hole up and stay until spring. Now I leave you."

3. Wi-sak-a-chak and the Chickens and the Coyote

Wi-sak-a-chak was on a journey; he came across some prairie chickens; they were young ones in a nest. The old one was away getting food. "What is your name?" he asked. "What is your name?"

"Our name," said one of the chickens, "is Pah-ha-yo."

"Is that the only name you have?"

"Yes," answered the chicken. "That is all. We have only one name."

"Everybody has more than one name," said Wi-sak-a-chak.

"No, that is all we have, Pah-ha-yo."

"Oh no, I guess you have more names. Surely you have two names."

"Yes, we have another name." answered the chickens.

"What is it?" asked Wi-sak-a-chak.

"O-kos'-ko-he-wah-ses' " (To scare anything).

"Oh hoh!" he laughed. "Why have you got that name? You can't scare anything."

Then Wi-sak-a-chak dunged on the chickens, right on their heads.

"You can't snare us that way," said the chickens. Pretty soon the old woman chicken came in.

"What is the matter?" she asked. "You are covered with filth."

"Wi-sak-a-chak did it," answered the chickens. Then she was mad, the old chicken. She went to find all the other chickens to tell them about it.

And Wi-sak-a-chak went on his way. Pretty soon he came to a creek; it was not very wide, but it was quite deep. He stopped on the bank, and all the chickens were hiding along the creek in the grass and bushes. But Wi-sak-a-chak could not see them; he was dressed in buckskin leggings and moccasins and he had a buffalo robe over his shoulders. He stood for a while on the bank; then he lifted one foot and cried, "Se-pe" (river) and tried to jump across. But he could not, as it was too far; he called again, "Se-pe," and then he lifted his robe up over his shoulders and went back for a start, but just as he jumped all of the chickens flew into his face. He was so frightened that he jumped into the water. "Ah-hoe! Now I am all wet, but I am a good swimmer." He soon got to the other side and he was mad. After his clothes were dry he started along a narrow bushy trail which led up the mountain. Pretty soon he met a coyote. "Where are you going, Me-sem?" (my younger brother), he said.

"Where are you going, Wi-sak-a-chak?" asked the Coyote.

"I am going on a long journey," answered Wi-sak-a-chak. "You are the younger, go around and let me pass. I am older than you and I don't want to go around."

"No," said the Coyote. "I am the older."

"No, no," said Wi-sak-a-chak. "I am the older. I will sit down here and whoever is the older will sit a long time and the younger will go first." So Wi-sak-a-chak and the coyote sat down and I do not know how many years they sat there.

Finally the coyote said, "Wi-sak-a-chak, are you dead?"

"No," said Wi-sak-a-chak.

After a long time again, Wi-sak-a-chak said, "Coyote, are you dead?"

"No," answered the coyote, and they lay there about two more years, and there was nothing left of them but skin and bones. Wi-sak-a-chak thought the coyote was dead.

"Ah hah! Coyote, are you dead?" But the coyote would not talk; then Wi-sak-a-chak got up and shook himself. "Nobody can beat me," he said. "I'll have my way. I am very old; I am the oldest of all the animals." And he started again on his journey. "Oh! Poor coyote. He is dead."

But he had not gone far when the coyote got up and ran to him and said, "Where are you going, Mesem?"

"Nobody must call me Me-sem," said Wi-sak-a-chak, "for I am the oldest." And the coyote ran away for he was afraid Wi-sak-a-chak would kill him.

4. Wi-sak-a-chak and the Animals

Wi-sak-a-chak was a wise man; he could make almost anything. He was continually travelling and he could talk with all the animals and understand what they said. Buffalo, deer, elk and wolves; he called them all his younger brothers.

One day when he was walking along, he saw two buffalo bulls standing off by themselves. He sat down and watched them for some time. "I am hungry," he said, "but I don't know how I shall kill these buffalo, for I have no bow; only a knife." Then he began to make his way around to a clump of willows, so that he should have a better hiding place. From there he crept nearer. He then cut some of the willows and fixed them up so as to look like men. He put his shirt on one and on the other, his robe; then he set them up so that the buffalo could see them.

"I wish a little wind would come," he said. Pretty soon the wind began to blow and the willow men swayed back and forth, and it looked as though they were fighting. Wi-sak-a-chak put his knife in his belt and went quietly to the buffalo who were lying down together; and he had no shirt or robe. When he was close to the buffalo they became frightened and got up. "Hold on," he said to them. "I want to talk to you and tell you something." So they stopped; one was an old bull, the other was young.

"I think Wi-sak-a-chak is coming," said one of them in buffalo language.

"Hold on!" called Wi-sak-a-chak who came up panting for he had been running hard. "Look at those two people fighting; they want to kill. I guess you don't want to see people kill each other."

"Oh yes," said the younger buffalo. "I saw them fighting."

"Look," said Wi-sak-a-chak. "One is cut already on the breast; they sent me to find out which of you was the older."

"I am the older," said the old bull.

"You can't prove it," said Wi-sak-a-chak. "I am the older," said the old one again.

"I will try to find out for myself," said Wi-sak-a-chak. "I want to see your testicles; the one who has the bigger ones is the older." So he felt the old one's testicles and said, "I think you are the older." Then he got up close to the young bull and stabbed him in the belly. "You fools," he said. "I was only hungry; those are not men fighting there, they are willows. I fooled you," and he started to cut up the meat.

Near by were two birch trees growing close together. Wi-sak-a-chak went and stood between them and said, "Come together," and they came together and pressed him tightly. "He-he-ee," he said. "I want to eat lots." Then he said, "Let me go," and the trees returned to their former position. Just then a magpie flew past. "Ho, Magpie," he called. "Now you will go and tell all the birds and come back to eat that meat. Don't you touch it. It is mine." But the magpie flew away and called all the birds and animals; eagles, crows, rabbits, gophers, coyotes, wolves and others.

"Don't eat my meat," called Wi-sak-a-chak, but just then the trees came together again, for he had not moved out from between them. They held him fast so that he could not get away. When all the meat had been eaten and there was nothing left but the bones, the trees let him go. He was very angry and he cut and whipped the trees. That is why the bark on this kind of tree is marred.

Wi-sak-a-chak picked up the bones and put them on a large flat rock; he then took a round stone and pounded the bones very fine. Then he boiled them and made bone grease. He put it in a bladder and threw it over his shoulder. The grease would not freeze. Pretty soon he came to a big river which he could not cross. "I'll make that bone grease freeze," he said, and he tied a string to the bladder and threw it into the river and it floated down the stream.

Before long he saw a muskrat swimming towards it. "As-tam, Me-sem," (Come on, my brother) he called.

"I don't want to," answered the muskrat. Maybe you want to harm me."

"Oh no, I do not want to harm you. I want to tie my grease to your tail and have you swim around with it and make it freeze; then we will eat it." So the muskrat let Wi-sak-a-chak tie the bladder to his tail and he began to swim around.

"I want to tell you something," called Wi-sak-a-chak again.

"All right," answered the muskrat, "tell me, but don't scare me; I am easily frightened. Then I dive into the water." Then he came closer; Wi-sak-a-chak sat on his heels near the bank.

"Come close, come close," he said, and the muskrat kept swimming around in a circle, sometimes close to the shore and then farther out in the river. If the man moved he became frightened and dived. "I think I will scare him," said Wi-sak-a-chak to himself. Then he called out, "Come right up close to me. "Don't be afraid." But when the rat came quite close, he shook his robe and cried, "Ah-hah."

The rat dived and the bladder broke and all the grease was spilled and spread out over the water. "Oh, hoh, you have spoiled my grease." But the muskrat went into his hole and Wi-sak-a-chak did not see him again.

Then all the animals came down and ate the grease off the water. Wi-sak-a-chak put his hands into the water and licked them off. "I want to eat a little myself." But the wood rabbit ate a good deal. "Hold on," Wi-sak-a-chak said to him. "You eat a good deal. You are getting too fat. You are not smart. You are too easy to kill. I don't want you to be fat." So he took the rabbit and squeezed the grease out of him and made him poor. "You stay in the woods," he said. After he had eaten the grease, he called out:

"Come on, my brothers, I want to tell you what you shall do; where you shall live and what you shall eat. You rabbits, eat sticks. You wolves eat all kinds of meat—ducks, gophers, chickens, buffalo—all kinds. Just the same, you coyotes, you eat all kinds of meat. You buffalo and all animals who have horns, eat grass. You elk, moose and blacktails eat sticks and grass and live in the mountains; you beavers eat sticks too, and live in the water; just the same you muskrats. You bears are too mean; you shall eat roots and hole up in the winter. But do not eat people meat. You must not kill people. All you birds eat the things on the ground. Do not eat meat except you crows. Hawks and eagles, you may eat meat."

5. *Wi-sak-a-chak and the Fox*

One day Wi-sak-a-chak was walking along the shore of a big lake. It was in the season of the year when the ducks and geese shed their feathers and cannot fly well. It was a dry season and the lake was low.

He went carefully through the brush so as not to frighten the birds; he had a large sack on his back. Finally, he came close to the edge of the water. "Ducks," he called.

"Wi-sak-a-chak, what have you got?" they called.

"Pa-so-kwa-pa-se-mo-na." (Blind dancing), he replied.

"You can't make a dance with us," said the ducks.

"All right," he answered, "I will make one." And he built a big long dance lodge with three fires—one in the middle and one at each end. Then he called, "Ho-he-oo! Astam Me-sem, come on all my brothers."

And they all came to the big pow-wow. All the ducks and geese came in from the lake and sat in the lodge. "I want to tell you something, my brothers," said Wi-sak-a-chak. "My dear brothers, I want to tell you something." And he began to sing.

"Pa-so-kwa-pa-se-mo-na Na-pa-che-wo-tan
Pa-so-kwa-pa-se-mo-na Na-pa-che-wo-tan"

All the ducks and geese began to dance. After a while he stopped singing and began to talk. The next time he sang, they danced the Blind Dance. Nobody looked; they danced with their eyes shut. The fat ones he made to dance on one side of the lodge and the poor ones on the other, and none of them saw what was going on for it was the Blind Dance. Wi-sak-a-chak sang and danced with them. He seized the fat ones and wrung their necks, and he killed a great many. But he did not kill the poor ones. Se-kep, the mud-hens, danced alone, and pretty soon they saw what Wi-sak-a-chak was doing. So they called, "Look out! Wi-sak-a-chak will kill us all." And they all ran for the lake. Wi-sak-a-chak ran after them seizing all he could and wringing their necks. He kicked the mud hens and broke their legs. That is why they have crooked legs today.

"I am hungry," he said. "I will make a great feast." So he made a big fire and put in all the birds he had killed. "I will walk around so that my belly will get very empty. I want to be plenty hungry." He had not gone far when he met a lame fox, who had hard work walking. "Fox, where are you going?" he asked.

"I am looking for something to eat," the Fox replied.

"I will run you a foot race," said Wi-sak-a-chak. "And the winner can eat all the ducks and geese which I am roasting."

"I can't run," answered the Fox, "for I am lame. I have a sore leg."

"Never mind, I will tie stones to my ankles." So Wi-sak-a-chak tied a large stone to each ankle.

"Which way shall I go?" asked the Fox.

"We will run around the lake to the place where the fire is. I will go around to the right. You can go the other way. It is shorter. I will go the long way because you are lame."

"Who-hoh!" yelled Wi-sak-a-chak, and they started. The poor fox could hardly run at all, and Wi-sak-a-chak laughed, but when he had got part way around he saw the fox running hard. Pretty soon he was out of sight; he reached the fire before Wi-sak-a-chak and ate all the birds. He ate everything but the legs. These he fixed up so that they stuck out the way they were, fixed the fire and went away. He felt good.

Before long, Wi-sak-a-chak came and everything looked all right.

241

"Ho, you big fool, to run a race with me. I am too fast," and he took hold of one of the legs which was sticking out of the fire. But it came out easily. "I cooked it too much," he said, and he seized another. It also came right out. Then he looked into the fire and found nothing, for the fox had eaten everything already. He was mad. "I will kill you, Fox," he cried, and he set out on the trail. And he cried because he had lost his meat. He tracked the Fox to his den, and found him apparently asleep. But the fox was watching from between his paws, and he saw Wi-sak-a-chak coming. Wi-sak-a-chak had in one hand a big club to kill the fox. "Hold on!" he said to himself; and with his other hand he took hold of the hand which held the club. "Hold on or you will spoil the skin. It will make a fine cap."

"Stop," he said, again holding back his hand. "Hold on. I will tell you something." So he started a fire all around the fox, but the fox was watching. When the fire got close to him, he got up and said, "I am sorry."

"You ate all my ducks and geese," Wi-sak-a-chak said. But the fox jumped through the fire and ran away, and he was not burned. Then Wi-sak-a-chak cried.

6. *Wi-sak-a-chak and the Wolves*

It was while his mother was still alive. One day, Wi-sak-a-chak left her. He went away. After travelling some time, he met some timber wolves, a great many of them.

"My brothers," he said, "which way are you going?"

"We are hunting," they answered.

"I will go with you," he said.

"All right," answered the wolves, "but we find it hard work to make a living." They were camping on a prairie.

After a while, one of the wolves said, "The best way to cover our brother is to lend him a robe to cover himself with." But Wi-sak-a-chak had no robe for himself.

"We will make a bed for our brother," said the wolves. "You can sleep with us." They slept in a circle with their tails together and some of them put their tails on Wi-sak-a-chak's back to make him warm. After a while one of the wolves said, "My brother, are you warm enough?"

"Yes," answered Wi-sak-a-chak. "I am warm now." But the wolves stank. "They stink, those wolves," muttered Wi-sak-a-chak to himself, for he slept close behind them.

Then one of the wolves asked, "Wi-sak-a-chak, what did you say?"

"I did not say anything," he answered. "I only said that my brothers have warm robes, good warm robes. That is what I said."

In the morning they went away together. About noon the wolves said, "Who is the best hunter?"

The chief man of the wolves was Wah-yo (no hair on the tail). One of the wolves started away on a moose trail. He followed it a short distance and killed the moose, and the others were behind with Wi-sak-a-chak. When Wi-sak-a-chak and his companions came to the place where the moose had been killed, they found nothing but blood and bones, no meat. The first wolves had eaten it all.

"You dirty thieves. You eat lots," said Wi-sak-a-chak. "What shall I eat?" 'What did you say?" asked one of the wolves.

"I said nothing," he answered. "I only said my brother is a pretty runner, that is what I said." For he covered what he said. He did not want the wolves to know that he spoke meanly of them. Then all the meat that the wolves had eaten came up out of their mouths. They made fresh meat.

After they had made camp, one of the wolves piled up some sticks and then jumped over them. They began to burn quickly. Wah-yo did it. That was the way he made fire. He was a good hunter. He was the head man of all the wolves. He was the chief. "Who can make some bone grease now?" he asked. "I can make bone grease", answered one of the wolves, and he began to chew the bones and make grease. "Do not look at me," he said. "Nobody shall watch me, while I make bone grease this way." And all the wolves held their heads down so as not to see him make the grease. But Wi-sak-a-chak watched him from under his arm, while he chewed the bones. And the wolf hit him over the eye with a bone. "Ooo," cried Wi-sak-a-chak, for he had been hit right over the eye.

"Ah! You were watching me," said the wolf. "That is the reason I hit you."

"Oh no, I was not watching you at all," said Wi-sak-a-chak.

The next morning, they went hunting again, and it happened just as it had the day before. The chief, Wah-yo, the great hunter, killed another moose. In the same way again, the others coming up, found nothing but blood and bones, as the first wolves had already eaten the meat.

"Who will make some bone grease now?" asked the chief.

"I will make some grease," answered Wi-sak-a-chak, and as he started, he said, "Let no one watch me. All my brothers, do not look at me. You must not see me while I make the grease." But one wolf, the one who made the grease the day before, watched him from under one leg, which he held up a little. Wi-sak-a-chak took a large bone and hit him on the ribs.

"Well, Wi-sak-a-chak, you hit me," said the wolf.

"I guess you were watching me. No one can watch me that way while I am making grease."

"Oh, no, I was not watching you," said the wolf, "but you hit me."

The next morning as they started out again, Wi-sak-a-chak said, "I think, my brothers, I will leave you. I am ashamed at what my brothers have told me. Show me that way you have for making fire."

"All right," answered the chief wolf, "I will give you just a few." And he gave Wi-sak-a-chak two trials to make fire that way. He gathered together a pile of sticks and jumped over it. That was the way he made fire.

After he had left the wolves, and walked a short distance, Wi-sak-a-chak shook himself. "I am very cold," he said. "I am very cold." So he collected a pile of sticks and jumped over it and made a fire. But he did not warm himself. He left the fire burning. He only wanted to know if he could make a fire that way. And he went on a little piece, not far, only a short distance, and he found a large heap of dry sticks, already piled up. The wind had done it, I guess. Well, he jumped over it that way again and made a fire. And he started on again. He jumped over, but they would not burn now.

It was all gone what (power) he had possessed. He did it three times, two times were good, but the third time was bad.

So he turned back to find the wolves again. And he cried. When he found the place where he had left them, he began to track them. But he could not catch them. He could not find them again, those wolves.

7. *Wi-sak-a-chak Robs an Old Man's Traps*

Wi-sak-a-chak was travelling. He was always travelling; he found a big dead tree, a poplar tree. "I think I can make something out of that tree," he said. So he made many things from the tree, a hunting knife, a long double-edged knife, a bow and arrows, an axe, a spear, and many other things. After they were all finished he sat down to think.

"I wish I could find something alive that I could fight with," he said. So he walked along the edge of a river. After a while, he saw a bear on the other side and the bear saw him. Then Wi-sak-a-chak yelled across the river to the bear, "Who is that over there with a crooked back?" That made the bear angry. She jumped into the river and swam across. Wi-sak-a-chak took off his leggings, moccasins, and robe. "Hah!" he cried, "If you want to fight, I am ready for you," and he jumped into the river. When he was near enough, he shot at her with his arrows, but they all broke. And the bear kept coming closer, and when he was about waist deep in the water they met and Wi-sak-a-chak seized her by the ear and struck her with his best knife. It broke and he threw it away. "If I had only one knife, you could kill me," he said, "but I have more." And he struck her with his other knife. It also broke. They all broke for that kind of wood was not good to make weapons of. The bear dragged Wi-sak-a-chak into shallow water; he still hung to her ear. He was getting tired now. When he got ashore he ran away leaving all of his things—leggings, moccasins, robe—everything. After a while he came to a small clump of bushes. He ran around it. The bear was still chasing him for she was angry. Pretty soon he saw the tip of a buffalo horn sticking out of the ground. The bear saw it too and jumped aside every time she passed it for she was afraid of it. Each time Wi-sak-a-chak ran around the bushes he kicked it. After the bear had chased him all day, the horn came out. Wi-sak-a-chak picked it up and held it against his head and ran towards the bear. "Now I will hook you," he cried. The bear became frightened and ran and Wi-sak-a-chak chased her. She looked around and saw him coming with the horn on her head. Finally Wi-sak-a-chak gave up the chase. "Hoh!" he said, "When did you ever see me with a horn on my head, you fool? I have no horn."

After he had gone some distance he found some timber wolves, ten of them. "My brothers," he said. "I would like to live with you because I am alone all the time. I want to see how you live." So he went along with the wolves. They came upon a large camp of Indians. The Indians made a great many traps to catch wolves and coyotes, and Wi-sak-a-chak was with the wolves.

In the morning an old man went out to look at his traps. He found nothing in them. Wi-sak-a-chak had picked down the traps so that the wolves could eat the meat. "I think some man has done that," said the old Indian.

"I can see his tracks. Some person is with the wolves. I guess it must be Wi-sak-a-chak. I will try to catch him."

That night when the wolves were howling, Wi-sak-a-chak howled too, like they did, "Hoo-o-o-o." The old man was listening.

When Wi-sak-a-chak howled he said, "I think that is not a wolf. It is some person. It must be Wi-sak-a-chak, surely."

Then Wi-sak-a-chak called out, "If you use fat meat for bait, I will go into the trap. You can catch me that way."

The old man watched his traps that night. He set a great many in the brush. There were a great many wolves. Someone was with them. The old man had a friend with him; they hid together in the snow among the bushes.

"I think that is Wi-sak-a-chak all right," said one.

Then Wi-sak-a-chak said, "Tas-dwa Me-sem" (hold on, my brother), and he took a stick and knocked down a trap. The old men then saw that it was surely Wi-sak-a-chak.

One took up his bow and arrows and said, "Is that you Wi-sak-a-chak? I want to shoot you." Then Wi-sak-a-chak was frightened.

"I will shoot you," said the old man. "What are you doing around here? You spoil all my traps and take my meat."

"Hold on, my brother," said Wi-sak-a-chak. "Hold on, I want to tell you something."

"Better get away or I will shoot you," said the old man.

"All right, my brothers," said Wi-sak-a-chak. "Maybe some time I will help you in some way," and he went away.

The old man went home. "We saw Wi-sak-a-chak just now." They told the others. "He did it. He broke down my traps and took my meat. He was with the wolves."

8. Wi-sak-a-chak Trades Berries for Feathers

There was a man who lived by himself and he had lots of berries. He would trade these berries for eagle feathers only; he would take nothing else. He seldom saw anybody. He had a fine lodge. A bow case and quiver was tied to each pole around the inside. For pegs he used eagle feathers, just tail feathers, and feathers stuck up from the outside all around the lodge. But he did not have enough; he wanted lots more but he did not know where to get them.

One day Wi-sak-a-chak came to this camp. But the man was not home, so Wi-sak-a-chak went into the lodge and sat down. Towards evening, pretty near night, the man returned. He came with a big black-tailed buck on his back. He left the deer outside end entered his lodge. He saw old Wi-sak-a-chak there but he did not talk to him at all. Wi-sak-a-chak was afraid. He thought this man was angry. Then the man untied a sack of berries and ate four of them. He did not talk to Wi-sak-a-chak at all. He did not even look at him. After a while the man made a sort of a jump and he rubbed one of his legs. Then he jumped again and rubbed his other leg. Then he jumped again and rubbed one arm. Then he made another jump and rubbed the other arm. Then he spoke to Wi-sak-a-chak, "Hello, my brother, you have come?"

And he shook hands with him. "Now, my brother," he said. "You go out and skin that deer and make a roast so we can eat." So Wi-sak-a-chak went out and skinned the deer and made a big roast. Then he said, "My brother, I would like to stay with you here."

The man said, "Yes, I will be glad to have you stay here with me. But you want to do right. Do you know where I can get some more eagle feathers?"

"Yes," answered Wi-sak-a-chak. "Sure, my brother, I know where you can get them. I know a girl who lives by herself, who has lots of feathers."

And the old man asked, "Well now, my brother, will you take some of these berries and go and make a trade for them?"

"All right, my brother, I will go," answered Wi-sak-a-chak. And the man gave him a little sack full of berries.

"When will you be back?" he asked.

"I don't know," answered Wi-sak-a-chak. "It is quite a long way off where that girl lives. I do not know when I will get back, but I will try to get here." So Wi-sak-a-chak started off. He had not gone very far when he stopped. "Oh my, but I am awfully tired," he said to himself. "I am going to try it. I am going to try some of these berries. I don't know whether it is true, when a person gets tired and eats some of those berries, it rests him. That is what my brother said. So I will try it now, right now. I am very tired." So he ate some of those berries. They tasted good. A while after he had eaten them, he began to jump, jump high. "Now," he said. "I can go. I can travel now. I am not tired at all. So those berries are all right. It was true, my brother was right. Now I will go." So finally he came to the lodge where the girl lived. "Oh hello, my sister, do you live here all by yourself?"

"Yes," she answered.

"How long have you lived here, my sister?"

And the girl said, "I do not know. As far back as I can remember, I was here. I am here yet."

"Now, my sister," said Wi-sak-a-chak, "you have lots of eagle feathers."

"Yes, I have a great many," said she.

"I came to make a trade with you. I brought some berries."

And the girl said, "What kind of berries?" and he showed her. "Yes, those are the kind; I have wanted some for a long time. I knew there were some, but I did not know where to get them. Come in, come in, my brother."

So Wi-sak-a-chak went into the lodge and he gave the girl a lot of berries, but he did not give her all he had; he kept some for himself. And the girl said, "Well, my brother, I will give you these feathers. I have many more but I give you lots of them." So she gave him lots of feathers and he started back, back to his brother's camp.

When he had travelled about half the distance, he said, "I am tired, I will eat these berries again." And he sat down to eat and he ate too many. He jumped so high that he lost all the feathers he had. Then he fell down and hurt himself, because he jumped so high. Then he started on. When he reached his brother's lodge, he was sick. "Oh, my brother," he said. "I am pretty near dead."

"What is wrong? What is the matter, my brother?"

"Oh," Wi-sak-a-chak said, "I had the eagle feathers; I found that girl's camp and when I was coming back, I met two Wes-tah-pa-wak (giants) and I fought them. They were pretty stout, my brother. Well, when I get better, I will go again. I will go after more feathers."

"Well all right, my brother, you can. You can go again when you get better."

So when Wi-sak-a-chak had recovered, he said, "Ho, my brother, I am all right now; I will go again." So the man gave him some berries; he gave him a different kind, not the kind he gave him the first time. So Wi-sak-a-chak started off with some berries again. When he had been on the trail for quite a time, he said, "My, but I am tired; I will eat some more berries. Maybe my brother gave me a different kind this time." So after he had eaten some of them, he found that they had a different taste altogether. They had a rather bitter taste, those berries. "I knew he wouldn't give me the right kind this time," said Wi-sak-a-chak as he continued his journey. "But I will go anyway." So he came to that girl's camp again and he gave her the berries.

"Have you got the same kind of berries this time?" she asked.

"Yes, I believe these are better ones."

"I will taste them first," the girl said. "I am afraid these are not the right kind."

Wi-sak-a-chak said, "You do not have to taste them, they are the same kind."

But the girl said, "I must. I have got to taste them. I must be sure you are giving me the same kind."

"They are the same kind, I tell you," said Wi-sak-a-chak. "I am not lying."

"No, I will taste them before I let you have those feathers."

"All right," said Wi-sak-a-chak. "Taste them." So the girl tasted them.

"These are a different kind altogether. They are not the same kind," the girl said. "I cannot give them to you. I will not give you any more feathers. I have given you some once already. I gave you lots. Then you come back with a different kind of berries and want some more. I cannot do it. You want to cheat me. What did you do with those feathers I gave you? You must have given them to someone."

He said, "Yes, they were not for me. I gave them to my grandfather. My grandfather wanted them."

"What does your grandfather do with those feathers?"

"Oh, he makes lots of arrows."

"And what does he do with those arrows?"

"Well, did you not hear of that war?"

"No, I hever heard of that war anywhere."

"Oh, there are lots of wars—that is—where my grandfather is going with his band of Indians."

"What is your grandfather's name?"

"Oh, my grandfather's name is Pe-kwat-ta-tao (Big Toad). That is my grandfather."

"Your grandfather cannot go anywhere. He cannot run. You tell him I will not let him have them. I do not like your grandfather. I would like to see him. I would kill him, your grandfather. He is the one who killed my father and my mother."

So Wi-sak-a-chak started off. He could get no more feathers. He went back and looked for the feathers he had lost. He found a few but some were nearly spoiled. At last he reached his brother's camp and brought the feathers and gave them to him.

"Oh, my brother," said the man. "These are no good."

"Well, they are the only kind the girl has now. She gave me the only kind."

"All right," said the man. "You do not have to go any more."

Then Wi-sak-a-chak said, "My brother, I am going away now. I am going to some other country. Someday I might meet you again." He shook hands with his brother and started off.

9. *Wi-sak-a-chak and the Chief's Daughter*

One day Wi-sak-a-chak was travelling along and he was alone. Finally, he came to a camp, a large camp of Indians. Some children were playing around the camp. He asked them who the chief was. The largest boy answered,

"This boy; his father is chief."

"Is that all?" asked Wi-sak-a-chak.

"No," answered the boy. "There are two other big chiefs, and there are others too, but the head chief is this boy's father."

So he went to the chief's lodge. He found out the chief had a pretty daughter, just one; he also had some sons. Wi-sak-a-chak then went away. Pretty soon he came to an old camp ground. It was very large. There used to be a great many Indians there. He found a small piece of robe. It was very old, and about as large as two fingers. He took it up and shook it. "Ho," he said. "I wish I had this when it was new." And then the robe was new. He did it when he shook it that way. Then he found a piece of tanned skin, buffalo skin. In the same way he picked it up and shook it. "I wish I had this when it was new," he said again, and it was new. He found a piece of a knife, the sharp edge. It was about as long as a finger. He picked it up and shook it in the same way. "I wish I had this when it was new." And he made it into a new one. Whenever he found things, he made them new in that way—a bow, arrows, and other things. He also found an old horse—so lame that he could hardly walk. Then he said, "I wish I had this horse at the time when he was young." And then he went to the camp again. He rubbed white mud and yellow mud onto the horse and made it into a pinto horse.

And he went to the camp again after that girl, the chief's daughter. He asked the chief to give him his daughter as his wife. It was the first time Wi-sak-a-chak had seen her in his life. The girl liked him for he was a fine appearing man, and he had a good horse and good clothes. So he got the girl and she went away with him. After they had gone a long distance, they camped and they started to make a bed.

Now Wi-sak-a-chak had scars on his rump. Everybody knows that. The girl saw them after he had gone to sleep, for he pulled his robe over his head and she saw the marks. "I think that is Wi-sak-a-chak," she said. "I think that is surely Wi-sak-a-chak."

"Is that you, Wi-sak-a-chak?" she called aloud.

"No," he answered, "I am not Wi-sak-a-chak. I am another man." But the girl knew that he was Wi-sak-a-chak and she drew her robe around her and set out towards home. She was crying.

"All right," said Wi-sak-a-chak. "I got a proud girl, the chief's daughter. I fixed her."

The girl went home to her father. When she came to his lodge, she said, "My father, you have caused me shame. You gave me to Wi-sak-a-chak, my body." But the people in the camp all laughed.

"That proud girl. She is married to Wi-sak-a-chak." And they all laughed because she had been so proud.

That is all.

10. How Wi-sak-a-chak Shamed the Chief's Daughter in Marriage

One day when Wi-sak-a-chak was walking through the woods he found an elk's head. It was full of maggots and flies were buzzing around. He sat down and watched them. "My brothers," he said. "What are you doing here?"

"This is the way we make our living and raise young ones," answered the flies.

"I would like to do what you are doing," he said. "Let me do that."

But the flies said, "It is very hard to do this. I would not do it."

"Never mind," said Wi-sak-a-chak. "Let me do it."

"All right," said the chief man of the flies, and Wi-sak-a-chak became very small and crawled up on the head back of the antlers. He began to buzz; after a while he ceased to hear anything. All the flies had gone, and the maggots too. They had grown up. Then he got up and shook himself; he was a man again. But he could not get his head out of the elk skull, so he walked along with the skull on his head. He held it up with his hands; he could not see anything. Pretty soon he came to a large camp; children were playing near by.

"He, he!" cried a boy. "A bull elk is coming."

For Wi-sak-a-chak walked right into the camp. He could not see anything. When he heard the children yell, he began to run and all the camp ran after him. "Chase him, chase him," they cried. He ran into a lake and swam like an elk. Some of the men ran around the shore to cut him off; the banks were rocky. When he got across he heard them yell and turned back again.

"Kill him, kill him," they called. As he was running back into the water he fell down. The skull struck on a rock so hard that it broke. Wi-sak-a-chak was free, but all his hair came out. He was very angry. "Hoh!" said the Indians. "We nearly shot you.

"I wanted to eat; that is the reason I got my head stuck," said Wi-sak-a-chak.

Then he went on until he came to another large camp. He saw some children playing around. He asked them where the chief was. "That is his lodge," they answered. "That big one in the center of the circle."

So he went into the tent, but the chief did not know he was Wi-sak-a-chak. "How my boy, where did you come from?"

"I came from far away," answered Wi-sak-a-chak. He had already seen the chief's daughter; she was a very pretty girl. The chief also had a son.

"What is your father's name?" asked the chief.

"I don't know. He was killed before I was born."

Wi-sak-a-chak liked the girl very much. He said to himself, "I think I will try and marry that girl." And he called the chief's son his brother-in-law. After he had gone out the young man said to his father, "I don't know why he called me his brother-in-law."

After a while Wi-sak-a-chak saw the young man alone. "I have two sisters," he said. "I wish you would come with me. I will give you my sisters, but I would like you to give me your sister."

"My sister does not belong to me," said the young man. "She belongs to my father and mother. Better ask them."

Now Wi-sak-a-chak had scars on his buttocks from the time he had burned himself. The chief noticed the scars. "I think that must be Wi-sak-a-chak."

"My brother-in-law," asked Wi-sak-a-chak. "what kind of meat does your father like best? What kind of animals?"

"I like bear meat best," answered the chief.

"All right," said Wi-sak-a-chak, and he started off hunting. He had not gone far when he found a hole, like an old badger hole. He stopped over it and kicked; then a small black bear came out. Wi-sak-a-chak knocked him down, and carried him back to the chief's lodge. He threw the bear down inside.

"Hi, hi!" (thank you) said the chief, and Wi-sak-a-chak sat there. He was proud because he had killed the bear. "Tell me, my brother-in-law," he said again, "what kind of meat does your father like best? I am a good hunter."

Finally the chief said to his wife, "What do you think about that young man?"

"I had rather not give my daughter to him," she answered.

"He is a good hunter," said the old man. "He can keep her well. I think I will give her to him. I have only one daughter, but I will give her to him."

"All right," said the old woman.

"I will help my daughter to him," said the chief. The girl was proud and at first did not want to marry Wi-sak-a-chak, but finally she consented.

"My wife," he said to her. "What would you like to eat? What kind of meat do you like best?"

"I like moose meat," the girl answered.

"All right, I will go hunting early in the morning. I can't go now; it is too late." That night he slept with his wife. Early in the morning he said to her, "I am going hunting now. Watch for me."

So he started off. He did not go far before killing a moose; he could do anything. He took the meat back to the lodge. "Here is that meat," he said as he threw it down. His wife boiled some Sas-kwa-toon berries for him; he ate alone for he was a proud chief now. The chief had given all his property to his son-in-law.

Wi-sak-a-chak lived with his wife for some time. He generally hunted all day and he came home at night. One morning the girl got up while Wi-sak-a-chak was still asleep. He had pulled the robe over his head, part of his body was bare, and she saw the scars on his buttocks. The scars from the burns. Then she woke him.

"Better get up and eat," she said. After he had eaten and gone away the girl went to her father. "I don't want to live with that fellow any more," she said.

"How is that?" asked her mother. "What is the trouble?"

"I think he is Wi-sak-a-chak. I saw the scars where he was burned."

Then the old woman said to her husband, "I think it is Wi-sak-a-chak surely."

And the girl was ashamed, because she had married Wi-sak-a-chak. "There were many good young men who wanted to marry me, but you would not give me to them. You gave me to Wi-sak-a-chak. I don't want to stay with him any more. I will kill him tonight; I will put an axe near my bed. After he is asleep, I will chop his head off."

But Wi-sak-a-chak suspected something, for he knew everything. He knew already what the girl had said. When he came in she began to joke with him. "This is the first time she ever acted that way," he thought. He went to bed and pretended to go to sleep, but he could see through his robe. Pretty soon she lifted the axe to strike him, but he struck it so that it fell to the ground without cutting him. "I am smart enough," he said and went out. "You bad girl I've got you already." She began to cry. The old woman cried too. She was sorry she had given her daughter to Wi-sak-a-chak. The chief's son was very angry.

"I will do the same thing to him; I will go to his camp and marry his sisters," he said. So he left his father and mother and went off to find Wi-sak-a-chak's sisters. After a while he found his mother's camp, but Wi-sak-a-chak was not there. The girls lived up in a very high tree that had been peeled off and was slippery. Anyone who could climb up to the girls could have them for his wife. The old woman had a long pole many times the length of a lodge pole which she used to put things up to the girls. So the young man came into the camp and asked about the girls. "If you want to talk with them," said their mother, "climb up there. You can have them if you can get them."

The tree was very slippery, but the young man started to climb. He had a sharp bone in each hand. At first he got along pretty well. The Wi-sak-a-chak came home. "Hoh!" he said. "Who is that fellow? What is he doing?"

"He is going up there to get your sisters," answered his mother. "He asked me and I gave them to him if he could get them. I am sure he cannot reach them. The tree is very high."

Wi-sak-a-chak blew on the tree and made it still higher. The young man was getting tired and the bones were making his hands sore. All at once he stopped and said to himself, "Now I remember, I can fly, but I don't know how far." Wi-sak-a-chak sat at the foot of the tree and looked up.

"Ha, ha!" he laughed. "Pretty soon he will come down, O-pe-pe-kwa-ka-na-ya-tak (Carry-Whistle-in-a-Bag). Surely, he cannot catch them."

But O-pe-pe-kwa-ka-na-ya-tak knew a great deal, like Wi-sak-a-chak. So he flew up and jumped into the place where the girls were. "Well," he said, "I have come after you. Wi-sak-a-chak gave you to me."

"I guess not," said one of the girls. "He did not know this about us, our brother."

"I have talked to your brother already. I want you to take off all your clothes. I am going to put you down." So he made them take off their clothes, and he dropped them down.

Wi-sak-a-chak looked up, "He-he-e-e, O-pe-pe-kwa-ka-na-ya-tak is coming down. You fool, you can never reach my sisters anyhow." Just then the girls dropped down near Wi-sak-a-chak, and they were naked. He got up and he was greatly ashamed for his sisters. He was very angry.

"O-pe-pe-kwa-ka-na-ya-tak," he cried. "I will kill you. For you have put me to shame by treating my sisters so." But O-pe-pe-kwa-ka-na-ya-tak flew back to his own country. Wi-sak-a-chak cried.

"My boy," his mother said. "Have nothing to do with that young man. Keep away from him or he will kill you. He has beaten you now and you cannot get the best of him anyhow."

"All right," he said. "I caused him shame for his sister. I treated him in the same way. I put him to shame first."

II

1. *Mas-to-sewa-kp-pe-ke-e-kat (He is Raised with Two Buffalos)*

One day they were moving camp. A dog was trotting along dragging a small boy on a travois. As they were passing some buffalos the dog ran away and disappeared among the herd, dragging the boy with him. The boy's father and mother hunted a long time, but could not find him. At night the dog came back, but there was no sign of the travois or the boy.

The parents cried, they were very sorry; they hunted everywhere for four days, but they could not find him. Then the man went to his father, who was chief of a big village. "My father," he said. "I have lost my poor boy; I have lost him for good."

But the boy was safe; he was alone on the prairie with two buffalo bulls. He rode on the head of one of them. The buffalos talked continually with the boy, and called him their grandchild. After a while one of the buffalos said, "My grandchild, are you hungry?"

"Yes," he said, "I am hungry."

So the old bull took a piece of cud out of his mouth, and mixed it with some Sask-wa-toon berries, and made some pemmican. "Eat that," he said.

Whenever the buffalos stopped, the boy jumped off and played around, climbing on them and sliding down their sides, but one of the old bulls did not like the boy very well; so one time when the boy jumped off his back he shook himself. Then the other bull said, "Don't do that my friend, make your heart good. He is so poor, the little boy, I like him first rate." And he said to the boy, "My grandchild, do you see anything?"

"No, nothing," he answered.

Then the old bull said, "I think there is somebody not far off, pretty close."

"No," said the boy. "I see nothing excepting a great many buffalos."

"That is what I mean," answered the bull, "the buffalos." After a while he spoke to the boy. "My grandchild, I am going to leave you. I am going among the buffalos, and make a big time among them. I am going to make a place for you to stay." And he made a kind of nest in the top of a big tree and made the boy climb up into it. "Don't come down," he warned. "Many girls, buffalo girls, will call you, maybe, to come down and have a good time. But don't come down. Stay where you are. Maybe after a couple of nights I will come and see you again, if I am not killed. Don't go any place. Stay in the nest." So the two buffalos went away and disappeared among the buffalos.

After a few nights two buffalo girls came along and stopped under the tree, and they called to the boy. "Better come down and we will have a good time together." But the boy answered nothing. "If you don't come down, I will knock the tree down," and she ran against the tree, and tried to shake the boy down. But she could not and soon went away. After that came four others. "You had better come down," called one. "I will take you for my sweetheart." The boy would not answer. "If you don't come down, I will knock you down," she said.

But the boy sat still on top of the tree, looking down. He was making a bow and some arrows. The cow hooked the tree so furiously that she knocked a piece off, and the boy began to be afraid. Then another cow said, "You high-toned boy, one of your grandfathers is killed already. One is alive," and they went on. A few days afterwards all the buffalos were gone.

Two nights after the buffalos had disappeared, one of the old bulls came back, the one who had been so kind to the boy. He was wounded and very thin for he had been fighting. "I think my grandfather is coming," said the boy.

When the bull was close under the tree, he looked up and said, "My grandchild, you had better come down, I am nearly dead; look at me; see how bad I am."

So the boy came down. "Where is my other grandfather?" he said.

"He was killed, the poor fellow is dead."

"Do you think you can show me where he is lying?" asked Mas-to-swa-ko-pe-ke-e-kat, for that was the boy's name.

"Yes, I can find it," answered the bull.

"Then show me where he is, my grandfather, for I want to go and see him." So they went and found him. He was full of maggots already. Mas-to-swa-ko-pe-ke-e-kat was very sorry, and he took lots of dirt and put it over the bull. Then he took an arrow and shot it straight into the air over the dead bull.

"Hoh! Get away from here, I might hit you. Look out, my grandfather," and the old bull got up and shook himself and walked around.

Mas-to-swa-ko-pe-ke-e-kat then went ahead to look for good grass for the old bull. Finally he found some. "My grandfather," he said, "better stay here; is plenty good grass."

After a while August came. It was beginning to be fall. One day one of the bulls said, "My poor grandchild, your father and mother are very poor. They have no clothes, no robes, no moccasins and no leggings, they cry for you. You had better go and see your father now, but I will give you something before you leave us." So he gave the boy a buffalo robe with the hoofs and horns on. "I want to tell you something," he continued. "Go straight that way, toward the rising sun. Go fast. Before sundown you will come to a steep hill. Go straight up to the top and then you will see a man. That is your father."

So the boy went as he was told and met a man on the hill, and he was crying. "My father," said Mas-to-swa-ko-pe-ke-e-kat. "Do not cry; I am your son." For when he was lost he was a small boy, but now he was a young man, so the father wiped the tears from his face and saw his son standing before him.

"He looks just like my boy," he said.

"My father, do not cry. Look at me now. My father, I want to tell you something. Do not let any women see me, only the men. Tell some of the young men to put up a lodge in a place where the women do not come; tell all the young men to come out and meet me."

And the man went home and said, "I have found my boy who was lost; he has come home." He told the chief, and he called out in a loud voice. "Listen! Listen! My grandchild is coming now. You young men go and meet him."

Mas-to-swa-ko-pe-ke-e-kat was among them and no woman saw him. After he had gone into the lodge, he said, "For four nights no woman must see me, not even my mother or my sister. Only the men." So he stayed in the lodges and ate nothing but Sask-wa-toon berries.

After sundown when he was sitting alone with his father, he said, "My father, get some fresh hay." So the man went out into the swamp and cut some fresh grass with his knife and took it back to the lodge. He put it down near the boy.

"My son wants to make a bed," he thought. Then he lay down to sleep before the door for he wanted to keep his boy. They two were alone in the lodge. Finally he was awakened by a sound like a bull eating, so he looked out from his blanket and saw a young bull eating the grass. For the boy had changed himself into a bull, but in the morning when he awoke he found him a man again, eating Sask-wa-toon berries.

"My father," he said. "Tell the Indians to make a pound."

So they built a pound and someone went after the buffalo, and a great many were driven into the pound. They killed them all for they were nearly starved. For three nights they did the same thing. One night Ma-che-ke-wes said to Mas-to-swa-ko-pe-ke-e-kat, "Ko-sak (a woman with two husbands) better come out; there is lots of fun at the pound, lots of good looking girls."

"No," he answered. "I will wait for one night more, I don't want to go now. After one night, all right, I will go."

"Better come with me tonight and see the girls," said Ma-che-ke-wes. "You can pick one out for your sweetheart."

Then the father said, "Better quit talking that way to my boy. After one night all right. Only one night."

254

But Mas-to-swa-ko-pe-ke-e-kat said, "All right, I will come out; I will take my bow and spear." So they went to the pound, and all the women and girls looked at him.

"Ho! He is fine looking, that young man. He is the best looking of all." But he walked along and hid his face in his robe. When he got to the pound he climbed up and sat on top; after a while he began to shake.

Then his father began to cry. "I found my boy; I think I shall lose him again."

A great many tried to hold the young man but they could not; he arose straight into the air. "My father," he said, "I am going to leave you, I am going to my grandfather. If you hear anyone talking of a person half bull and half man, it is I."

And they never saw him again.

2. Sta-pat and the Big Knife

Many winters ago an old chief lived among his people. His name was Sta-pat; he had four sons and two daughters. Although he was quite old he was still very strong and active, and he was very much feared by all the Indians. But he was so blood-thirsty and cruel that he had no friends; everybody hated him greatly and were always watching for a chance to kill him, but he was so wary and watchful that no one had yet dared attempt it. He had a very large knife with a long double-edged blade, which he always carried with him and with it he killed many people. It was a fine old knife and Sta-pat prized it greatly. It was elaborately decorated and from the handle dangled many kinds of feathers—eagle, hawk, swan and others.

When a hunter returned to camp with game, old Sta-pat always found it out for he never relaxed watching. He would go to the hunter's tent, cut off the best parts of the meat and carry them home. If the man made any objections the big knife would finish him. If the man had a very nice daughter, Sta-pat would take her and make her his wife, and no one dared say a word against it for fear of the great knife. So old Sta-pat had eight or nine wives and many of the young men were angry. Kam-set-awa-ses, or Big Child, was his eldest son and he helped his father in all that he did. But the youngest son had a good heart and did not like his father's ways, so one day he said, "No-ta-we (my father) you had better quit this business. I am sorry you have killed so many people already, for nothing. Nobody can be good friends with you, for their hearts are all bad towards you now." But these words only angered Sta-pat, and he would not listen to the good advice of his son. So Sta-pat ruled over his town with a heavy hand, and all his people would have been glad of a chance to kill him.

Finally some of the young men became restless. They had put up with too much from the old man. Two cousins lived in the village. They were brave young men and good hunters. Sta-pat had robbed them too often, so one day one of them said, "Mes-chas (my cousin), I will kill that old man. He killed my father."

So the young men took their weapons and went out and killed a fine fat moose. Then they prepared a great feast and cooked the best parts of the meat. Before the guests came they cached a bow and some arrows under a pile of blankets at the side of the lodge. Then the elder of the cousins said, "I don't want to go in. I will watch outside with my bow." So the other young man gave the feast alone. Pretty soon all the guests came and among them was Sta-pat.

When he saw that the elder cousin was not there he said to the other, "Where is your cousin?" and he was very angry.

"He is sick and stayed home in his lodge," answered the young man.

Then the old man got up and walked out of the tent, drew his great knife with the feathers hanging from the handle, held it up ready to strike and called out, "As-tam, As-tam, come out here, I want to kill you." And all the people were very much afraid. But just as he raised his arm, the young man who was waiting outside the tent, shot him in the side with an arrow. Sta-pat dropped his knife and fell to the ground.

"Come and help me," he called to his sons. But none of them would help him.

Even Big Child said, "I cannot help you, you have killed too many people already."

So Sta-pat died and not even his favorite son would help him or avenge his death. The youngest son was glad that his father was killed, and he gave many fine presents to the young man who killed him. He said to him, "I am glad. You cannot blame me. He did it himself. I will take you for my brother. I am not sorry you killed my father."

That is all.

3. *Ghost Story.*

There was quite a large camp. One man told his brother, "Let us move away from here. Let us go somewhere else and stay for the winter."

"All right," said his brother. So they went. There were three of them; the man and his wife and his brother. They had horses; they went a long way off from the camp and lived there. After the middle of winter, the younger of the brothers said, "I am very lonesome. Tell my sister-in-law to make me some moccasins. I am going away. I am going back to the camp we left." So the man told his wife to make some moccasins.

"My brother is going away. He is lonely."

So after his moccasins were finished, the young man packed his blanket and grub and started off. After nine days he came back to the camp. When he got there it was late. It was getting dark. He heard drums and singing and children playing, and he saw the lights of the camp; but when he got closer, he could see no lights and he could hear nothing. There was no more noise, so he stood around; he did not know what to do. Finally, he saw a light in one lodge, and he went in. There was a man lying down there. After a little while, he saw a boy enter. This little boy, when he came in, had some dried meat; he was going to roast it. So the man sat down and watched the boy—what he was doing. He roasted the dried meat and looked at the door once in a while. He talked but the man could not hear anyone answer him.

"Hold on, my cousin," the boy said. "Wait until I have roasted my dry meat. Then I will go out."

The man did not know what to do. There was something wrong. What was the matter with people who make no noise? After he was in the lodge awhile, he heard noise again; all the camp was talking and singing. He was pretty tired and went to sleep. In the morning he went out and looked around; he could see nothing; could hear nobody talk. He went back into the lodge and the boy woke up.

Then he asked the boy, "Boy, what is the matter with these people?"

And the boy said, "Everybody is dead except myself."

The man went around and taking the boy along, searched the whole camp. Sure enough, everybody was dead. Then he went to work to bury them. It took him quite a while to bury them all, for there were a great many of them. And so just the two of them lived there, he and the boy, and they did not know what to do. So they decided to stay until spring.

"There are lots of horses," said the boy. "If we can get them all, we will be all right. They are all over; nobody has looked after them since these people died."

At night time there was plenty of noise; they could hear the children playing, the women talking, and the men singing; but in the day time they could hear nothing. When they went about they could see nothing that could make a noise. Now spring came and the snow went off.

One night he heard someone say, "Now we will go home; get ready. We will go home." So he heard the people all over the camp; some talking, some singing, others crying; all kinds of noises, and they started off toward the south. The next night and after that the man never heard them any more. The ghosts had all left; no one was there but himself and the boy; just the two.

Then he told the boy, "Now we will go around and get all the horses we can find." So they went hunting horses, and they gathered all they could find.

"Now," said the man. "We will go and look for the other people."

"All right," said the boy. "We will go."

So the man rode on ahead and the boy followed, driving the horses. The first people he met were his brother and his wife.

When he saw the horses, his brother asked, "What is the matter? What is the trouble?"

And the young man said, "Do you remember the camp we left? Well, everybody is dead. There was no living person there, only this boy."

Then the older man said, "Well, we will have to find the other people and tell them that their relatives are dead." And he asked the boy, "What was the trouble? Of what kind of sickness did they die?"

"I do not know," answered the boy. "One night we all went to bed and the next morning when I got up there was no one living but I. Everybody was dead."

So they went to look for the other people and when they had found them, they told them, "Nobody belonging to that camp is living; all are dead." The people did not believe it, and they called the boy, and he told the whole story; how they all died but him. Now that is the last.

4. Wah-to-wo-wah-ses (And How Chiefs Came to be People and Not Animals)

There was a large camp. The Bear was chief. Everytime he heard of anyone having good meat, he sent his wife or daughters and said, "Get that meat. I want it." All the people were very poor. They could not get good meat to eat. Every time a man returned from hunting, the chief sent his wife or daughters to get the meat and fat and bring it to his lodge. So when any of the people had any good meat, they had to hide it.

One day an old woman was scraping a hide, a buffalo hide. She picked up all the scrapings (Wah-too) and made them into a ball and made soup of it. When she had done that she put some of the Wah-too inside her lodge. When she went back in she found a boy there in the lodge. "Hoh, my grandchild," she said. "You are Wa-to-wo-wah-ses," (he came for the scrapings).

He said right away, "I am hungry, my grandmother."

The old woman said, "Ah, my grandchild, I have nothing to give you; I am poor, I can hardly get anything and when I do, the Bear is here, the Chief."

The next morning the boy said, "My grandmother, give me some sinew. I am going to make some snares."

So the old woman gave it to him. Her lodge was full of holes. It was an old lodge. Wah-to-wo-wah-ses put a snare in every hole in the lodge.

After he had finished, he said, "My grandmother, go out and visit somewhere. Do not stay long. Come back pretty quick." So she went out. After a while Wah-to-wo-wah-ses took hold of one of the poles and shook the lodge. "Yoah, Yoah," he cried, and he caught a great many snow birds, lots of them; in every snare he caught one. Then he took them off.

When she returned, the old woman saw all the snow birds.

"Now, my grandmother, clean these birds," he said. "We will have a good feed. They are all fat," said the boy. So the old woman cleaned and boiled the birds.

"Now, my grandchild, we will have a good meal, something good," said she.

While the birds were boiling, the Bear smelled them. "Go over to that old woman's lodge," he told one of his daughters. "That old woman has something good. If there is anything there, bring it over. I want it. That old woman is not fit to eat anything good." So one of the girls went, one of the Bear's daughters. When she entered the lodge, she saw the snow birds boiling; the kettle was full.

"My grandmother," she said. "I am after your kettle here. My father sent me to get it." So the old woman told the girl to take it. When she reached her father's lodge, the Bear asked her what it was.

"Birds," said the girl, "and all fat. I saw a big boy in her lodge. I don't know where she got him."

After the girl had gone the old woman began to cry. But the boy, Wah-to-wo-wah-ses, said, "Do not cry, I will get them."

"Oh, my grandchild, do not go. The Bear will kill you."

"No," he said, "I will go. I will go and get them." So he went out, the boy, and went to the Chied Bear's lodge. He had a big lodge. He had two sons, grown men, and two daughters.

When Wah-to-wo-wah-ses entered the lodge, he told the Bear, "I came after my birds."

The Bear told his daughters, "Catch him and throw him out." So one of the girls threw him out. Then Was-to-wo-wah-ses got up and went into the lodge again.

"Say," he said. "I came after those birds. They belong to my grandmother."

And the Bear's older son said, "Better give them to him, my father. You had better give them to him. You do not know what kind of man he is."

But the Bear said, "No, I will not give them to him. They are too good. I will eat them myself." So he told his daughter, "Throw him out, throw him outdoors."

The girl said, "No, I will not do it; you must put him out yourself." So the Bear got up and seized the boy and threw him outside. Now, Wah-to-wo-wah-ses' nose was bleeding; he was bloody all over his face and breast; he had hardly any clothes. So he got up and went in again.

"I want those birds. I came after them. They belong to my grandmother. I am going to have them."

The chief's oldest son said, "My father, I tell you, you had better leave him alone. Let him have the birds."

"No, I will put him out this time, and he will not come back again."

Wah-to-wo-wah-ses was angry now, and when the Bear tried to catch him to throw him out again, he seized the Bear by the arm and broke his wrist.

Then the Bear quit and Wah-to-wo-wah-ses took the kettle and went out. The old woman was glad now, and they ate the birds. "My grandmother, the Bear made me angry and I broke his arm," said the boy.

Then the Bear's son said, "I told you, my father, to let him alone, but you would not heed me, and you see now what he has done to you. You have been Chief here for years and years and nobody has ever treated you like this before. Now you see what he has done to you that Wah-to-wo-wah-ses."

"My grandmother," said Wah-to-wo-wah-ses. "You go over and see Chief Bear and tell him if he will give me one of his daughters, I will doctor him. I will fix his arm." But the old woman did not want to go. She was afraid of the Bear. "You go over there," he said. "If he hurts you, I will kill him." So the old woman went. The Chief was suffering from his wrist which was broken, and the old woman went into the lodge.

"My grandchild sent me here. He told me to tell you that if you would give him one of your daughters, he would fix your wrist," said the old woman.

"All right," said the Bear. "I will give him one of my girls." So Wah-to-wo-wah-ses went to doctor the Bear. He went into the lodge and took hold of the Bear's arm and rubbed it a couple of times and the Bear was well.

"Which one of my daughters do you want," he asked. "Either one who wants me," he answered.

The older girl said, "I do not want him, I do not want any Wah-to-wo-wah-ses. I do not like him because he has a big belly and a big head."

"I will take him," the younger girl said. "I do not care if he has a big belly."

So he married Chief Bear's daughter, Wah-to-wo-wah-ses, and he did every-thing he could think of to make the girl angry. When he saw he could not anger her, he told her, "Tomorrow you make a sweat lodge and when you have finished, tell me, for I want to take a sweat bath." So the next day his wife made a sweat lodge, and told him when it was ready. "Try and get me a piece of otter skin," he told her. "Even a small piece will do." So she asked her father for a piece.

"Have you a piece of otter skin?"

"Yes, I have," answered the Bear. "What do you want with it?"

"Your son-in-law wants it, just a little piece." And so he gave it to her, because he was afraid of Wah-to-wo-wah-ses.

Then Wah-to-wo-wah-ses went into the sweat lodge and he told his wife, "Get me your father's rattle. I want to sing."

She went to her Father's lodge and said, "Wah-to-wo-wah-ses wants your rattle, that good one." So the Bear gave his daughter the rattle.

"All right," he said.

Then she gave the rattle to her husband and he went into the sweat lodge and started to sing. He was making medicine; he made some clothes for him-self. From that piece of otter skin which he had, he made everything—leggings, shirt, robe, bow case and quiver—all cut of that piece of otter skin. When he had finished, he said to his wife, "Open up the lodge." When he came out his wife saw a fine looking man. He was not too dark and he had long hair and he put on his otter skin clothes.

Then he told the Bear, "Now, I will go out. These people are all too poor. I am going to get some buffalo. When they are all killed, those buffalo, you must not do what you have been accustomed to do heretofore."

So Wah-to-wo-wah-ses started out. After a while he returned driving a bunch of buffalo and he drove them into a corral, Pe-te-ko-han. Everybody helped himself. Chief Bear did not get everything now.

Then Wah-to-wo-wah-ses said, "Now, Bear, you will be a bear no longer. You will be a person like the rest of them. When you were Chief, the people were poor all the time. After this there will be a chief from among the people. You will be a Bear no longer." For in those days the Chiefs were animals, like the bear, wolf and others. After this, people were chiefs.

5. *Mis-ta-ta-o-wa-ses (Big Belly Boy)*

Far up in the North Country there was a large camp. The head chief was very powerful and everyone feared him. He had two daughters and a son, the son was the youngest.

It was winter and all the people were very hungry, for the hunting was poor.

One day the chief said, "I am going to pull out. I am going to a place where the hunting is better, so they broke camp. But all did not go. One woman who was about to give birth to a child was left behind in the deserted camp. The camp was in a clearing and there were woods all around. A few days afterwards a boy was born. He grew very fast; one day he fixed some sticks like arrows.

"Don't go away," his mother told him. "Stay near me." So he played around the camp and when he wandered towards the woods his mother would call, "Don't go that way."

"I don't know why my mother won't let me go any farther," he said, but he played around and kept close to his mother.

One day, however, he said, "I am going to see the place my mother keeps me from." So he went into the woods. He looked around and came back.

Once he asked, "My mother, have you lived alone always?"

"No," she answered.

"Who camped here then? It looks like a camp circle."

"There used to be many people around here."

"Where have they gone, those people?" he asked again.

'The last time I saw them, they were going towards the west," answered his mother.

"My mother," he said. "Let us go and camp in the woods." So they moved their lodge into the brush. The next morning the boy said, "My mother, if you will help me I will make a pound." So they made a pound. Every morning the boy went out and blew his whistle and all kinds of animals came into the pound—buffalo, elk, antelope and deer. They all came into the pound when he whistled; they killed the animals and made lots of dried meat and pemmican. Then the boy said, "My mother, I guess you have enough food now. I am going to leave you; I am going to find those people."

His mother began to cry. "Better stay home," she said. "Maybe you will freeze to death, winter is coming on."

But the boy said, "My mother, I am going to make you a kind of stone lodge." He took a little round stone and blew on it; it soon became very large—as large as a lodge. Then he put all the food inside.

"My mother, go in," he said, so she went in, and she was crying. "Well, my mother, I am going to put that big flat stone up for a door; nobody can take it away but I. I am going to leave you for good. Maybe, if I live, I will come and see you once."

So he started away next morning. He travelled towards the West. He had camped twice. It was morning. He was walking along when he heard something behind him; he looked around and saw a crow, so he said to the crow, "Tell me where are those people?"

"I am going that way, follow me," answered the crow and flew on towards the west. The boy followed but soon lost sight of him.

When it was nearly sundown he saw the crow on the top of a hill. It was the same crow, but he flew off again towards the west. Now the sun had nearly sunk out of sight; the boy found a feather which had dropped from the crow. Pretty soon he came to some woods; it was dark and he could no longer see, so he camped. It was cold that night and snow fell.

In the morning he saw some old tracks which were nearly covered by the snow. He put his feet into the tracks. "He has the same kind of feet as I have," he said, but soon he lost the tracks for it snowed all day. He was walking along with his head down when he saw a weasel near his feet looking up at him.

"Hoh," said the weasel. "Here is my friend. Come with me to my place."

So the boy followed him. He saw a great many holes and weasel tracks in the bushes.

"What will I do?" he asked. "The holes are too small, I cannot go in."

"Close your eyes and don't open them," the weasel said. So he closed his eyes.

Shortly after, the weasel said, "My friend come inside." When he opened his eyes he found himself in a great lodge, and there were an old man and his wife and ten sons, twelve in all. "I want you to stay here four nights," the old weasel man told him. Then they all began to sing; the old man gave him a great many presents—a bow and arrows, a buffalo robe, leggings fringed with winter weasel skins, horn head dress and other things. After four nights another old man came into the lodge. "I want you to stay four nights with me, I will give you many presents and clothes."

"I am glad you will give me many things," said the boy.

"All right," said the old man. "I will take you for my son." The youngest son of the weasel family said to him, "I know well that you want to get married, you are looking around for a girl."

After he had stayed there four nights the boy said, "I am going now. I will see you again, my father."

So he started out again. Finally he came to a large camp. It was the same village to which his mother had belonged. He cached the things which the weasel people had given him in the snow among the bushes. Just outside the big camp he saw a little old lodge. It was full of holes; an old woman lived there all alone; he went into the lodge and stayed with the old woman until it got dark.

Then she said, "My Grandchild, better go home, it is too dark."

"My Grandmother," he said. "I have no home. Where I sleep is my home."

Then she took him in her arms. "My poor child," she said, for he was still very small, although he knew as much as a man.

He saw the chief's big lodge in the center of the circle, and someone was singing there. "How is that?" he asked. "They sing every night now."

"The chief does it," she answered.

"What is he making, that he sings that way?"

"The hunting is poor; everybody is hungry. The chief will give his daughter to anyone who brings any animals into the pound—buffalo, elk, deer or any kind of animal."

"I can get some buffalo myself," said the boy.

He was still very small, and the old woman said to him, "Don't go anywhere, my grandchild, maybe you will freeze out there."

In the night he said, "My grandmother, I am hungry."

"My poor child," she said. "Don't talk that way. You make me feel sorry. You make me cry," and the old woman began to cry.

In the morning, the boy said, "My grandmother, better get some wood. There is not much left." After she got ready he asked, "My Grandmother, have you any sinew?"

"Yes, I have some. I will give you half." She thought he wanted to eat it.

And he made little nets out of the sinew over all the holes in the lodge. He went outside the door and blew his whistle and a great many little snowbirds flew into the tent. When they tried to fly out of the holes they were caught by the neck in the sinew nets. He cleaned them quickly and put them in the kettle to boil. There were enough for them to eat twice; after a while the old woman came in with the wood. "My Grandmother, come in and eat; I am hungry."

Then she began to cry. "I wonder where I can get something to eat," she said.

After they had eaten a part of the birds, she wanted to save some for the next meal. "No, no, my Grandmother," the boy said. "Eat it all now. I will kill some more." Then they heard the singing again. "I am going to see the chief," the boy said.

"No, better not, he is a great chief. He is high toned, he might put you out."

"I am going anyhow," so he went to the chief's tent. He opened the door and looked in. The chief's son was lying against some robes, fixing Sask-wa-toon berries in a wooden dish. All the rest were singing. Then he went in; he went to the back of the lodge in front of the chief's son. "What have you there?" he asked, and he took up the dish and drank.

One of the men tried to put him out, but the chief's son said, "Never mind the poor boy." Then the boy went out. That was a sign that he was going to kill something.

When he got back to the old woman's tent he said, "My Grandmother, I am going out tomorrow and kill some buffalo."

"My grandchild," she said. "Better stay here maybe. If you go out you will freeze somewhere on the prairie."

"No," he answered. Before he went to sleep he said, "My Grandmother, after you get up in the morning, better tell the chief that I have gone to fetch some buffalo." And the old woman put her arms around him after he had gone to sleep. In the morning the boy got up, put his calfskin robe around him and went back to his cache. He put on the clothes that the weasel people had given him. He was a large boy now. The old woman was still asleep and knew nothing of what the boy was doing.

At sunrise a man from the camp went up on a hill to sing. "Wa-yah!" he said. "Lots of buffalo are coming." The whole camp was still asleep, but they were soon up when they heard that the buffalo were coming. They looked out on the prairie and saw them coming in a bunch. Someone was running along on foot driving them. After they had all gone into the pound the boy came around to his cache. He put away his good clothes and put on his old ones.

The chief thought his singing had brought the buffalo. The boy asked the people who had brought the buffalo.

"The chief did it," they answered.

The chief gave the old woman an old cow. It was nothing but skin and bones. He kept the best for himself and the other people. After the boy had helped the old woman carry the meat to the tent he said, "How is it that you did not take one of the best cows?"

"That is the only one the chief would give me."

"Never mind, my Grandmother, bring some clean grass from the swamp where the people have not trodden it down."

Before she went he had her pile the meat on one side of the lodge and cover it over with the hide. Then he got four pointed sticks. He painted each stick half red and half black. Two of them had black butts and red tips; the other two had red butts and black tips. He then took up the four sticks and struck the hide four times with the butts and four times with the tips.

Pretty soon the old woman returned. "Come in, my grandmother and see your meat," he said. So the old woman came in and turned back the hide. It was all tanned fine and soft. The meat was all fat.

"Where did you get that?" she asked. "I think some kind hearted woman tanned it for me." That night there was a great feast, and the people were no longer hungry. "Now, I am going to tell the chief that I will do it again tomorrow," said the boy, and the next morning he started out again.

When the old woman got up she missed the boy. "I am ashamed for talking that way about him; that he can't do anything for he is too small," she said to herself. Then she to the chief. "I want to tell you something."

"All right," he said. "Tell me what you want to tell me."

"My little grandchild, he has gone after more buffalo, the same boy who brought them yesterday. He has gone after them again."

At sunrise the same man went up on the hill again. He saw a great many buffalo. Then the chief came out and began to talk. "Listen my friends, I want to talk a little. This old woman's grandchild, the same boy who brought the buffalo yesterday, has gone to fetch some more." That is the way he talked; he talked loudly. All the people were watching now, for many buffalo went into the pound. After they had skinned all the cows, the chief said, "Say, my daughters, better get ready. Take all your robes and clothes and moccasins and marry that boy."

The chief's son then gave plenty clothes and many present to the boy, and he called him, "Mes-ta-ta-o-wa-ses" (Big Belly Boy). The chief gave him a big new lodge near the center of the circle.

The chief's boy said, "Now I will stay with my brother-in-law." That night when it was time to go to bed they put up the Indian bed. Mes-ta-ta-o-wa-ses lay down between his wives, the older one on the left, and the younger on the right. But the older girl did not like her husband and she moved as far away from him as she could. The younger slept close, so he said to the young girl.

"I think your sister doesn't like me very well."

"That girl is foolish," she replied. "I am going to do something to her," he said, so he defecated in the bed.

"Oh, you dirty boy," said the older girl. "Many nice young men wanted to marry me, but my father would not let them."

Then they cleaned the bed, the older girl left and went home to her father. "I won't be married to him," she said. "He acts awfully."

Then Mes-ta-ta-o-wa-ses said to his wife, "Tell me if you like me. Tell me truly."

"I don't care if you defecate in the bed again, I will wash the bed. I will stay with you," she replied.

In the morning he said, "Make me a sweat lodge."

"All right," said the girl, and she made a sweat lodge. She put a lot of stones in it and poured some clean water on them, and they both went in, but the older girl would not go. She stayed with the father.

Then Mes-ta-ta-o-wa-ses said, "I am going to change it now." He began to sing and wash himself. He washed his face and hands with clean water, also his wife. Then he passed his hands over his wife's hair, and said, "I wish my wife had long hair and myself too. I wish my wife to be nice looking, not big; not tall, medium. Just the same myself." When they came out of the sweat house they were both fine looking. Mes-ta-ta-o-wa-ses was grown up now.

Then he said, "My wife, I am going to do this way. I am going after buffalo. Tell your father. If you see anyone come to the front of the lodge on the east side, it is I. Don't be ashamed. Come to me. If you are ashamed, you will kill me."

In the morning all the Indians were yelling. Someone was coming behind the buffalo. The girl saw a man coming on the east side of the front of the pound. He had a bow and spear, "I don't believe it is my husband," she said. "He is too fine looking. I am not ashamed." She had made some Sask-wa-toon berry[1] drink for her husband. She had put it over some burning sweetgrass to give it a sweet flavor. As he came along he was the finest looking man of all.

She went up to him, "Take this," she said and she handed him the bowl of drink.

"Come up here and sit by me," he said.

"I can't, it is too high." He held out his hand, she took it and he lifted her up, and set her to his left.

Then the older girl said to her father, "Give me some Sask-wa-toon berries. I will give it to my husband."

"Better not," said the chief. "You don't like him. He makes you ashamed."

"Never mind," she said.

"Then take some other berries; I don't like to spoil Sask-wa-toon berries."

When she got the drink made she went to Mes-ta-ta-o-wa-ses. "Take this," she said. "Help me to get up."

"I won't help you," he answered. "Come up. You have hands." She climbed half way up and then fell and spilled the berries all over herself.

"Why not take me up?" she said. "I spilled all the berries for nothing."

"Give me an arrow," he said to his wife. "Now what would you like to make a robe of, a cow or a bull?"

"A yearling bull," she replied.

"All right," he said, and he gave his wife the bow and arrow.

"No, I can't kill it," she said, but she shot the bull and killed him.

Then the older girl said, "Let me do that too."

"No," said Mes-ta-ta-o-wa-ses. "I will kill one for you, you can't kill one." As the buffalo ran around, he killed an old bull. "Skin it," he told her,

---

[1] The Sask-wa-toon berries mentioned in this story as well as in several of the other narratives, are the ones referred to as service berries (Amelanchier alnifolia).

but he helped his other wife, and they carried the skin and meat to their lodge. Everyone was praising him.

"You had better go away for awhile," he told his wife. Then he hung the hide on a string in the lodge. He used his sticks again, and the hide was tanned.

Mes-ta-ta-o-wa-ses lived for some time with his wife in this village. Finally a boy was born, but he became gloomy. He would sit all day leaning over looking at the ground without speaking. He was thinking of his mother, whom he had left.

"You make me sorry," his wife said. "You never talk."

"I am sorry for my mother," he replied. "I am going back."

"I am going with you," she said.

"No, I don't want you to go with me. I will come back after a while."

So he started back, but his wife followed him. The baby was crying for his father. He saw them and waited, "Better go home," he said.

"No, I like you too much."

"Well, if you like me so much I will tell you something. I am going through a narrow pass. If you see anything don't be frightened; don't look behind, maybe you will meet something." When she passed by some high rocks a big buffalo came and tried to hook her. Mes-ta-ta-o-wa-ses had changed himself into a buffalo. The woman was frightened.

"Ah, hah!" cried her husband. "Once more I will try you, don't be frightened." So again they came to a narrow place in the trail. A big bear came towards the woman. He was walking on his hind legs. This time also, the woman was frightened.

"You are foolish," said her husband. "I can do nothing, my boy, I leave him. You know what I have done. Just the same my boy, you cannot stay with me any longer. I am going." The woman cried and Mes-ta-ta-o-wa-ses disappeared in the sky.

APPENDIX B

Language

It may be somewhat surprising to find, in a treatise such as this one, a section on the language of the Cree. Instead, however, of its being a discussion of language from the linguistic point of view, I shall treat here some of the material concerning the written form, for it has certain religious overtones. Since the Cree are the only Plains tribe with a written language, it is worthwhile, I think, to see how it developed. The Cree account differs entirely from that of the published sources.

In the beginning, there was only one Indian language and all of the people everywhere spoke it. That language was Cree. A verification came not too many years ago when a Blood Indian died and went to the land of the dead. He had known the Cree here on earth and could understand their language. His spirit came back to the earth some time after his death and told his relatives and friends that the only language spoken in the land of the dead was Cree, and for all of the Indians here to learn Cree while they were living if they wished to be able to understand the language in the hereafter.[1]

According to the Montana Cree, the spirits came to one good man and gave him some songs. When he had mastered them, they taught him how to make a type of ink and then showed him how to write on white birch bark. He was told that he must not put down any bad words, for there was great power in his writing. Hence he must exercise every care in the subject matter that he wrote. For a long time, he possessed this ability to write and guarded his secret carefully.

The man grew old. Finally, another spirit came to him and gave him further instruction. This spirit wrote down the names or the initials of all the spirits. When that was done, the spirit showed the old man how to make a little book out of birch bark and how to fasten it onto a piece of wood. In this book, the old man wrote what amounted to a Cree Bible under the direction of the spirit. He recorded all of the things that had happened from the time of Creation down to the present. He faithfully detailed all of the teachings of *Ki-sei-men'-to* so that there was a record of how the Creator wanted His people to live properly. Toward the end of the instruction period, the spirit mentioned the Wind and said that the Wind was the last of the strong spirits. It can teach man many things, said the spirit, who also warned that the Wind can destroy. The old man put all this material together in his little birch-bark book and returned to his people. From time to time on his way home, he stopped and read all of the material.

---

[1] Personal interview, Raining Bird, December 30, 1959.

CREE LANGUAGE
TABLE OF CHARACTERS

INITIAL OR PRIMALS

▽	△	▷	◁
e	i	o	a

2. MEDIALS

∨	∧	>	<
Pe	Pi	Po	Pa
U	∩	⊃	⊂
te	ti	to	ta
ᚅ	ᚏ	J	ᒐ
tʃe	tʃi	tʃo	tʃa
ᖃ	P	ᑯ	b
ke	ki	ko	ka
ᒋ	Γ	⌐	L
me	mi	mo	ma
ᓀ	σ	ᓄ	ᓇ
ne	ni	no	na
ᔑ	ᒥ	ᔈ	ᔈ
se	si	so	sa
ᐸ	ᐳ	ᐻ	ᐳ
je	ji	jo	ja

3. FINALS OR TERMINALS

m	⊂	P	l	ai	ᔈ
n	⊃	+	/	ov	o
s	∩	k	ᔈ	ASPIRATE	‖
h	–	ʃ	z		

FIGURE 3. Cree Script showing the syllabic form of their writing. The characters are from Peeso's unpublished manuscript and from my own informants. Symbols for pronunciation are those of the international phonetic alphabet.

When the old man returned to his camp, he taught the people how to read and write. The Cree were very pleased with their new accomplishment, for by now the white men were in this country. The Cree knew that the white traders could read and write, so now they felt that they too were able to communicate among themselves just as well as did their white neighbors. More than that, they were particularly proud of this splendid record, directly from a spirit who had dictated the teachings of *Ki-sei-men'-to*.

Time went on. The old man died. Before his death, however, he gave his book to one of his friends. No one knows just what happened from then on, but some years later a half breed secured the book, took it to the missionaries, and read the material in it to them. The missionaries dismissed the good teachings contemptuously and were interested only in learning how to read and write the text. The half breed, who could read the script, taught the missionaries the form. Soon, the missionaries began using this method to write down their Bible, and then started teaching that material to the Cree. Some time later, the same white people claimed that they had invented the form of writing that the Cree use. "That is not so," says Raining Bird

<ᒉ ᐊᐳᐣᏫᔦ ᓂᐧᐁᐧᐤ ᐁ ᒪᕒᐊᐧᑕᐦᐊᑐᐦᐧᐃᐧ ᐤᔦᔦᐳᓂᐊᕐᐞ

ᒫᑫᓇᑭᐧᐳᐟ ᓂᐦᒉᕒᐧ

1 ᐧᐁᔦ, ᑦᐂᐣᐣᒪᐦ, ᑰᐊ ᓂᒧᓐᐊᐦ, (ᐤ ᒪᕒᐊᐧ-
ᐊᒪᐧᐅᐦᑊ) ᐊᓓᐊ ᐤᔦᔦᐳᓂᐊᐧᐊ ᐅᑭᔦᕒᐧᐊᐧᐊ ᐳᐦ-
ᓚᐳᐟ ᑫ ᐊᔦᔦᑊᐦ ᑫ ᒑᐅᐨᐊᐤ, ᑦᐊ ᑫ ᓂᐤᔦᐦᕒᐧ
ᓇᐧᐃᐧ ᓂᐦᔦᐦᐧ ᑫᐧᐞᐧᐞᐧ:

2 ᒐᕒᑫᒪᐧᐃᐧᐧ ᑭ ᑫ ᐊᔦᑫᐧᐤ, ᑦᐊ ᑭᔦᐣ-
ᐃᐧᐞᐧᐞᐧ ᐳᐦᓚᐳᐟ ᑫ ᒑᐅᐨᐊᐤ ᐅᐧᐞᐧ, ᑦᐊ ᑫ
ᓇᐧᐃᐧᐤᐢᐧᐞᐧ ᓂᐦᔦᐧ ᑫᐧᐞᐧᐞᐧᐧ:

3 ᐃᑫᓈᐤᐧ ᒐᕒᐊᐧ ᒍᐦᔦᐧ ᑫ ᐊᐦᓈᑊᒪᐧᐞᐧ
ᐳᐦᓚᐳᐟ ᑭᔦᐊᐧᐤ ᐊᐧᐞᐧ, ᒐᕒᐊᐠᐣᐢᐧ, ᑓᐞᐧᐧ ᑫ
ᐊᐧᐞ ᐤᐞᐧ ᐊᐣᐞᐧᐞᐧᐢᐧᐞᐧᐞᐢᐤᐧᐞᐢᐤᐧ, ᑭᐧᐞᐧ ᑭ ᒐᐧᐞᐢᐤᐧᐦ-
ᒍᒐᐧᐣᐧᐧᐞᐤ ᐊᐦᐣᐦᐤ ᐤ ᐳᓂᐊᐳᐢᐧᐤ, ᑦᐊ ᐊᓕᐧ
ᐤ ᐊᐧᐞ ᐦᐧᐧᐞᐤᐧ ᑫᐤᐞᐧᐞ ᑫ ᐃᑭᔦᐞᐧᐞᐤ ᐤ ᐤᐧᐞᐧ-
ᕒᐸᐧᐣᐧ;

4 ᐤᐞᑦ ᒫᑫ ᒐᕒᐊᐧᐤ ᓇᐦᔦᐤᐧ ᑭ ᒪᒪᐧᐨᐞᐊᐊᐤ
ᐳᐦᓚᐳᐟ ᐅ ᐨᔦᕒᐧᐊᐧᐢᐧᐞᐢᐤᐧ, ᑭ ᑦᐤᐊᐧᐞᐤᐧᒍᐊᐧᐢ-
ᓂᐊᐧᐞᐧᐞ ᐊᐧᐞ ᑦᐊ ᑭ ᒐᐧᐞᐢᐤᐧᐞᐢᐤᒍᐊᐧᐞᐢᐤᐊᐧᐞᐢᐧᐞ.ᐞᐧᐞᐞᐤ
ᐞᐧᐧ<ᒐᐣᐞᐊᐧᐞ ᑦᐊ ᐊᔦᕒᐞᐊᐧᐞᐢ ᐊᓃ ᑫ ᐊᐧᐞ
ᐊᐳᐣᑫᐢᐧ;

5 ᐊᓂᓃ ᑫ <ᐦᐨᐅᐊᑊᐢᐞ ᐤ ᐳᐣᐳᐊᐞᑦᒉᐊᐧᐞᐢ
ᐊᓂᓃ ᐳᐦᓚᐳᐟ ᑫᐞᐤᐧ ᐅᐣᐧᐤᐤ·ᐊᕒᐊᐧ· ᐅᐊᐧᐣ-
ᐞᐞᐧᐤ·ᐧᐞ, ᑫᐨ ᐤᐊ ᐊᐣᐞᐧᐅᕒᑫᐊ·ᐠᐧ ᐳᔦ-
ᓚᐳᐟ ᐅ ᒍᐊᐧᐊ·ᐊ·ᐣᐧᐢ, ᐊᓂᓃ ᑭᐞᐊᐧᐞᐤ ᑫ ᐅᐞᐞᐦ
ᐞᐞ·ᐨᐞᐞᐥᐤᐣ:

6 ᐤ ᐊᐞᐨᐞᐞᐢᐤᐤ ᐊᓂᓃ ᐤ ᕒᐤ·ᐦᐞᐤᐠ ᐳᐞ-
ᓚᐳᐟ ᑭᑭ ᓇᐨᐊᐧᐊᑫᐞᐧ ᐊᐞᕒᐞᐞᐤᐧ ᐊᓂᐳ ᑫ
ᕒᐞᐣᐤᕒᐞᐞᐢᑭᑫᐞ·ᐤ:

7 ᑭᐞᐊᐞ ᒫᑫ ᐨᐣ ᑫ ᐊᐞᕒᐞᐊᐞᐊᐢ·ᐊᐢ ᑭ
ᐊᐞᕒ ᐊᐞᐞᐊᕒᐊᐞ, ᐊᐣᐪᐦ ᑫ ᓇᐧᐞᐞᐞᐞᐞᐦᐞᐞᐧ ᐞᐞᐧᐞᐞ
ᐞᐞᕒᐳᐞᐞᐢᐧ ᑫ ᐤᐊᐞᐤ·ᐞᐞᐞ·ᐞᐤ ᑫ ᐤᐤᐦᐣᐞᐞᐧ· ᐅ ᐞᐞᕒ
ᐤᐞᕒᐞᐊᐧ,

8 ᐤᑫᐦᑊᐤᐥ ᐊᐣᐤᐤᐥ ᑫ ᐅᐣᐞᐞᑊ ᐳᐞᐊᐞ·ᐞᐞᐤ·ᐞᐞᐤ
ᐊᐞᐳ ᐤᑫ ᑫ ᐳᐣᐊᐢᐞᑊ ᐳᐦᓚᐳᐨᐞᐞ·, ᑦᐊ ᐊᐞᐳ
ᐤᑫ ᑫ ᒐᐧᐞᐢᐤᐧᐞᑊ ᐅ ᕒᐞᐞᐞᐊᐞᐞᐤ ᑭ ᓇᐧᐞᐞᐞᐞᐞ-
ᕒᐞᐞ ᐞᐞᕒ ᐞᐞᐤᐞᐞᐞ:

9 ᐊᐳᑭ ᐞᐞ ᑫ·ᐨᐞᐤᐊᐢᐞᐞᐤ ᑫᐳᐞ ᓇᕒᐞᐞᐥᐞᐞᐊᐞᐞᐤ·ᐞᐞ
ᐤᐨᐣᐨᐞᐤᐊᐞ ᑫ ᓇᐧᐞᐞᐞᐞᐞᐞ ᐊᐧᐞ, ᑦᐊ ᐤ ᐊᐞᐞ
ᐞᐞ·ᐨᐞᐞᐢᐤᐞᐞᐞ ᐤ ᑫᐣᐳᐤᐊᐞᐞᐊᐞᐞ ᐤᐞᐞ;

10 ᐊᐣᐪᐦ ᐤᕒᐨᐞᐞᐳ ᑭᑭ ᐞᐞ·ᐨᐨᐊᐞᐢᐞᐞ ᐊᐞᐊ
ᐤ ᑫᐊᐞᕒᐞᐢ, ᑦᐊ ᑭᑭ ᐳᐣᐤᐞᐞᕒᐞᐞ ᑫᐞᐳᐞ
ᐊᐞᐊ ᑫ ᒐᐧᐞᐞᐞᐨᕒᐞᐞᐞ (ᕒᐞᐞᐞ ᐊᐞᐞ ᓇ ᒑᕒ ᒍ-

FIGURE 4. Page photographed from the Cree Bible. (Publication facts on bible unknown as title page is missing. Date on fly leaf written in longhand reads 1885.) The material on this page has been identified by Mrs. Florence Standing Rock as being from the First Epistle to the Thessalonians.

emphatically.[2] "The white men got the material from that breed who stole it."
Quite naturally, this account differs from that recorded by printed sources.

[2] This view of the primacy of the Cree language, given me by Raining Bird on December 30, 1959, suggests to some degree what Brinton wrote: "The Cree language is built on a few simple unchangeable radicles and elementary words, denoting being, relation, energy, etc. It has extreme regularity of construction, a simple negative, is wholly verbal and markedly incomparative, has its grammatical elements better defined than most of its neighbors, and a more constant phonetic system. For these and similar reasons, we are justified in considering it the nearest representative we possess to the primitive tongue, and unless strong grounds to the contrary are advanced, it is proper to assume the purest dialect is found nearest the primeval home of the stock." D. G. Brinton, *The Lenape and Their Legends*, Library of Aboriginal American Literature (Philadelphia, 1885), quoted in F. E. Peeso, Unpublished Ms.

All writers seem to be in agreement that the Rev. James Evans, superintendent of missions for the Hudson's Bay territories and representing the Wesleyan Missionary Society of England, invented the Cree syllabic script in 1840. Discussing the development, Peel says,[3] "He used a variety of triangles, angles, pothooks (at first ten in number but later reduced to nine) each with four positions—up, down, left, and right—to depict the musical language of the Cree... The use of each of the nine symbols in four different positions gave the syllabary a menemonic quality which helps to explain its success." The first recorded printing using the syllabic form was completed on November 11, 1840, when three copies of the hymn, "Jesus My All to Heaven Has Gone," was done with type made from the lead lining of tea chests. The printer's ink had been ingeniously prepared from lamp chimney soot mixed with sturgeon oil, while the press was a fur bailer. By 1861, with the help of three mixed bloods, they were able to publish the complete translation of the Bible into Cree syllabic. The actual printing of this volume, however, was done in London.[4]

As other religious denominations reached the Cree, they too adapted the Cree syllabic for their use. The Church of England sent Archdeacon James Hunter to Saskatchewan in 1844. He married Jane Ross, daughter of Donald Ross of the Hudson's Bay Company and a Cree woman who had taught Jane the syllabic form. Mrs. Ross, assisting her husband, worked on the Book of Common Prayer which was published in 1854.[5] The first Roman Catholic missionaries to use the Cree syllabic were Oblates stationed at Moose Factory and Alban. Father Jean Laverlochère, OMI, began translating prayers and hymns while his successor, Father André Garin, published the "Catéchisme, recueil de prières et de cantiques à l'usage des sauvages d'Alband, (Bai d'Hudson)," in 1854. He followed this publication with a selection of prayers in 1856, and a translation of sermons in 1859.[6]

Peeso found the Cree whom he met to be thoroughly conversant with the form. In his unpublished manuscript he says,[7] "The Crees have a written language composed of syllabic characters by means of which they carry on an extensive correspondence among themselves. Nearly all read and write readily for the characters are so simple and comprehensive that a person of ordinary intelligence can learn to read and write it in a few days."[8]

---

[3] Bruce Peel, "How the Bible Came to the Cree," *Alberta Historical Review*, Vol. VI, No. 2 (1958), p. 15.

[4] *Ibid.*, p. 16.

[5] *Ibid.*, pp. 16–17.

[6] *Ibid.*, pp. 17–18.

[7] F. E. Peeso, Unpublished manuscript, p. 25.

[8] The Cree script or syllabic is not the only form to which this language has been reduced. Father LaCombe, well known early priest to the Plains Cree, published a Cree-French grammar in phonetics rather than syllabics in 1874. Writing about this grammar, Hugh Dempsey, Secretary of the Historical Society of Alberta, said: "Actually this priest (Father LaCombe) was a diligent worker but had received only a limited education. The man who really did most of the work was Father (then Brother) Constantine Scollen. He was a scholarly Irish priest who was exposed to

Among the Montana Cree today, the form is used exclusively by the older inhabitants of the reservation, although some of the younger people are not too interested in learning it. "It is very easy to learn," says Joe Stanley.[9] "The next time you stay here for two weeks, I'll teach you how to read and write it." Practically all of the correspondence between the Montana Cree and their Canadian friends or relatives is written in the syllabic form. Several families subscribe to a church magazine, *The Cree Review*, which is published monthly by the Oblate Fathers at Lac LaBic Mission in Alberta. This periodical is printed entirely in syllabics.

Perhaps no one will ever know the complete story of the invention of the language. Evans' sources are now obscure. Before one completely disregards Raining Bird's account, two factors should be considered. In the first place, the writing does not look like anything a white man, and especially an Englishman, would invent. In the second place, an interesting speculation arises concerning the possibility that the Cree might have developed their own written form—much as Sequoia did for the Cherokee—by what Kroeber calls "stimulus diffusion." Writing about Sequoia's accomplishment, Kroeber says:[10] "That Sequoya's feat was however a genuine and single-handed invention is shown by two facts. Not one of the characters has the same value as in English; and all the characters denote syllables, not letter sounds. We have thus a true and real invention, with a high degree of originality; and yet we also have the assurance that but for the influence and example of the alien culture, the invention would never have been made."

Without detracting from the struggle and hardship and ingenuity of the Rev. Mr. Evans, it does not seem too incredulous to believe that the Cree may have developed a written form of their language based on knowledge of the white man's printed word. They had been in association with the white man for well over two hundred years by the time Evans joined them. His feat in reducing the syllabic form to print, especially under the difficulties he had to experience (type from lead lining, ink from soot and oil, press from a bailer), gives him proper recognition. But the actual form, it seems to me, might well have been original with the Cree.

---

a considerable amount of jealousy because he was learned and non-French. The method used by Father Scollen in gathering material for this dictionary and grammar was as follows:

He would go out from the mission with a party of half-breeds to cut wood. When lunch time or a rest time came, he would point to certain objects and give the word in English. The half-breeds would then say it in Cree. Father Scollen would write the word on a chip of wood and go on to the next word. At the end of the day, he would gather up the chips and take them back to the mission where the information would be transcribed into his notes."

An old Oblate priest nearly one hundred years old at the time, gave this information to Mr. Dempsey several years ago. Personal letter to the author, January 20, 1960.

[9] Personal interview, June 12, 1961.

[10] A. L. Kroeber, *Anthropology* (New York: Harcourt Brace and Co., 1948), pp. 369–370.

ABBREVIATIONS

AA	American Anthropologist, Menasha, New York.
AHR	Alberta Historical Review, Calgary.
APAM	Anthropological Papers of the American Museum of Natural History, New York.
ARBAE	Annual Reports of the Bureau of American Ethnology, Washington, D.C.
B	The Beaver, Winnipeg.
BAMNH	Bulletins of the American Museum of Natural History, New York.
BBAE	Bulletins of the Bureau of American Ethnology, Washington, D.C.
CC	Christian Century, Chicago.
CUAAS	Catholic University of America Anthropological Series, Washington, D.C.
E	Ethnos, Stockholm.
FCMP	Field Columbian Museum Publications, Chicago.
GFT	Great Fall Tribune, Great Falls, Montana.
INMAI	Indian Notes Museum of American Indian, Heye Foundation, New York.
JAFL	Journal of American Folklore, Boston, New York.
LAAL	Library of Aboriginal American Literature, Philadelphia.
MAAA	Memoirs of American Anthropological Association, Menasha.
MJ	Museum Journal, Philadelphia.
NMCAS	National Museum of Canada Anthropological Series, Ottawa.
PAES	Publications of American Ethnological Society, New York.
PAMAE	Proceedings of Annual Meeting of the American Ethnological Society, Seattle.
PM	Primitive Man, Washington, D.C.
PROHS	Papers and Records, Ontario Historical Society, Ottawa.
T	Tomorrow, New York.
UCP	University of California Publications in American Archaeology and Ethnology, Berkeley.

BIBLIOGRAPHY

Books and Articles

Benedict, Ruth
  1923. The Concept of the Guardian Spirit in North America. MAAA XXIX.
Bloomfield, Leonard
  1930. Sacred Stories of the Sweetgrass Cree. NMCAS 11.
  1934. Plains Cree Texts. PAES XVI.
Brinton, Daniel G.
  1885. The Lenape and their Legends. LAAL V.
Burg, Margery
  1932. Much Accomplished Among Rocky Boy Indians on Reservation. GFT, July 3.
Cadzow, Donald
  1927. Smoking Tipi of Buffalo-Bull the Cree. INMAI IV.
Cameron, William B.
  1950. Blood Red the Sun. Calgary.
Clements, Forrest
  1931. Plains Indian Tribal Correlations with Sun Dance Data. AA XXXIII, 2.
Collier, Donald
  1944. Conjuring Among the Kiowa. PM XVII, 3–4.
Cooper, John M.
  1933. The Cree Witiko Psychosis. PM VI, 1.
  1934. The Northern Algonquian Supreme Being. CUAAS, 2.
Denny, C.
  1944. Blackfeet Magic. B CCLXXV, 2.
Densmore, Frances
  1918. Teton Sioux Music. BBAE 61.
DeVoto, Bernard
  1947. Across the Wide Missouri. Boston.
Dixon, Roland B.
  1905. The Northern Maidu. BAMNH XVII.
Dorsey, George A.
  1905. The Cheyenne, Vol. II: The Sun Dance. FCMP 103.
Dorsey, James Owen
  1889. Teton Folk-Lore. AA, Old Series, 2.
Durkheim, Emile
  1915. The Elementary Forms of Religious Life. London.
Dusenberry, Verne
  1955. The Northern Cheyenne, Montana Heritage Series No. 6., Helena.
  1958. Montana Indians and the Pentecostals. CCLXXV, 30.

1959. Vision Experiences Among the Pend d'Oreille Indians. E 1959: 1–2.

Firth, Raymond
1951. Elements of Social Organization. London.

Flannery, Regina
1944. The Gros Ventre Shaking Tent. PM XVII, 3–4.

Frazer, Sir James George
1949. The Golden Bough. Abridged edition. London.
1951. The Magic Art and the Evolution of Kings. New York.

Freud, Sigmund
1957. The Future of an Illusion. New York.

Goddard, Pliny Earle
1919. Notes on the Sun Dance of the Cree in Alberta. APAM XVI.

Graves, Robert
1960. Food for Centaurs: Stories, Talks, Critical Studies, Poems. New York.

Grinnell, George Bird
1920. Blackfoot Lodge Tales. New York.
1923. The Cheyenne Indians. New Haven.

Hakluyt, Richard
1904. The Principal Navigations. Glasgow.

Hoebel, E. Adamson
1960. The Cheyenne: Indians of the Great Plains. New York.

Howard, Joseph Kinsey
1952. Strange Empire. New York.

Hultkrantz, Åke
1953. Conceptions of the Soul among North American Indians. Statens Etnografiska Museum, Monograph Series Publication No. 1, Stockholm.
1957. The North American Indian Orpheus Tradition. Statens Etnografiska Museum, Monograph Series Publication No. 2, Stockholm.

Kroeber, Alfred L.
1948. Anthropology. New York.

Leach, Maria (ed.)
1949. The Standard Dictionary of Folklore, Mythology and Legend. Vol. I. New York.

Linderman, Frank B.
1929. The American. New York.

Linton, Ralph
1943. Nativistic Movements. AA XLV.

Lopatin, Ivan A.
1960. Origin of the Native American Steam Bath. AA LXII.

Lowie, Robert H.
1909. The Assiniboine. APAM IV, 1.
1922. The Religion of the Crow Indians. APAM XXV, 2.
1931. Supernatural Experiences of American Indians. T XI.

Malinowski, Bronislaw.
1955. Magic, Science and Religion. New York.

Mandelbaum, David G.
1940. The Plains Cree. APAM XXXVII, 2.

Mooney, James
1898. Myths of the Cherokee. ARBAE XIX, 1.
Murphy, Robert
1958. Mundurucú Religion. UCP XLIX, 1.
Murray, Sir James (ed.)
1933. The Oxford English Dictionary. Oxford.
Murray, Margaret A.
1921. Witchcult in Western Europe. Oxford.
Pearce, Roy H.
1953. The Savages of America. Baltimore.
Peel, Bruce
1958. How the Bible Came to the Cree. AHR VI, 2.
·Peeso, Fred E.
1912. The Cree Indians. MJ III.
Primitive Man
1944. Volume XVII.
Radin, Paul
1914. An Introductive Enquiry in the Study of Ojibwa Religion. PROHS XII.
1957. Primitive Religion: Its Nature and Origin. New York.
1960. The World of Primitive Man. New York.
Ray, Verne F.
1941. Historic Backgrounds of the Conjuring Complex in the Plateau and Plains. In: Language, Culture and Personality. Menasha.
Richardson, James P.
1913. Messages and Papers of the Presidents. New York.
Rodnick, David
1938. The Fort Belknap Assiniboine of Montana. New Haven.
Rossignol, M.
1939. The Religion of the Saskatchewan and Western Manitoba Cree. PM XI, 3–4.
Schmidt, Wilhelm
1933. High Gods in North America. Oxford.
Skinner, Alanson
1911. Notes on the Eastern Cree and Northern Salteaux. APAM IX.
1914 a. Bear Customs of the Cree and Other Algonkin Indians of Northern Ontario. PROHS XII.
1914 b. Notes on the Plains Cree. AA XVI.
1914 c. Political Organization, Cults, and Ceremonies of the Plains-Ojibway and Plains-Cree Indians. APAM XI, 6.
1914 d. The Sun Dance of the Plains-Cree. APAM XVI, 4.
1916. Plains Cree Tales. JAFL XXXIX.
Speck, Frank G.
1935. Naskapi. Norman, Oklahoma.
Spier, Leslie
1921. The Sun Dance of the Plains Indians: Its Development and Diffusion. APAM XVI, 7.
Stewart, Omer C.
1956. Three Gods for Joe. T IV.

Swanton, John R.
　　1928. Social and Religious Beliefs and Usages of the Chickasaw Indians.
　　　　ARBAE XLIV.
Taylor, John
　　n.d. The Witchcraft Delusion in Colonial Connecticut. New York.
Teicher, Morton I.
　　1960. Windigo Psychosis, A Study of a Relationship between Belief and
　　　　Behavior among the Indians of Northeastern Canada. PAMAE.
Thompson, Stith
　　1956. Motif Index of Folk Literature. Vol. III. Bloomington.
Thwaites, Reuben Gold (ed.)
　　1896–1901. The Jesuit Relations and Allied Documents. Cleveland.
Turney-High, H. H.
　　1941. The Ethnography of the Kutenai. MAAA LVI.
Umfreville, E.
　　1790. The Present State of Hudson's Bay. London.
Voget, Fred
　　1951. Acculturation at Caughnawaga: A Note on the Native and Modified
　　　　Group. AA, LIII.
Watetch, Abel
　　n.d. Payepot and His People (as told to Blodwen Davies). Saskatchewan
　　　　History and Folklore Society, Saskatoon.
Wissler, Clark
　　1912. Ceremonial Bundles of the Blackfoot Indians. APAM VII, 2.

Documents

Constitution and Bylaws of the Chippewa Cree Indians of the Rocky Boy's
　　Reservation. Washington: Government Printing Office, 1936.
Maine Historical Society Collections, Series 2, IV, 1889.
Official Correspondence Relating to Admission of Montana as a State into
　　the Union including Proclamations and Official Address of Joseph K. Toole.
　　Compiled by R. P. Stout, private secretary to the Governor. Helena, 1892.
Report of the Commissioner of Indian Affairs. Washington: Government
　　Printing Office, 1894.
Report of the Commissioner of Indian Affairs for 1935. Washington: Govern-
　　ment Printing Office.
Senate Reports. Vol. 4, No. 821. 54th Congress, 1st session.
Survey of Conditions of Indians in the United States. Hearing before a Sub-
　　committee on Indian Affairs. Part 23, Montana. U.S. Senate, 72nd Congress,
　　1st session.
Tentative Roll of Rocky Boy Indians, May 30, 1917. Office of Sub-Agency,
　　Rocky Boy's Sub Agency, Box Elder, Montana.
U.S. Statutes 38. No. 807.

Newspapers

The Anaconda (Montana) Standard. January 19, 1896.
The Cut Bank (Montana) Pioneer Press. August 1, 1901.

The Fort Benton (Montana) River Press. August 24, 1887.
The Great Falls (Montana) Tribune. November 9, 1887; June 6, 1894.
The Havre (Montana) Plaindealer. June 7, 1894; December 21, 1912.
The Helena (Montana) Independent. June 26, 1896.
The Montana Daily Record (Helena). August 1, 1901.

Unpublished Materials

Brief on the Rocky Boy's Reservation. A duplicated report prepared by the
 Bureau of Indian Affairs for planning purposes only. October, 1956.
Dusenberry, Verne
 Unpublished Northern Cheyenne Field Notes, 1956.
 Unpublished Assiniboine Field Notes, 1958.
Gray, Raymond
 History of the Cree Nation. W.P.A. Writer's Project, January 16, 1942.
 Unpublished typewritten manuscript.
Hultkrantz, Åke
 Class lectures, Brandeis University. Summer, 1958.
Peeso, Fred
 Unpublished manuscript of material collected and written, 1905–1912.
The Promised Land. Typed coverage of problems on the Rocky Boy reserva-
 tion. No date or author given. Manuscript loaned by George Denny, Secretary
 of Tribal Council, September 1, 1960. On file at Tribal office.

SUBJECT INDEX